GRAYWOLF FORUM 2

*Body Language*

GRAYWOLF FORUM ONE
*Tolstoy's Dictaphone: Technology and the Muse*
Edited by SVEN BIRKERTS

GRAYWOLF FORUM 2

# *Body Language*

## Writers on Sport

*Edited by*
GERALD EARLY

GRAYWOLF PRESS : SAINT PAUL

Publication of this volume is made possible in part by a grant provided by the Minnesota State Arts Board through an appropriation by the Minnesota State Legislature, and by a grant from the National Endowment for the Arts. Significant support has also been provided by Dayton's, Mervyn's, and Target stores through the Dayton Hudson Foundation, the Andrew W. Mellon Foundation, the McKnight Foundation, the General Mills Foundation, the St. Paul Companies, and other generous contributions from foundations, corporations, and individuals. To these organizations and individuals we offer our heartfelt thanks.

Additional support for this publication was provided by the Patrick and Aimee Butler Family Foundation, the Star Tribune/Cowles Media Company, and the Lannan Foundation.

James A. McPherson's essay, "Grant Hall," was published in *DoubleTake*, Winter, 1998.

David Foster Wallace's essay, "Derivative Sport in Tornado Alley," was published in *A Supposedly Fun Thing I'll Never Do Again* (Little, Brown & Co., 1997).

Published by Graywolf Press
2402 University Avenue, Suite 203
Saint Paul, Minnesota 55114
All rights reserved.

www.graywolfpress.org

Published in the United States of America

ISBN 1-55597-262-4
ISSN 1088-3347

2  4  6  8  9  7  5  3  1
First Graywolf Printing, 1998

Library of Congress Catalog Card Number: 97-70216

Cover photograph: Douglas Dearden
Series and cover design: AND

# Contents

. . . . . . . . . .

# Introduction

. . . . . . . . . .

You can't judge people by what they do. If you judge them at all,
it must be by what they are.
   EILEEN WADE in Raymond Chandler's *The Long Goodbye*

I dreamed of Ted Williams
leaning at night
against the Eiffel Tower, weeping.
   GREGORY CORSO, "Dream of a Baseball Star"

Muscle and pluck forever!
   WALT WHITMAN, "Song of the Broad-Axe"

The appeal of sports, especially of high-performance athletics, in the
main for the participant and the spectator, is that they permit us to
judge people exactly and precisely by what they do. Sports tell us that
people *are* inevitably and irrevocably what they *do*. This greatly simplifies life because it greatly simplifies meaning and the search for it. We
might still be interested in motives, the athlete's own in doing what he
or she does, or our own (if we are not the athlete but the spectator), in
why we should be interested in what the athlete does. But the primary
interest is in a moment of action, in a moment of execution that either
fails or succeeds. That the action is not merely physical, but indeed an
extremely strenuous, intensely ritualized rendition of a highly developed physical skill, a kind of superphysicality, makes it all the more definitive because meaning becomes, in this way, strikingly specific and
discernible, explicit and self-evident. The body is not simply given an
artistry, an expression, like dance, but a goal. Sports do not etherealize
the body but make it even more concrete.

Sports are about the finality of the consequences of an action or a set of actions, the immediate and intractable drama of making a mechanically physical but deliberative choice upon which one's fate, starkly imminent but darkly unforeseeable, rests. Thus, sports make human life, above anything else, a metaphysical expression, intelligible as both a higher purpose and as an absurd futility in ways that religion, for instance, cannot. While sports carry the majestic power of ritual and ceremony, and with such events as the Olympics, the World Series, the Super Bowl, the NCAA Basketball Championship, the Kentucky Derby, the Master's Golf Tournament, Wimbledon, and the Indianapolis 500 have given us a powerful set of movable feasts that gives them much in common with religion, high-performance athletics is not religion. Or perhaps the paradox of sports is that they give us all the trappings of religion while being the antithesis of it.

First, sports are about play, about doing something for the fun of doing it, for its re-creative or competitive potential, which, it seems, is the antithesis of the creeds of monotheistic religions that would, rightly or wrongly, deny their believers *that* level of self-absorption that ultimately would not lead to greater consciousness of God. Or has the fun been drained from sports once they become high-level competitions? As sports have increasingly become a form of work, are they no longer a true form of play but only an ironical kind of play, an indication that in this postmodern, post-Christian age it is impossible to distinguish work from play and therefore impossible for us to find true refuge from either one or the other? If that is the case, sports are an expression of our own confusion and of the failure of religious expression in the world since we now have spaces, symbolized by where sports are performed, that are neither sacred nor profane yet both. Are sports a heroic reflection of the human quest for excellence or a further sign and expression of our desperation, our anxiety, our unhappiness in this world? There is something inherently sinful about sports, for there is something inherently pagan and inherently pointless about them as well. In the West, particularly, this sense of contradiction that surrounds sports might very well be related to the fact that sports are a physical expression, a celebration of what the body can do. We, in the West, have always felt ambivalent about worshipping the body,

.   .   .   .   .   .   .   .   .   .

although we have generally felt less disgust about the body and carnality, despite our puritanical inclinations and our hypercritical morality, than has been typically expressed in Eastern mysticism. We do not think the body to be a bad invention, we simply think the mind to be a better invention. In our culture, those who are characterized by their physical presence, such as women and blacks, are seen as gifted in their way, but distinctly inferior; women are inferior to men because men are smarter, blacks to whites because whites are smarter. It is also interesting to note that in our culture, sports, with few exceptions, are downloaded as expressions or activities in popular culture, not high culture. In this way, sports can be, by turns, intensely popular and easily dismissed. Popular culture is where all our sensuality is packaged and sold, largely, though not exclusively, on the fuel of white women's bodies and the putative sensuality of Negro men, so it is a natural location for sports. For the cynical among us or for the stubbornly puritanical, sports are thus a sign that we either worship the wrong gods or are so debased as to worship no gods at all—the same complaint by the highbrow about popular culture itself.

Indeed, in this regard, an important set of questions about the significance of play in our culture arises: What does organized play mean? What form of game-playing is sports? Why do we associate game-playing with children when virtually all of our professional sports, when the idea of play as an *organized* activity are adult in origin? Why is it the case that the entire concept of sports, both amateur and professional, in the world today was created by one small country, nineteenth-century England? Why have we, the industrialized and nonindustrialized modern world, the left and the right, the capitalist and the collectivist, professionalized our games, as did our Greek and Roman forebears, to such a passionate extent? And if sports can represent the ideology of both the colonizer and the colonized, the communist and the capitalist, the bushman and the urban dweller, even men and women, what, at the root, are the human values that sports truly reflect? In short, how does play become both an expression of politics and the transcendence of politics? It is not my intention to answer any of these questions, nor did I compile this book of essays with the thought that such questions would be answered. I think these questions suggest the incredible magnitude of sports and organized play in our lives and how an understanding, not necessarily an appreciation, of sports, is essential in understanding how modern life is structured and how human desire is sublimated. In some intriguing, even compelling, ways, the essays here consider these questions, or consider these questions boiled down to three questions: What is our strange and glorious province of play, where, ironically, merit reigns without mercy? How does one enter it? How does one escape? For what is our play but an expression of our restlessness, of our fitfulness as human beings, "the great unrest of which we are part," as Whitman said.

But even more important than sports and the meaning of play in human culture, than sports and its relationship to religion is the connection between sports and science. Sports are a science made accessible, for John Hoberman in *Darwin's Athletes* is right when he says that the triumph of sports in the modern world, as the modern world's most powerful expression of itself in search of its humanity, is the triumph of the rationalism, the method, the quantification, the engineering mystique of science. Simply put, sports are about providing a context for the demonstration of the rationally engineered human body. This does not answer the question entirely but does come close to suggesting something about the values that sports represent and reflect in the modern world. Sports are not a science, but it would not be possible to play and enjoy sports today without science. Sports are all the things religion and science as mystery and measurement aspire to be in the realm of the human imagination, heroism and accessibility writ large; and so, in many ways, for ordinary human purposes of expression, sports are better than either. In this way, I think sports are ideal subjects to write about. They are magnificent junctures of spectacle and explanation, of ritual and reason.

Indeed, we might take writing about sports in this country for granted because there is so much of it. A mountain of books comes out each year about sports, ranging from ghostwritten autobiographies by athletes to trite advice books by famous coaches; from a variety of books by fans—from reference to anecdotal—to dozens of books by journalists—from biographies, to histories, to "contemporary issues"

. . . . . . . . .

such as sports financing. Even academics have gotten into the act (have been for a while, actually), with, for instance, a new academic biography about Babe Didrikson (appropriately lesbian feminist in denouncing male hegemony) and a new academic examination of race and sports (appropriately liberal in denouncing white hegemony).[1]

Of course, virtually every daily newspaper in America has a sports section and a staff of sportswriters. So, there is endless reporting about, commentary on, analysis of sports on all levels in the United States. We are constantly informed about the boys and girls who perform sports, and the men and women who either perform them or who teach them. News about sports can be easily ignored but not so easily evaded. But so much of this journalism is disposable, which has led many of us to think in two mistaken ways: that sports are such tawdry spectacles that they are worthy only of disposable commentary and that sports themselves are disposable because they are trivial human activities. The first thought misses the very vital point that day-to-day events in high-performance sports competitions are, indeed, *news*, to be gathered and presented in a highly professional way, in the same way that other aspects of popular culture such as film, music, and theater are. The writing itself may be disposable, a reflection of our disposable popular culture, but there is, ironically, an act of preservation in making something newsworthy that means, in effect, we have made something a part of our history, a reference point, a defining instance, something that must be returned to by future generations if they are to understand us and themselves. With the exception of our politics, nothing comes as close to being recorded almost completely as an epic narrative in our news as our sports. The second thought confuses the *content* of sports performance with its *meaning*. The goal of any particular game or even of any particular sports season is trivial, but the fact that it is being played and being supported by a huge corporate and technological apparatus is not. Teams and individuals may be beaten, but the kingdom of sports is unstoppable.

On the other hand, there have been several first-rate writers who have written brilliantly about sports: Joyce Carol Oates, C. L. R. James, and Stephen Jay Gould, to name the most prominent. There have been very good sports journalists, too, from Grantland Rice to

A. J. Leibling, from Robert Lipsyte to Ralph Wiley. Yet it is surprising how few of our very best writers have written at all about sports. Perhaps many feel that one must be a fan, an aficionado, in order to write about sports. But one hardly has to be a fan of any other segment of popular culture—film, music, television—to write about it, to criticize it, to wonder about it as a human activity. And sports have penetrated our lives in deep and complex ways, certainly as richly complex as film or popular music—hardly any one of us can claim we have not been touched by sports at all, even casually. And certainly by fewer than six degrees of separation we are all related to an athlete or a wanna-be athlete. This interaction between the casual observer or participant and sports needs to be explored more by good writers who are not necessarily fans of athletics. That is the idea behind this collection: I asked several very good writers if they could write personal essays about an encounter with a sport and what that encounter meant. I purposefully sought writers, in most instances, who had not written about sports at all or had written only very little about them. I went out of my way to choose writers who were not sports fans or who felt ambivalent about sports, or, if they felt a passion for sports, could detach themselves from it. The result is not simply a collection of well-written essays but a collection of some importance, of some moment, about sports as an ironical cultural expression of loss through gain or victory through defeat.

Sports, finally, are about the fear of a world of chaos. Sports are about our hope for our order of things and, paradoxically, our realization that our hope will be dashed. This is why, ultimately, sports are such powerful attractions. What attracts us is the contradiction of trying to find a sense of permanence in such an ephemeral, contrived, minor expression of the human will. Thus, buried in the activity of play itself is innocence and experience, triumph and tragedy. Think of our current fitness craze in this country, actually dating back to the early days of vegetarianism and "physical culture" in the antebellum nineteenth century. What does this craze reflect but our fear of aging and death and our innocent hope that, if we train like athletes, cling to their habits, we can retain our youth, our health, our bodies against the relentlessly encroaching chaos of our unstoppable decline and unbeing. O, that we should believe that our bodies are made in the image of God

.   .   .   .   .   .   .   .   .   .

and that we must be trapped by these flimsy, bedeviling devices, and that we should be *conscious* of our entrapment! The body is the last frontier. Perhaps the body has been, in truth, the only frontier, and our history has been merely the projection of the various insecurities that we feel about our bodies, about our physical presence. If this is so, sports may be the greatest religious experience, the most refined and profound encounter we can ever hope to have with the reality and the unreality of ourselves. This collection shows the intensity of and affection for sports and play that lie in our very ordinary, commonplace, sometimes amusing, sometimes troubling encounters with them. Perhaps Gregory Corso expressed the overall sentiment of these essays best in a line from his poem, "Dream of a Baseball Star": "God! throw thy merciful pitch!"

GERALD EARLY
*St. Louis, Missouri*
*30 July 1997*

## NOTES

1. Susan E. Cayleff, *Babe: The Life and Legend of Babe Didrikson Zaharias* (Urbana: University of Illinois Press, 1995) and John Hoberman, *Darwin's Athletes: How Sport Has Damaged Black America and Preserved the Myth of Race* (Houghton Mifflin, 1997).

GRAYWOLF FORUM 2

*Body Language*

# Confessions and Self-Justifications of a Sports Fan

. . . . . . . . .

*by*
PHILLIP LOPATE

## 1. ATTITUDE

I have been a sports fan all my life, and expect to continue in my enthusiasm or "dependency," come what may, till death or senility. By this, I mean that I cannot imagine any set of seedy events that might occur in the professional sports I follow (chiefly baseball and basketball, but also some football, boxing, and tennis) that might alienate me from them. When, a few years ago, the pundits were opining that the American public had been "turned off" to baseball by the season-shortened shenanigans of union-busting owners or greedy players (depending on one's view), and speculated that the sport should try to market itself more agreeably to these wavering fans, I knew they were talking about a different breed of rooter from myself. I have no choice in the matter: The baseball season gives shape to my year. I could no sooner boycott it because certain owners are capitalist jerks than I could refuse to buy those supermarket products that are manufactured to make a profit. I can't imagine not wanting to watch an Albert Belle, Barry Bonds, or Robby Alomar play ball, regardless of their character flaws. Nor am I drawn especially to "bad boys": I followed as avidly the efficacious moves of straight-arrow types like Julius Erving or John Havlicek as I do those of Dennis Rodman. In short, I watch sports for something other than role models.

My sports jones began in childhood. I was one of those nerdy kids who disguises his incipient intellectuality, or makes it more socially

3

respectable, by memorizing batting averages. I read every baseball book in the Young Adult section of the library, and in this way came to know almost as much about historical figures, such as Walter Johnson and John McGraw and Christy Mathewson, as I did about those living idols, Don Newcombe, Jackie Robinson, Roy Campanella. Past or present, they were all gods to me.

We are told that the huge contracts of ballplayers have broken down the essential trust, the symbiotic (however Mittyesque) identification between fans and players. I grew up rooting for that famed (sometimes I think too famed) Brooklyn Dodgers team of the fifties; and I am here to tell you that I never identified with the gods of the diamond, however much Carl Furillo or Gil Hodges may have lived in the same borough as I. I worshipped them, yes, but they were as much above my identification when they made $20,000 a year as today, when they make seven million. Perhaps because my own athletic prowess has always been so limited, I never saw professional ballplayers as anything but divinely Other.

Now, I can only laugh when a sportscaster refers to some professional team as "blue collar" because they bang and dive for balls around the net. How can you lump a quintet of millionaires with a bunch of guys on the assembly line? But I don't *resent* them for making a million dollars, or feel that their enormous paychecks have cut the ethical legs out from under the sport. No, I watch them doing what I cannot, and I get swept up in the narrative of the game.

I watch sports largely for the convergence of narrative, character, and situation—its novelistic attributes, you might say. (Bottom of the eighth, two on: Will they ask the strikeout-prone, duck-billed Darryl Strawberry to bunt?) Because the development of plot is important to me, I have to watch whole games and follow teams for entire seasons. It amazes me when people say that the only important part of a professional basketball game is the last ten minutes. What they miss is the rise and fall of energies, the way some players will start hot in the first half and cool off in the second, or vice versa. And they miss the doldrums, which have their own meditative value.

The other night I was watching a New York Knicks game, which they won, to my great satisfaction, beating a talented Atlanta Hawks

. . . . . . . . . .

team, and I was surprised to hear the sportscaster remark apologetically that there hadn't been much in the way of excitement. Actually, no more than five points had separated the teams for the first three quarters, so I wondered what he meant by lack of excitement—what standard was not being met? Perhaps the fact that, from the middle of the last period on, the denouement was not really in question, made him bored, even as it made a team partisan like myself quietly happy.

I note that most current newspaper reporting of sports focuses on the last sequence of plays, to the exclusion of all that went before. When you read an account of a sports contest, there is none of the sense of rising and falling fortunes that seems so important when you are at the game. The impact of TV news, with its highlights of the go-ahead point, has conditioned the way games are reported and, by extension, perceived. Beyond that, sports are reported almost entirely from a human interest angle (player returning against his former team does well or badly), with virtually no descriptive analysis of the physical components that go into an individual athlete's style.

In recent years, the moralism of sports commentators has also turned me off—not to athletics itself, but to these Sunday sermons on sociology and ethics. The self-righteous, puritanical tone of sports writers about, say, Pete Rose's gambling or Dwight Gooden's substance abuse has made me question the rules themselves. Why *should* athletes be tested for drug-taking, and suspended if they are found to have indulged? Since I don't believe taking drugs should be treated as a criminal offense in the first place, it would be hypocritical of me to apply a different standard to sports figures. And until it is proven that smoking marijuana or snorting coke gives an unfair performance edge to an athlete (which I strongly doubt), I see no reason to suspend drug-taking players. As for gambling, I cannot understand banning a man like Pete Rose from baseball when he places bets on other sports. If his gambling has nothing to do with the outcome of a game he is participating in, why consider it an offense?

Short of allowing them to beat up on refereees, let the players play. That's my philosophy. There are lots of individual ballplayers around the country whom I keep my eye on, but essentially I root for the local teams. Some say: How can you continue to support a team when most of the personnel changes every few years, either through trades or free agency? Easy. Just as one's body transforms its cells every seven years, yet the core of one's identity remains the same, so the players come and go, but the team's Platonic essence stays intact: The Cowboys are the Cowboys, the Steelers, the Steelers. Of course a team's fortunes are altered through additions and subtractions, but that is only another way of saying that the history of the franchise waxes and wanes, as it should.

There are different circumstances that give each team its enduring character, such as continuity of ballpark, ownership, local demographics. No Met, for instance, has ever won a batting crown. I used to think that a player had only to be traded to the Mets for his batting average to dip thirty points. Was it the ink in the uniforms that sapped their strength? More likely, Shea Stadium is simply not a good hitters' ballpark, because of its mound, wind patterns, and dimensions. The St. Louis Cardinals will always have speedsters, just as the Los Angeles Dodgers will always do their best to attract Mexican ballplayers. Loyalty to the mystique of a team and loyalty to certain players are not necessarily at irreconcilable cross-purposes; just as in our work life, we can continue to root for certain colleagues, even if they jump to another institution or corporation.

## 2. DISAPPOINTMENT

Again and again I have turned to sports for a reasonable distraction, and they have invariably served me in that modest function. When I was writing my first novel, *Confessions of Summer*, I found myself mentally overheated at the end of a workday; and to unwind I took in a lot of basketball and ballet. After a while the two spectator events began to merge in my mind's eye: I would watch Bob MacAdoo setting himself for a jump shot and superimpose Peter Martins lifting Suzanne Farrell. This is by way of saying that sports possesses an abstract enthrallment having nothing to do with who wins or loses.

But of course, the fiercer emotions related to athletics are touched off only when the outcome matters. In my case, sports have proven an excellent school for disappointment. My chagrins as a fan have branded me far more deeply than my triumphs. Statistically, to root for a local team is to encounter loss much more commonly than success. Being a sports fan is in part a way of coming to terms with failure. It is said that gamblers are addicted to the experience of losing, which is why they cannot quit when they are ahead. So with sports fans.

Two particular basketball games, in which the teams I was rooting for lost, scarred me as keenly as certain deaths or career disappointments. I was already over forty for both, and should have known better. The first involved the University of Houston's meeting with North Carolina State in the NCAA final. I had never been much interested in college sports, so that, when I went to work for the University of Houston in 1980, I was ripe for the picking. Suddenly my employer was fielding that marvelous team, Phi Slamma Jamma, that included Hakeem (then Akeem) Olajuwan, Clyde Drexler, and some very decent sidemen who never made it to the NBA. Olajuwan, still new to basketball at that time, played with an infectious enthusiasm and joy that was beautiful to behold; and Drexler was already the epitome of inventive grace and speed that earned him the knickname "The Glide," and put me in mind of an earlier "Clyde," Walt Frazier.

The previous year, the University of Houston had lost the championship to a stronger team, Georgetown (with young Patrick Ewing, coached by the great John Thompson); but now we were up against a weaker adversary, North Carolina State, and we fully expected to triumph. Helen, my girlfriend at the time, had set the table with candles and champagne for a celebration dinner, in anticipation of victory. (She was as fanatic a Cougar fan as I—even more so, being a native Houstonian. She was also the sweetest, most considerate, classy woman I had ever dated; we had been going out for a couple of years, and were expected to get married someday; I was working up to a proposal, even as I experienced an interior uneasiness that such a wonderfully kind lady might not be entirely suited to a gruff, malicious type like me.) In any event, we watched as the Cougars led for three quarters, and we brought the champagne to the table—and then, inexplicably, they blew it. Phi Slamma Jamma had one Achilles' heel, their dim-witted coach, Guy Lewis, he of the checkered towel, and whether it was Lewis's dumb strategy of running out the clock the last ten minutes, or some death wish on the part of the players themselves, momentum shifted to the canny North Carolina State men, who knew how to take advantage, and who stole the game with a three-point shot in the final seconds. Helen and I looked down at the tablecloth and candles, unable to face each other: The sickly grief we felt is indescribable.

I wonder, had the Cougars won, if I would have been carried on a wave of well-being toward Helen and proposed to her then and there, and might be married to her now.

The second utterly heartbreaking basketball game occurred in the final of the NBA play-offs between the New York Knicks and the Houston Rockets. Again Hakeem Olajuwon was involved, but this time I had returned to my New York roots and was 100 percent for the Knicks (led by my once-Georgetown enemy Patrick Ewing). This time the two teams were evenly matched; they had played to a 3–3 tie. No one could accuse Pat Riley of being a stupid coach; yet again I had the sensation of being stuck in time-stops-still molasses, doomed by one-dimensional strategy. This was the game in which John Starks took shot after shot, hogging the ball and hitting nothing. Every time I watched Starks square his shoulders and send up a clinker, I felt like Scottie Ferguson in *Vertigo*, trapped in a repetition-compulsion nightmare brought on by the endlessly circular defects of one's character. I was Starks, the arrogant street kid who cannot learn from his own limitations; I was Riley, the Armani-wearing fatalist who believed that you had to "play out" the hand that was dealt you, and leave with the gal that brung you. . . . This time I watched the game with two neighbors, visiting Danes from across the street who had caught Knicks fever, and who, when it was over, slunk away with that binger's sense of disbelief and guilt. The guilt was perhaps explained as: Had we really invested so much of our psychic energy in this foolishness? Yet there was also a film noirish edge to our shame, as though we had unwittingly committed a criminal act together. We had fallen for an unsuitable love object, a femme fatale with the eyes of John Starks.

One of the most ridiculous sports disappointments I ever experienced occurred not during a defeat to my team, but a victory. It was 1986. I had already had the good fortune to witness at the Astrodome what

. . . . . . . . . .

was in some people's opinion the single most exciting baseball game: the extra-inning finale between the Mets and Astros. Now the Mets were in the World Series, and my new girlfriend, Bonnie, came down to Houston to watch the climactic games with me. Bonnie, like many non-sportif New Yorkers, had been swept up in Mets mania, and found herself an obsessive devotee of Keith Hernandez, Gary Carter, Strawberry, Gooden, Mookie, etc. The Red Sox had a 3–2 edge in the Series. All would have gone nicely if the weather had cooperated; but it rained, the sixth game was postponed and moved to Saturday night. This posed a conflict: I already had tickets Saturday night to the premiere of a friend's symphony at the Houston Philharmonic. Actually, he was not quite a friend, but a warm acquaintance, the friend of a true friend of mine, a poet who was passionate about music—and who expected me to attend the premiere.

Here may be the place to point out that, in the arts community to which I belong, I know many people who have zero interest in sports, and who look askance at anyone who does. Many of these friends have no idea of my addiction. It would take too long to explain it, and I have no interest in trying to justify so baffling a habit or to convert them. An additional fact was that the poet, the composer, and their respective boyfriends were gay. Of course there are many gay sports fans, but these men were the sort of Wildean gay aesthetes who had not the least scintilla of curiosity about baseball. I wanted to keep their good opinion of me, and did not wish to flaunt my traditionally "manly" obsession in their faces.

In the end, I decided that the duties of friendship took precedence over the imperatives of romance and fandom, and so I told Bonnie we would have to attend the concert instead of staying home to watch the most important game of the year. Bonnie was a good sport; we drove to Jones Hall, with the game on the radio, and parked the car. As it happened, my friend's piece was the third on the program. We excused ourselves from Brahms, Schubert, and ran around trying to find some bar nearby with the World Series on. I don't know if you've ever been in downtown Houston, but its corporate headquarters turn ghost town on weekends; there were no bars within several blocks of the hall, and even the parking attendants (perhaps in revenge against the Mets for

· · · · · · · · ·

breaking the Astro fans' hearts) were not watching the game. Except for one, who told us the Mets were losing. We rushed back to the concert in time to hear my friend's symphony, which sounded in my admittedly distracted frame of mind like bombastic neo-Expressionism.

When the concert ended, we maneuvered the party of three gay couples and us to a restaurant/bar I was fairly sure had a TV. A very choppy time followed, in which postmortems of the concert and gossip about the art world were punctuated by Bonnie or me, unable to disguise our obsession any longer, leaping up to find out what was going on. This was the famous ninth inning in which Bill Buckner booted Mookie Wilson's single (which I did not see, by the way: I only heard a roar of disbelief go up at the bar, then rushed up to ask what had happened).

What I can never forgive myself for is that I not only missed one of the most celebrated World Series games, but denied poor Bonnie, who had flown down expressly to share the Series with me, the chance to see it. For me, after all, there will be other years, but Bonnie will never again get as swept up in baseball as she did in the fall of 1986. And, since I broke up with her three months later, through no fault of her own, her sacrifice was all the more in vain.

## 3. MAGIC

I am not otherwise superstitious, except when it comes to sports. Then I believe I can affect the outcome of a game by the purity of my heart (or lack of same), and the complicated workings of my karma as it intersects with the poor team that has fallen under my aegis. I regard myself as the equivalent of one of the Greek gods in Homer, who can affect the outcome of a battle up to a point, before His or Her own shortcomings play into the mix.

I vividly remember one of my more telling interventions. The New York Yankees and the Boston Red Sox were fighting to eliminate each other in a one-game division play-off, since both teams had finished with the exact same number of wins (ninety-nine) by season's end. It was the first time in thirty years that two teams had ended up tied for first in the American League; and it came about because the Red Sox had self-destructively blown a fourteen-game July lead and let the Yan-kees pass them, then pulled themselves together and caught up on the last day.

I was rooting for Boston because, I suppose, I felt sorry for the Red Sox, the way they'd suffered a nervous breakdown in the second half and started having dizzy spells in the outfield and missing the cutoff man; and because the Red Sox have traditionally been the favorite of writers (although some of that literary bathos about Bosox misfortune is tiresome beyond belief); but mostly because I had grown up a Dodger fan and a Yankee hater. The Yankees were considered the team of money, the Republican bankers who opened their wallets and bought up all the good free agents, while the Red Sox seemed more like old-fashioned working-class underdogs. Never mind that the Red Sox were also one of the wealthiest franchises, which bought up free agents and kept players loyal with fat contracts. In a showdown game, it is myths, not facts, that square off. We must honor the myths.

It was Rosh Hashanah and the public school where I worked was closed, so I had nothing in my way, nothing to do all day but get set for the big afternoon game. I watched the pregame show, during which the Yankee sportscasters made smug, asinine comments such as: "The Yanks may have the edge in starting pitchers. Young Ron Guidry's got ice water in his veins, but Boston's Mike Torrez is an emotional-type Latin player and he's liable to fall apart if the Yanks can get to him early. Whoever gets on the scoreboard first will have a decisive advantage."

The game started, and I was quietly pleased when Boston's Carl Yas-tremski, who at forty was regarded as so aged by the sportscasters that they openly suggested he retire, lined a home run into the bleachers to give the Red Sox a one-run lead. Then big Jim Rice, Boston's slugging star, added another run to their lead with a single up the middle. Mike Torrez was tooling along, cool as could be: The crybaby sportscasters were acting like every Yankee fly ball should have been a home run but was held up by the tricky Aeolian winds at Fenway Park. And Ron Guidry, "Louisiana Lightning" as they were fond of calling him, didn't seem to be pitching his sharpest. It was getting toward the sixth inning, and the usually chatterbox Yankee announcers were growing quieter. This could be it.

I started thinking, What if New York *didn't* make it into the World Series? Sure, the Yankees were a bunch of assholes, but they were also the hometown team, and if they lost it would be bad for commerce; the city wouldn't get that extra tax money; cabbies and hotels would suffer. I hadn't minded Boston taking the lead, but now they were acting cocky. I don't know what came over me but I began rooting for the Yankees.

They were still behind two to zip when they got two men on with singles, and up came Bucky Dent, their runt of a shortstop and my least favorite Yankee. He was a mediocre hitter and had lousy defensive range. I felt sorry for the once-superb shortstop, Phil Rizzuto, who had to watch him daily from the sportscasters' booth. So this punk got up to bat and fouled a ball off his foot and the trainer had to run out and spray some anesthetic on his ankle. It was pathetic. I said: "Oh, all right, let the little shrimp hit a home run." So on the very next pitch Dent swings and hits one into the net for the cheapest three-run homer you ever saw. Watching him trot around the bases, the picture of vanity — it sickened me to think what I had done. But I had to do it: I was a New Yorker even before I was a defender of the working class.

The Yankees picked up a few more insurance runs, and I started to lose interest in the game. Then, just to liven things up, I switched my magic to the other side. Sure enough, Boston came back with two clutch runs to tighten the score, 5–4. Mind you, I didn't want Boston to win, just to give the Yankees a good scare. Show them what gallantry in defeat looked like.

The stage was set for the bottom of the ninth inning: The weaker part of the Red Sox lineup would be at bat. All right, let a few of these singles hitters get on, I thought, and give big Jim Rice, their best hitter, a chance to crack one out of the park.

So, wouldn't you know it, both Burleson and Remy get on base somehow. At this point I unplugged my magic. I decided I would not root for either side; I would neutralize my powers, and drift with Fate. My only allegiance would be to historical inevitability. Someone had to lose, someone had to win: I was only a nonpartisan observer, like the Swiss. So Jim Rice, the black Hector, with 135-plus runs batted in, came to the plate. I had to bite my lips to keep myself from giving him

. . . . . . . . . .

the edge, because I really liked Jim Rice, his scowl, his focus, his warrior's calm demeanor. Rice fouled off a few, then lined a long fly ball to right field, missing a home run by not much, and smacked the top of the dugout in disgust. That left only one out remaining, in the person of the future Hall of Famer, Carl Yastremski. Yaz, who had gone on record earlier saying this was the single most important game in his twenty-two-year career, had already driven in two runs with a homer and a single. He was fittingly the Red Sox's last hope. He faced Goose Gossage, the Yankees' fireball reliever. Gossage got him to hit an easy pop-up to Graig Nettles at third. The Yankees ran onto the mound and hugged each other. The Yankee sportscasters acted as though they had known it all along. I snapped off the television set, with a Big Apple-patriotic, but empty, feeling in my stomach, not sure I had done the right thing.

# My Pirate Boyhood

. . . . . . . . . . . .

*by*
VIJAY SESHADRI

In October 1960, when the Pirates beat the Yankees in a World Series
that ended with a legendary home run, my parents and I were living on
Electric Street, in Ottawa. My father, after being awarded his American
Ph.D. in physical chemistry, had returned to his native India to collect
my mother and me and move us to Canada, where he was to take up a
postdoctoral fellowship with that country's National Research Coun-
cil. I have a tape of that last and most famous game of the 1960 Series,
the first World Series that I have a memory of. The tape was given to me
by a friend at work after he heard me lamenting over the fate of the Jim
Leyland Pittsburgh Pirates—a team that allegorized certain dementias
of our era by winning three straight division titles in the early nineties,
only to fall short of the pennant each time, and then to see itself deci-
mated by the economics of contemporary sports. I've played this tape
many times over the last three years, rehearsing its rhythms and antici-
pating, with a tension that familiarity only intensifies, the famous
home run—second baseman Bill Mazeroski's solo shot that opened
and closed the ninth, beating the Yankees 10–9, still the only home run
to decide a championship in the bottom of the ninth of the seventh
game of a Series. My interest in this game has something to do with the
satisfaction it provides: It must be one of the most spectacular baseball
games ever played. But it has much more to do with the fact that this
game marks a point in time when my life pivoted, when what I might

14

. . . . . . . . . .

have become began to be subsumed by what I became—half-alienated and half-assimilated, a hyphenated American and a Pirate fan.

My father maintains that he decided to leave India when he did because to do the kind of work he wanted to do he would have had to go to the north (we come from Bangalore, deep in the south, where the culture resembles the culture of North India as little as Italy's culture resembles Sweden's), and that he felt if he had to go north he might as well go all the way. I happen to know for a fact that my parents' desire to see me have a great academic career in science was crucial to their setting out on their long journey to another civilization, but I've never challenged this explanation my father gives for his motives. Not having had a great academic career in science—not having had a career in science at all—I'm naturally uncomfortable when I think about what they gave up. Bangalore must have been a hard place for my parents to go so far from when they did—not the megalopolis of today, where a lot of the world's computer software is being written, and where the newborn, capitalist, high-tech India chafes against the India whose problems seem intractable, but a gracious garden city, one of Asia's most beautiful. My parents were born into a community with deep roots in that region. They had only just stepped out of the old Indian world, the world that antedates the arrival of the British, and even of Islam, to the Subcontinent.

Considering how far they stepped, it's surprising how surefooted they were. In the mythology of my family, those years in Ottawa are described as being filled with possibility. My mother is the keeper of this myth. She was pregnant through much of that first year, giving birth to my sister just before the Kennedy Inauguration—an event greeted in Canada with the same hopefulness as elsewhere (including India, where you can still go into a sweet shop in an out-of-the-way village and find a framed photograph of the thirty-fifth American president hanging in a place of honor and garlanded with marigolds). The Inauguration, my sister's birth, her own strength and youth, and a new life in the New World have combined in my mother's memory to weave a powerful aura around those years. To this day, she will walk out of a room if anything bad is being said about the older members of the Kennedy clan.

The Kennedy years. Our Ottawa neighborhood was bounded on one side by my school, my fifty-cent barbershop, and the Parliament buildings near the river; and on the other by a little commercial strip with an I.G.A. and a fifty-cent movie theatre. The people who lived around us were named Matherson, Campbell, Jones. Their religion was nonconformist and their game was ice hockey. I never took to the hockey, though I played a lot of it. I possessed a talent for the religion, though. My parents had the residual piety that characterizes even the most agnostic Indians of their generation, and a God-is-a-diamond-with-many-facets attitude toward doctrine. When the mother of a friend of mine asked if I could accompany her son to Sunday school, my parents said yes, and I became a valued member of a Christian congregation. I might have been valued because I was seen as a heathen ripe for conversion, but I doubt it. Those people were generous and unintrusive and enlightened. They had a reticence and dignity appropriate to their climate and dispensation. I'm sure they liked me as much as they did because I was a loud and contented hymn singer, and almost letter-perfect in learning the Bible stories. My favorite story was the one about Joseph, who was depicted in our Bible reader wearing his coat of many colors while his jealous brothers circled around him, getting ready to throw him into the pit. My favorite hymn was "O God, Our Help in Ages Past," whose first stanza,

> O God, our help in ages past,
> Our hope for years to come,
> Our shelter from the stormy blast,
> And our eternal home.

still calls up for me an image of sticklike, barely discernible human figures toiling over an immense, featureless landscape.

My parents' attitude toward Christianity was refreshingly nonsectarian: they also sent me to Mass occasionally with our next-door neighbors, a Quebecois family who had moved to Electric Street about the same time we did from Hull, on the Quebec side of the Ottawa River. I squirmed through Mass, but the children of that family were my best friends, and they and their father were the ones who introduced me to the pagan worship of baseball. Of all the people I knew in

.  .  .  .  .  .  .  .  .  .  .

those years, their father is the only one whose face I can recollect without an effort of memory. A decade and a half later, my mother, who
keeps in touch with everyone she has ever been close to, told me that he
had committed suicide, a piece of news that gave what I remembered of
him a strong, graphic, permanent clarity.

His face was long, saturnine, and classically Gallic looking, with
bushy, emphatic eyebrows and a heavy forehead, which contributed to
the image I have of him as always scowling, even when he smiled. I was
never afraid of him—he was extremely kind to us children—but he
clearly had an uncontrollable nature. He coached a peewee baseball
league team that I played on with two of his sons and he drilled us mercilessly. Long after we were expected home for dinner, he had us out on
the field chasing fungoes or learning to slide away from the bag. He gave
elaborate lectures about baseball history, and about the game's finer
points: the position and function of the cutoff man, the proper proce-
dure for a rundown, when to bunt and when to swing away. And he was
competitive to the point of instability. During a game in the spring of
1961, while disputing a call at second base, he abused the umpire with
such sclerotic profanity that our team not only was made to forfeit the
game but was kicked out of the league entirely.

I don't know whether his being a Quebecois among British Canadi-
ans contributed to his volatility, but his family was set apart from the
social life around them. His children didn't go to public school with the
rest of us, but to a parochial school nearby. Other than myself, their
playmates were exclusively French-speaking kids from beyond our
street—kids who were perceived, unfairly but inevitably, as tougher
and more unruly and less hygienic than the rest of us. In October 1960,
I spent a lot of time in their backyard, playing catch with my first mitt
and shinnying up the smaller of their two maple trees. It was there that
I first heard about a city called New York, the mighty Yankees who
lived there, and the great contest then taking place to the south. The
whole family were Pirate fans. Their father listened to the games in the
afternoon and told us the results around dinnertime. And when the
Yankees were brought to ruin at the hands of their improbable opponents, he had us rake up the fallen maple leaves in a pile, which he
lighted to make a bonfire for us to dance around in joy and vindication.

The next August we moved to Columbus, Ohio, where my father joined Ohio State's chemistry department. When asked where I come from today by people who expect to hear the name of a place in India, I say Ohio and go on to describe my classic Ohio boyhood—tree fort building, crawdad hunting, fishing for bluegills with dough balls—and the streams and woods and railroad tracks near where we lived.

Actually, my Ohio boyhood was classic only in its overall unhappiness. Disastrously for my athletic and social development, I had exhibited a degree of intellectual precocity while in Canada, and had been skipped two grades. As a result I was forced to play with kids who were larger and more coordinated than I was, and I became one of those forlorn, benchwarming children who are a source of pity and terror to their peers. Baseball was the worst, because I always had dreams of baseball glory. (Well into my twenties, in fact, I would fantasize miraculous chains of events that led me to the pitcher's mound in a big-league game.) When I got to bat, it was usually because I was small and could be relied on to draw a walk; when I was sent out to field, it was usually *way* out, to left or right.

There were more complicated problems, too. Small, brown, bespectacled, alien, and saddled with a name that others thought was unpronounceable, I was an easy target for the casual cruelties of childhood. On a baseball diamond during a game at the lunch recess in the spring of 1964, I was informed, by a kid half again my size, that I was, if I remember his words correctly (and I do), "nothing but a nigger." (About a year later, this same kid did me another injury. While fooling around on the railroad tracks near our house, I fell and gashed my leg to the bone on a spike protruding from a railroad tie. Coming across me as I hobbled home, he half-carried me the rest of the way, robbing me of the satisfaction of feeling contempt for him and prematurely introducing me to the hopeless complexities of experience.)

I didn't respond well to the social pressures I was encountering. I began to do badly in school, which was upsetting, to say the least, to my father. I became delinquent and secretive. The sport I excelled in was pyromania. One day while playing with candles and Ohio Blue Tip matches—which I liked because you could light them on the seat of your jeans, the zipper of your fly, even your teeth—I accidentally set my bed on fire. Firecrackers were illegal in Ohio, but I used my paper-route money to buy them from Ohio State students who smuggled them in from Kentucky and carried on a brisk contraband business. The ones I liked best were the big ones—the cherry bombs and, best of all, the M-80s. (My soul still thrills horribly when I see an M-80, with the evil little fuse sticking out of its side.) I threw them like depth charges into unpeopled swimming pools, and on weekends staged elaborate, solitary pyrotechnics at vacant construction sites near where we lived. When I was ten, after weeks of pleading, I persuaded my mother—a soft touch when it comes to her children—to buy me a BB gun. My father made her take it back the next day. I mourned that gun for years, and it was a long time before I recognized how shocking it must have been for my father, who grew up in an intellectual climate imbued with the presence of Gandhi, to come home and see his son cradling a not lethal but nevertheless dangerous replica of a Winchester repeating rifle.

Apart from interdiction and incarceration, my parents—disciplined, hardworking exemplars of immigrant virtue—didn't know what to do with me. Life had become more complicated for them, too. It is sometime in the mid-sixties that I date the beginning of my mother's long return to the religion of her people. My father was wrapped up in his work. He wasn't neglectful—he would regularly descend from his nimbus of equations and attempt to guide my education. My tastes in reading ran to Hardy Boys mysteries, sports biographies of people like Red Grange, and a book that I can't recall the title of but that I read again and again, which told the story of a girl and a boy who had various adventures on a tropical island, and who eventually grew up to become Queen Liliuokalani, the last native ruler of Hawaii, and her prince consort. My father tried to tempt me with more edifying material, chiefly the American naturalist fiction that he had read in college—*The Grapes of Wrath*, *Studs Lonigan*, Dreiser's Frank Cowperwood trilogy. Mostly, though, he preached the gospel of science, telling me stories that revealed the human side of figures like Einstein and Fermi, and describing the careers of renowned twentieth-century Indian mathematicians and physicists such as Srinivasa Ramanujan, S. N. Bose, and C. V. Raman.

In those years before the Immigration Act of 1965 abolished the rigid quotas imposed on Asian immigration, there were hardly any other Indians around. Dressed in her sari, with her bangles, and with the *bindhi* that signified her married status placed carefully on her forehead, my mother could be spotted a mile off. These days the smell of Indian spices—of cardamom, asafetida, fenugreek, black mustard seed, and turmeric—makes me ecstatic with expectation. In those days these same smells, emanating from our kitchen and wafting through the corridor of our apartment building, made me wince with an immediate, intimate, olfactory awareness of how different we were. At a parents' day at Crestview Junior High School, I pretended not to notice my mother when she came to look in on one of my classes—an act for which she has never forgiven me, and which she still holds up to me as an example of my ingratitude.

Columbus was (and still is) a football town, but it also had a Triple A farm club, the Jets, at that time a part of the Pirate farm system. It was understood that the town orbited the Pirate sun, and in the summer of 1967, when we were preparing to leave Columbus and move to Pittsburgh itself (my father was advancing professionally, which seemed to involve an ongoing nomadism), my Pirate boyhood began in earnest. By this time, my isolation had become as much a state of mind as a social fact. I had two friends, classmates of mine, but I was twelve and they were fourteen. The gap between a slighty chubby, indistinct, prepubescent twelve-year-old boy and a teenager of fourteen is enormous. I still had a fetish about my firecrackers, while my friends had moved on to *Playboy* centerfolds and shoplifting. They performed, or claimed they performed, secret acts with the girls of their acquaintance. I tried to keep up, but the hormones just weren't there yet. So I resigned myself to circling our neighborhood endlessly on my bike and spending hours learning how to do a back flip, a full gainer, and a half gainer from the diving board of the public pool a block away.

The strongest memories I have of that last summer in Columbus center on the passionate identification I developed with the Pirates' great right fielder Roberto Clemente. Clemente was flirting with a .400 average through the first half of the 1967 season, and getting the kind of national attention that he always craved. I watched him on TV whenever I could, and he was the first player from whose performance I derived a satisfaction I would call aesthetic. He was a compact, elegant, laconic presence on the diamond, spare and geometric, with a sprinter's legs. His fielding and throwing were legendary—even then he was recognized as one of the very best ever at his position. Among his peers, only Willie Mays, from whom he had picked up the famous basket catch when the two of them played winter ball in 1954 for Puerto Rico's Santurce club, possessed a comparable grace and aplomb in the field. He didn't have the marvellous Mays liquidity—everything about Clemente was angular and emphatic—but like Mays his movements left you with the impression that he lived outside his body and commanded it effortlessly from a great distance. He was a bad-ball hitter— about as far away as you could get, in the realm of greatness, from a student of the art like Ted Williams or a street-smart opportunist like Pete Rose—and a fierce, feral protector of the plate. With two strikes on him, he could foul off ball after ball, driving the pitcher crazy, until he got a pitch he could work with.

I used to follow the fluctuations of his batting average with an arithmetical intensity. Not content with the meager statistics that the paper provided, I built my own landscape of numbers around him, topographically dense and various, with interesting declivities and elevations. I waited every day for the afternoon paper, the *Dispatch*, to arrive. When I got my hands on the sports pages, I took them to the table in our dining alcove, where I had pencil and paper ready. I divided his at-bats into his hits myself and calculated his average out to six digits. Then I determined what his average would be if he went five-for-five the next game, or three-for-four, or three-for-three. I'd do this five, sometimes even ten, games into the future. I projected almost inhuman final averages for him—Rogers Hornsby's modern-day record of .424, for example—and then calculated backward, on the basis of four at-bats a game, the number of times he had to hit safely in the remaining games to reach it. If my sister disturbed me in the middle of my insane projects, I pounced on her with a fury.

This numbers mania subsided after a while, but my identification with Clemente went on deepening. I had to turn off the radio or the TV if he struck out. His successes transported me. I was at once shocked and satisfied when, in a game that August, he lined a drive back to the pitcher's mound and broke the leg of the awesome Cardinal right-hander Bob Gibson. Through the rest of Gibson's career, I felt toward him the solicitude we reserve for people whom we've injured without meaning to. The game that has pleased me the most in my years of following baseball was one between the Pirates and Cincinnati, a game that the Reds won 8–7. Clemente batted in all seven Pittsburgh runs, going five-for-five, with a triple and two home runs. I thought that this effort was incredibly poignant in its doomed and solitary heroism.

The only thing I relished about our move to Pittsburgh, which otherwise did not make me happy, was the fact that now I was in the Pirate home world. For the next three years, until I went to college in 1970, I was familiar with pretty much every game they played. I didn't get to the ballpark often though. My father couldn't tolerate more than four or five excursions a season, and I couldn't rely on friends because all through high school I refused to make friends. I was fed up with my parents' wanderings and sick of my ambiguous social status, and had decided to go it alone. So through those springs and sweltering summers, when the country was experiencing race riots, assassinations, and the divisions arising from the war in Vietnam, I could be found either in our basement, watching the one or two games that were broadcast weekly on TV, or lying on the floor in our living room, next to our Grundig radio, listening to the play-by-play relayed by Bob (the Gunner) Prince, the gravelly voice of the Pirates, and his sidekick Nellie King.

Clemente had an arthritic back—the result of a car accident in the fifties and the source of the physical frailty that became one of the causes of bad feeling between him and the baseball world—and after each pitch he would step out of the batter's box and whip his neck to the side, as if trying to realign his vertebrae. Though he could hit home runs, he was known for line drives, high averages, and two-hundred-hit seasons. This was upsetting to him, I believe, and to me, as well. I used to curse Forbes Field—that beautiful, now-vanished, old park, where the game was played the way it should be—because its spaciousness had forced him to relinquish power for the sake of average and to resist the temptation to swing for the distant fences. I also felt that his teammates let him down, although they were all fantastic ballplayers. Some of them—Willie Stargell, Matty Alou, Mazeroski—were stars in their own right, but nothing they could do was enough for me. I felt a general animus toward the Pittsburgh pitching staff, and a particular one toward Bob Veale, the gifted but wild Pirate fastballer, because he didn't have the control to be the stopper the Pirates needed. Clemente deserved better; he deserved Gibson or Ferguson Jenkins or Denny McLain.

I found his character as compelling as his play. Much of what I remember about him has been interwoven with the things I have read or heard over the years. But the aura he projected was unmistakable even then, and even to my relatively uninformed adolescent faculties. Moody, sensitive, forbidding, his coal black, faintly Aztec features usually scowling, he walked the earth feeling aggrieved and misunderstood. He had volatile relations with his managers, and his relations with journalists were bad until his very last years. I remember clearly that he was vocal about the effects of racism on his career—and vocal at a time when there were far fewer blacks in the major leagues than there are now, and when the reserve clause gave management enormous power over players. I found out later, when I read Phil Musick's biography, that he was convinced he had finished so low in the balloting for the 1960 MVP trophy because of the color of his skin, and so refused to wear the 1960 World Series ring. He had a running war with the press over the physical ailments that regularly kept him out of games. The local press was unsympathetic, and he would make matters worse with his responses to their provocations. When the broadcaster Dick Stockton suggested that he wasn't a team player, Clemente threatened to kill him if he came into the clubhouse. He had an inimitable way of giving ammunition to his detractors. Asked once how he was feeling before a game, he replied, "My bad shoulder is good, but my good shoulder is bad"—this in that thick Puerto Rican accent of his, which people were not above making fun of in those days, and which always gave me a pained sense of his vulnerability when I heard it in a postgame interview after he'd done something marvellous on the field. I interpreted him in a way that harmonized with my own social isolation: nursing a bitter, private grief for him, I projected onto him not only my dreams of glory but the feelings I had about my complicated social circumstances. I remember reading a story that left me with the impression that his social circle didn't extend any farther than the other Hispanics in baseball—Orlando Cepeda, the Alou brothers, Juan Marichal—and I was indignant.

My Pirate boyhood ended with Roberto Clemente's death, in 1972, in a plane crash off Puerto Rico while he was helping ferry supplies to victims of that year's earthquake in Nicaragua. By that time, other obsessions had come to join, and largely replace, baseball. I was eighteen, a junior in college, and deeply into the counterculture. I had all sorts of revisionist explanations of experience, some of which I applied to his abrupt departure from the world. Though I mourned him when he died, I didn't share the widespread opinion that his death was heroic. I thought it was unnecessary, even absurd. I suspected compensatory impulses at work in his disastrous humanitarian gesture, impulses that I ascribed to his social awkwardness. I now saw vanity as a driving force in his character (he was vain, but no more so than other players at his level of achievement). He had had a splendid World Series against the Orioles in 1971, finally becoming famous in the way Mays and Hank Aaron and Frank Robinson were, and I imagined that this grand justification of his talent had led him to commit an act of hubris, with its attendant consequences. He had come to see himself not just as a baseball hero but as someone with a mission to the world.

All this was unfair to him—he had grown up poor and wanted to give something back; it was as simple as that—but I'd been robbed of maybe two or three more .300 seasons and four or five hundred more hits. It took quite a while for me to recognize how perfect he had been for my peculiar, Indian adolescent romance of hero-worship—complex, human, uncomfortable in the world he lived in, but nevertheless astonishing and unequalled—and how much he had meant to me. Recently I saw in the news that they were demolishing an old skyscraper in Pittsburgh to make way for urban redevelopment—a skyscraper that had a gigantic mural of Clemente, along with other greats of Pittsburgh sports, on one side. On TV, the building was there, with the mural visible, and then it imploded in a column of dust that itself collapsed and

. . . . . . . . . .

spread out into the surrounding streets. There's another gigantic mural of Clemente, on a wall of a housing project at the edge of Harlem that is named after him. You can see it from the West Side I.R.T. local after it emerges briefly from its tunnel and runs on elevated tracks between the 116th and 137th Street stations. There he is, the Pride of Puerto Rico, facing the city. When I find myself on that subway line, I sometimes stand up in the car near the 125th Street station and look at him as long as I can.

When Clemente comes up in the bottom of the eighth, New York is ahead 7–5. The Yankees have already scored two runs in their half of the inning, turning a tense, unresolved 5–4 ball game into something a little different. The Pirates, in turn, dormant since the second when they scored the last two of the four runs credited to them at the end of the seventh, have, upon seeing the Yankee express getting ready to roll out of the station, suddenly come alive and have bounced back with a run. Gino Cimoli, a "handsome young man from the Golden Gate city of San Francisco," is already across, driven in by a Dick Grote single. At this very moment, Tony Kubek, the Yankee shortstop, is being taken in an ambulance to an emergency room, having been hit in the Adam's apple by a Bill Virdon ground ball bouncing wickedly off the hard Forbes Field infield. The eighth inning has been a long one, filled with pitching changes, colloquies, asides, hesitations, and ruminations, with players, managers, and coaches hitching their pants and squirting tobacco juice. But these delicious, quotidian baseball rhythms can't disguise the dread and nervous tension that has overcome everyone in the ball park. The 38,683 paid fans are up and roaring in the stands. They sound like an amplified gravel crusher, but they are, nonetheless, a civil crowd. They have given Kubek a fine standing ovation as he was escorted off the field and have done the same for Yankee pitcher Bobby Shantz ("Little Bobby Shantz," in the cheerfully insensitive description of the announcer) when he is pulled by Casey Stengel and replaced by Jim Coates after the Grote single.

Virdon is on third. Grote is on second. There are two out. Clemente fouls off the first pitch. (In the opinion of the play-by-play announcer, he is a little anxious.) He fouls off the second pitch, and does the same with the third, breaking his bat in the process. A momentary lull in the action, filled with the roaring of the crowd. The next pitch is a ball, low and outside. On the pitch after that, he hits a little dribbler ten or twelve feet to the right of first base. There is a play at first, but the Yankee first baseman, Moose Skowron, takes the ball to the plate, where Virdon slides in under the tag and scores the sixth Pirate run. Everyone is safe; Clemente is on at first, with an infield hit and a run driven in; the score is now 7–6. The next batter is the catcher Hal Smith, who has played only half an inning in this game, having replaced the starter, Smoky Burgess, yanked for a pinch runner in the bottom of the seventh. On a 2–2 pitch, Hal Smith hits a three-run home run over the left field wall, and Forbes Field explodes. Forbes Field, the announcer tells us, is "an outdoor insane asylum." The gravel crusher is deafening. "We have seen and shared in one of baseball's great moments," the announcer says. His partner adds, "This is one of the most dramatic home runs of all time."

When this game is remembered in the future, it will be remembered for the Mazeroski home run in the next inning. The home run will dwarf Mazeroski's brilliant career as a second baseman (he will win eight Gold Gloves before he's through and set the record for career double plays at his position), and it will sit like a dolmen in the landscape of Pirate and Yankee collective memory, obscuring, by its monumental presence, the intricate life that made it possible. People will inevitably forget that Mazeroski's shot was anticlimactic, that it unjustly and abruptly punctured a struggle of such dizzy equilibrium that it should have gone on, long into the extra innings, to end not in violence but in exhaustion and error.

But here and now the eighth inning seems to have lasted longer than the game itself. The announcers understand this, though they can't quite articulate it. They, along with the people in the stands, are having a hard time crawling out of the dream of the eighth. They can hardly make sense of the terrible top half of the ninth, when, with only three outs left to them, the Yankees claw back and tie the game. Events are outpacing their descriptions; their bag of superlatives has been empty for a while. They seem not to be paying attention to Mazeroski when he leads off the bottom of the inning and hits the second pitch over the

. . . . . . . . . .

left field wall, taking the air out of the game and the season. They are still back in the top half of the ninth, trying to grasp the fact that the Yankees, the mighty Yankees, the winners so far of eighteen World Championships, the team that at the end of the millennium will be acknowledged as the greatest professional sports franchise of the century, are back. They are still trying to absorb the fact that the game that everyone thought was over now has to be understood as being unfinished, and unfinishable.

# A Higher Plane

. . . . . . . . . .

*by*
WAYNE FIELDS

I.

In my remembering basketball begins twice. First, there are vague reminiscences of my youngest aunt playing in a small-town high-school gymnasium, only at the time—my fourth or fifth year—I was unaware that there existed places larger than Wyaconda, Missouri, nor did I realize that my aunt was a member of a team involved in a game with another team. Rather I remember thinking it odd to see her bounce a ball and run around in front of people wearing such peculiar clothes. In those days "girls" basketball was the most important athletic activity in places like Wyaconda, towns where graduating classes numbered in the low two figures and sports requiring more than five on a side were virtually impossible to offer. That I retain any recollection of that first exposure to the game, is due I am sure to my special fondness for that aunt and my amazement at the uncharacteristic cheering of an audience of normally reserved Midwesterners.

That is why I did not, a few years later, much associate my own play with the oversized ball I had inherited from my father with his sister and the game I had previously observed. My attention was almost wholly taken by the near impossibility of controlling a ball too large for my childish hands and the added complications of its being both slightly out of round and having a tear that exposed the rubber bladder and left a flap of leather to further frustrate my bouncing efforts. Memory here focuses more on equipment than skill, more on preparation

. . . . . . . . . .

than on play. Having a ball, no matter how deformed it might be, took you only half way. A basket was also required, and what stands out most vividly in my early basketball experience was my constant effort to find a suitable rim. Not that my standards were very high. I was unaware that there were specifications other than a general circularity to be met, and so I made do for a while with an old tire, split to provide an opening sufficient to allow the ball to pass through, nailed to a wall of my grandparents' barn. But the opening was never sufficient, and the end of all my effort was less a basket through which the ball could pass and more a nest on which, under the best of circumstances the ball might perch. Wire offered the most obvious solution but made such a fragile hoop that only a perfect shot or one entirely off target failed to bend it hopelessly out of shape. The only improvised goal that actually worked, predictably enough to all but my exacting mind, was a bushel basket with its bottom knocked out. This I eventually accepted but unhappily; it seemed so crude, so old fashioned and country hick-ish, and I wanted desperately to be up to date and—if I'd known what the term meant—sophisticated.

In any event in my own story this is how the game began, with an athletic aunt in a small-town gymnasium and the constant fretting about equipment, the search for an adequate hoop and the regular manicuring of the flap on my only basketball as I tried to bring it as close to round as possible.

The official story, that which puts my own into a larger historical and social context, is at once both parallel to my own and wholly different. But, as official stories so often go, this one grows more unlikely with every passing day, how Dr. James Naismith invented basketball in order to keep students at a Young Men's Christian Association Training School sufficiently exercised during the winter months, how he used peach baskets for goals, how the first players were required to "throw" the ball from the spot on the floor where they caught it, how the score often remained in single figures. Even after the associations of young Christians yielded the ball to more offensive college players and the point-a-minute teams of the thirties came along, the game remained quaint by modern standards. Part of the explanation is easy— the result of rule changes, taller and more athletic players, new coaching strategies—but there were other more subtle and probably more significant causes, matters both of play and sport. Whatever the reasons, basketball became a different game—"our" game—after the Second World War and, while baseball and football continue presumptuously to claim the title, established itself during those years as uniquely America's game.

The concept of play seems simple enough, even for children. For me, growing up, it was easily the most attractive of the three acceptable alternatives to work, the other two being sleep and church. Sport, on the other hand, was more difficult to grasp, since—according to all the best authorities—it required organization, practice, dedication. To my mind that made it seem very much like work, and in fact, while most of our official sports begin with play, they soon turn the better players into workers and the less good into fans, with the latter regularly complaining that the former do not play hard enough to deserve our loyalty or to earn their high-priced keep. But the changes in basketball as a form of play came about, for most of us born after 1940 because of changes in the sport; the game that, by the mid-fifties, we watched on television, was one much different from the one our fathers had played.

II.

Though baseball and football have been advertised more frequently as America's national sports, their claims are primarily those of sheer numbers of spectators and the pretentious pageantry they have invented for both the amusement of huge audiences and their own self-glorification. As outdoor games played on large chunks of real estate or in puffed-up structures with seating capacities far greater than any gymnasium, they have become preeminent crowd events and have produced annual spectaculars—a World Series and a Super Bowl—whose significance is measured in terms of a viewing audience of millions. By contrast, while basketball's own championships at both the collegiate and professional levels enjoy enormous television appeal, it is a more intimate affair, requiring only half as many players as its rivals, and with its action kept much closer at hand. Since Naismith designed it all

. . . . . . . . . .

for winter when, in pre-dome days, northern ball fields were snow covered and bleachers too cold for comfort, basketball games at every level are cozy affairs, played in rooms sufficiently warmed so that fans can watch in shirtsleeves and competitors can play in the silkier equivalent of men's underwear—or more precisely the sort of underwear common at midcentury. This informality, in contrast with heavily ritualized baseball and the armored combat of football, is part of the reason basketball has never appealed to the gurus of culture. It is an approachable sport, its underdressed competitors clearly human, its near continuous action undivided by the solemn interruptions marking changes in act and scene that football and baseball require. As a consequence it does not invite the reverential attitude so readily bestowed on those outdoor contests where a disembodied voice solemnly intones every down or at-bat with an epic pretension.

Yet nowhere in American sport were the social changes of the 1950s and 1960s more obvious than on the basketball court. As Ole Miss and Alabama and other Southern athletic powers integrated their football teams, little of the change was visible from the stands, so much were the players concealed under pads and clothing. Even major league baseball, despite being a warm-weather game, covers its athletes sufficiently to make racial differences nearly unrecognizable by spectators. But basketball flaunts its flesh, and it, above all other sports, revealed the changes taking place in American life and our sense of who we were in the second half of the twentieth century. It made evident not simply the presence of black people in America, but also the fact that traditionally all-white teams could only remain competitive by becoming more inclusive. While a few monochromatic teams rose to national distinction, these were increasingly all black, and the most successful programs were those in which blacks and whites were teammates, a situation that was also true for baseball and football, but not nearly so obviously.

Basketball yearbooks and encyclopedias give eloquent testimony to the change, less in their texts than in their pictures. Shots of plays, photos of teams, publicity portraits of All-Star teams uniformly reveal a sport to all appearances reserved for white males until the 1950s. The names in the early captions hint at the ethnic diversity of America—St. John's "Wonder Five" of the late twenties consisted of Begovich, Kinsbrunner, Posnack, Gerson, and Schuckman—but the sturdy young men in the team photo are all quite clearly of European ancestry. Then, after midcentury, the pictures change. Walter Dukes, Most Valuable Player of the National Invitational Tournament (NIT), looms large in the images of the 1952–53 season; and in the 1954–55 season, the one in which the modern game irrefutably declared itself, Bill Russell dominated the NCAA championships, while Maurice Stokes (playing for the fourth-place team) won the NIT's MVP award, and Si Green led all scorers in the championship game.

But more than color is exposed in these black-and-white photos; play is on a different plane, elevated by players—black and white—breaking free from the floor-bound sport of the older pictures. It has clearly become a game translated into the air, much of the photographer's frozen action now taking place above the rim. This is the play that postwar kids emulated, this soaring game that Oscar Robertson and Elgin Baylor taught us with their gravity-defying leaps. A part of the effect may well be the improved architecture and lighting that gave the game, whether seen in photographs or in person, an airiness it lacks in prewar photos, but there is a difference in the players, besides their changing colors and their increasing size, a lightness and grace that is harder to discern in other sports. Emphasis has shifted from the horizontal to the vertical, from deliberation to quickness. Set plays give way to an elaborate choreography, the game now an artistic performance marked by changing rhythms and tempos, bodies moving with balletic grace and precision, seven-foot centers pirouetting toward the basket, guards leaning backward into fadeaway jumpers, the *pas de deux* of a pick-and-roll, forwards leaping above the lane in elegant body-arcing hooks. All this makes for a new game, one exquisitely subtle and yet physically brutal in what it demands of body and will.

For those of us who played basketball after 1945 the attraction was no longer that of a warm winter activity—we played year round and mostly outside—it was rather this promise of breaking free, an anticipation of flight, of lifting our bodies to heights we would have thought

. . . . . . . . . .

humanly impossible except we had seen it done. The prewar players were, above all else, well grounded, crouching low as they moved the ball around the floor until the best shooter could launch a two-hand set-shot. Even their free throws, those low-dipping, underhand wrist shots, emphasized a gravity that seemed to require all of their energy just to get the ball into the air. After 1945, however, the game took a lighter turn and became increasingly a matter of improvisation, still played between the same lines, but on a different plane and with each player bringing to the old simplicity his or her personal complications.

## III.

As important as the postwar changes were for basketball as a sport, of far greater cultural significance was how it changed as a form of play, as a pastime engaging millions of Americans, far more at any given moment than can be found playing either of the other national pastimes. A simple count of hoops, a recognition of their ubiquity regardless of the economic or racial makeup of a community, rural as well as urban, testifies to basketball's importance for Americans (at least since the Second World War) and the degree to which it is embedded in our national experience.

The novels that best embody the masculine ethos of the second half of the twentieth century in America are John Updike's Rabbit Angstrom stories, and they begin and end, as does Rabbit's adult life, with basketball. "Boys," opens *Rabbit, Run*, "are playing basketball around a telephone pole with a backboard bolted to it. Legs, shouts. The scrape and snap of Keds on loose alley pebbles seems to catapult their voices high into the moist March air blue above the wires." And that is how it began for many of us, not just basketball, but our sense of a physical self and the changes we were undergoing. This was the game that literally measured us, established heights to which we could aspire and, sometimes, achieve in a fleeting moment that we would recall over years of decline and disappointment. It is a game whose trajectory matches that of our own bodies.

In my version of things, basketball became the most important game in America for Rabbit Angstrom's generation because of the Second World War and the departure of so many fathers from the boyhoods of their sons. Basketball is the only one of America's team sports that we could play alone. Unassisted, a kid can't learn to throw and catch, regardless of the shape of the ball, but he or she can dribble and shoot and develop the first and most basic basketball skills without anyone else around. That is why, somewhere in the early- to midforties—in the absence of fathers, uncles, and older brothers—hoops began to appear on telephone poles, barns, and garages, sometimes regulation rims but more likely makeshift affairs of the sort I constructed. It makes little difference for a game that requires only a ball and a hole carved out of air. And so, a decade after the war, signs of the game were everywhere, in urban alleys and suburban driveways and rural barnyards, evidence of kids whose out-of-school lives had not yet been neatly divided into official "activities" complete with coaches and chauffeuring moms, kids who played alone in the twilight in all but the coldest months, bouncing the ball erratically at first and then with the regular staccato of a more practiced hand, lofting shots wildly, using their entire bodies to compensate for still unrealized height and strength until the day that shooting, too, became a matter of control and finesse.

The modern game begins as a solitary affair, one kid, one ball, one hoop. Perhaps because my family moved frequently during my childhood (an itinerant life built around seasonal highway construction and winter returns to my grandparents' farm), I think of the game beginning in a necessary isolation, necessary because other kids weren't always around, but due also to a certain sense of propriety; a proper respect for team play that requires diligent individual preparation. This is a game in which, even under the best of circumstances, the risk of personal humiliation is exceedingly high, and it cannot be entered lightly. Before public exposure, the beginning player must work alone, practicing at the park or the schoolyard when the older kids have abandoned the asphalt courts, practicing in the alley behind the house, practicing wherever there is room to bounce a ball and no one to ridicule our first clumsy efforts.

. . . . . . . . . . .

When at last my father became a carpenter working at heavy construction, I took my own game to a new environment, one where older kids showed their stuff on playgrounds, one where comparisons could be made, distinctions in ability clearly drawn. This was no longer a peach-basket affair and demanded training of a sort I had not previously undertaken. After watching one evening (from a discreet distance) the play of others, I sat down at home and sketched out an accounting of myself, the strengths and weaknesses my personal preparation had to accommodate. I took a sheet of notebook paper and drew a line down the middle, marking the left side with a plus sign and the right with a minus. Then I wrote in the margin "Height." I checked the minus side. "Speed." Another negative. "Strength." Another mark on the right. This was bookkeeping that required only red ink. Then I wrote down "Quick" and managed to move the check to the middle of the page. Still, I recall the overwhelming sense of futility, but then I scrawled at the bottom of the page in my twelve-year-old's hand, "I am smart and have long arms and work hard and might grow." In the weeks that followed this painful assessment, I developed every move I could imagine that might help a not very fast, short kid outmaneuver a better-designed opponent, an opponent that I daily re-invented as I practiced running hook shots banked from the odd angles I thought taller players would concede to me, invisible defenders who skidded past my sudden stops as I learned to launch quick jumpers. Whenever in the day's failing light I could get a basket to myself, I practiced into the dark against my imagined versions of the players who had, earlier, held the court.

At this point in every player's development, basketball shifts from being merely a challenge to the flesh and becomes a test of the imagination. The whole game must be imagined in order to provide the singular work of dribbling and shooting with a context that will make of them the serious play that all serious sport is about. And always this individual rehearsing is for the eventual presence of others, teammates whose idiosyncracies must complement your own, allowing all the solitary pieces to come from the dull light of our private courts into the gymnasium of the real thing. This is a game in which the feint is as important as the completed gesture, and the subtle shifts of body, the slight turns of head, all the misdirections that will tempt an opponent into premature commitment, have been endlessly repeated before there is anyone to fool, part of the charade by which the individual prepares for the team play that lies ahead.

The repertoire of moves that characterize each player testifies to this loneliness in which the game begins and is the basis for subsequent success in the game. Though basketball requires continual improvisation, the basis of this adaptation remains the moves rehearsed alone, developed around the idiosyncrasies of the individual's body and talent. Eventually the results must be tested in actual competition, then revised or replaced, accordingly, in yet more private sessions. Much of what a kid practices in games of one-on-none has to be discarded in team play, thrown out because it is too fanciful with all its dips and exaggerated swoops and turns. And yet it is here the building blocks are first established. Basketball at every level is a matter of fundamentals, and the key is to repeat the same movements over and over but in new combinations and with the variations, made increasingly subtle, that cloak their basic nature. No matter how far the lean that pulls an opponent out of position, the same squared-up body must precede the shot. No matter the gestures that conceal actual intent, the arm has to return to proper alignment, the wrist must follow through. Solitary practice has a double purpose: to learn those parts of the game dictated by physics and the body (the common skills), and to develop sufficient originality to deceive a defender.

This imaginative practice provides the genius of modern basketball. The individual preparation that precedes team play is only as good as the self-created opposition, and in this peculiar partnership lies much of the explanation both of how the game is played and the importance it assumes for those who play it. The quality of the player created by solitary practice is determined, ultimately, by the talent of the invisible opposition he or she has been practicing against all those years alone. If they have prepared only by playing opponents slow enough of mind and foot to be fooled by the most obvious fake and to allow the most outlandish of shoots, real opponents will expose the mental sloth or dullness that, as much as any physical limitation, restricts their play. As the smart player improves so does the other self, the one silently contesting every effort.

The key to understanding as well as playing basketball is in the way players of all ages work alone, how intensely they focus on the task at hand, how elaborately they stage a performance that resembles some bizarre Kabuki danced out in silence and isolation. Kids, still too small to actually get the ball to the rim, learn the gestures of the game, mimic the fakes and drives of their favorite star in these elaborate routines in which they train their bodies for the moves that will eventually provide the signature of their game. As they grow their performance shifts from a stock of broad grimaces and outlandish gestures to the intricacies of dribbling, shifting the ball from hand to hand, and keeping the efforts of legs and feet coordinated with those of hands and arms. At this stage the degree of seriousness becomes obvious to even the most casual observer, the concentration, the endless repetitions. What was barely contained self-indulgence becomes a display of self-conscious discipline, subtilizing what had been extravagant and perfecting an economy of movement in slight feints that allows sudden bursts of redirected energy. Eventually what had been clumsy grows into a grace unique to this game; that which had been dissected so that each segment of a larger motion might be perfected is reconciled in the seamless fluidity of a drive to the basket or a jump shot from twenty feet out. No matter the level of skill a player eventually achieves or the teams he or she eventually joins, this private practice is never outgrown. NBA stars rehearse in the same way as kids on playgrounds; even in warm-ups amid the pregame hoopla, they isolate themselves to juke and fake against imaginary opponents before taking their shots.

One of the oddities of basketball is that players, on their own, practice only offensive moves, yet their eventual success depends upon their capacity to envision a defense they never develop for themselves until they participate in team play. Basketball solitaire is a game in which the visible player always has the ball, one in which even in failure—a missed shot, a double dribble—he or she remains in control, acting rather than reacting, going for the hoop rather than blocking someone else's way. The point of the game, always, is to get free, free from a defender—even an imaginary one—and, ultimately momentarily released from all that ordinarily holds us down, to leap higher than we ever have before and to hang at the zenith of that triumph for as long as possible.

IV.

The most obvious way to think of one-on-none basketball is as preplay, preparation for the real game, the teams for which this diligent practice will one day qualify you. That is the progressive American way, working our way up the ladder, building toward a larger arena and greater applause. And the uniqueness of basketball lies in the way that it eventually synthesizes all the improvisational skills, all the idiosyncracy developed in private with a group effort, a blending of individualism with community that fits our better notions of America itself—*plura* and *unum*. In few other activities do we see the one and the many so brilliantly combined, individuals containing themselves on behalf of a communal success, yet also encouraged to their greatest displays of virtuosity by teammates whose deft passes and high lobs make possible the moves and elevation that are the stuff of highlight reels and enduring memories.

Most of us first included others in our play with pickup games of one-on-one, another kid, sometimes a sibling, who blocked our path to the basket, lunged for the ball, in short found ways to uncover all our clumsiness simply through the imposition of a real body. Imagined competition always knows its place, accepts the role of second fiddle, but real opponents bring their own egos, and while they are never so graceful or gracious as our imagined defender, they are more troublesome precisely because in their clumsiness they are wildly unpredictable, they get in our way, cramp our newly discovered style. When kids start playing against other kids, regardless of the number to a side, a whole new set of skills—not counting defense—have to be learned. Second among these is how to read other players, how to size up both skill and attitude, how to gauge weakness as well as strength, in both teammates and opponents. But first is a form of self-knowledge, the equivalent of my childish accounting: an awareness of personal limits and abilities. In the solitary game, players can, in their heads, add inches to their jumps, imagine themselves swift off the mark; but competition requires honesty, teaches us how quick we really are.

Dr. Naismith, in good YMCA fashion, stressed the camaraderie of basketball, valued the way it taught young men to yield themselves to a group effort. Like all coaches and sports propagandists, he stressed the character-building function of team play. But this course of improvement begins less with the humility one learns from playing *with* others and more with that gained by playing *against* someone, an opponent who forces us to see ourselves as we are, not as we had hoped we were. Self-knowledge teaches both what we need to practice in order to become *and* what we can never be. The great divide of basketball, a moment no coach can greatly influence, comes when the young player either accepts what he or she is and makes the most of it or goes back to playing alone.

But with competition—even one-on-one—comes the need to play the defense we previously only imagined and even then in the second person. This is no small challenge since it goes against all our childish conventional wisdom. Our earliest tendency when someone has something that we want is to wrestle them down and take it away. But such directness, sensible as it may seem, is not what basketball is about. Property rights are taken very seriously on this court that both reflects and refines our general culture. It is illegal to use brute force to claim the ball, physical contact with the present owner being against the rules. Only the ball is to be touched, but this is a game governed by rules a venture capitalist can applaud. It is perfectly acceptable to claim property when the one in possession puts it at risk, that is to say releases it with a dribble, a shot, a pass in the hope of a gain to be duly registered on the scoreboard. And the rules require risk. Like the master in the New Testament parable, modern basketball demands that the "talent" be put into play, precludes simply hanging onto what one has. It demands that each team try to accumulate more, but this can only be accomplished by making the ball vulnerable to the opposition, making it possible for them to gain the very advantage you were seeking.

Risk assessment and management lie at the core of the modern game, reinforced by shot clocks and rules requiring that the ball be kept in motion. This is among the most difficult demands of team play: the rapid recognition of alternatives amidst constantly changing conditions and the ability to choose before an opportunity is lost. When to shoot or pass or dribble; when to fake and which way, when to take the outside shot, and when to drive for the basket: All of these decisions must be made in the smallest splinter of a second, based on a reading of a situation continually in flux. The addition of players until there are five on each side simply increases the extraordinary number of calculations required of each individual, a reading of opponents and teammates alike, alert for new opportunities as well as changing vulnerabilities. Defense, too, is a matter of anticipation and reaction, trying to think like the opponent and gain whatever advantage his or her game allows when nearly all the initiative lies in his or her hands, learning as the game progresses how to turn the tables through intimidation and deception. The statistical aspect of the game, learning to play not only within one's physical limits but also by the odds, requires coaching, a most difficult form of education precisely because it is being applied to play.

My first venture into team play came in the seventh grade under the tutelage of a tall, long-headed man whose feet so impressed us that we called him "Boats" behind his back. I remember him fondly for his immeasurable patience and the wry smile that seemed always to play around his mouth as he barked out commands with drill-sergeant gruffness. How he endured evening after evening of running twelve-year-old boys through passing exercises, endless grapevines that seldom made it from one end of the court to the other without becoming snarled in the most remarkable knots, layup drills—those simplest of exercises—in which we bounced balls off one another's feet or so mistimed our passes that teammates found themselves shooting beneath the backboard. One practice, Bernie Nolan, intent after several dribbling miscues, had his eyes so glued to the ball that he went past the basket and into the gym wall, knocking himself unconscious in his single-mindedness.

By ninth grade we had sufficiently mastered the game's minimum requirements and had grown to sufficient height to imagine ourselves much better than we were. That year, appropriately, our coach was a

.     .     .     .     .     .     .     .     .     .     .

foul-mouthed civics teacher who chewed tobacco. One evening the bravest among my teammates stole a bag of Redman from Coach's desk, and passed it around in the locker room. I'm not sure what exactly we had in mind, but I remember as we came onto the court, expecting stretching exercises and the usual night-before-a-game light practice, cheeks bulging and cockier even than usual, we were ordered to run laps, ordered to run all out until, one after another, we swallowed our wads of Redman and ran even faster to the locker room to puke it all up again. When, green-faced and queasy, we reassembled in the gym, Coach asked if there was a flu bug making the rounds, then opened a fresh pouch of Redman, and packed one cheek while half of the team rushed back to the toilets. The next night Bernie and I managed two flawless pick-and-rolls, and I made the first turn-around jumper of my career. Coach, in his surprise, offered to feed me tobacco the night before every game.

The game we learned while our bodies changed from those of children to those of adults was a team game. We resisted it, demanded the special indulgences of the old solitary play, frequently took the same old liberties, then slowly learned the privilege and pleasure of a cooperative game. Though it was never easy, at our best we accepted the superior talent of a teammate, sacrificed part of our ego so that he or she could soar above us to complete a maneuver in which we could only assist. We learned our limits and how to make the most of what we were rather than what we once imagined ourselves to be, setting picks, blocking out, playing tight defense. But for me the greatest challenge, always, was the anxiety created by constant movement, the never ending requirement to adjust and adapt. Unlike baseball and football where we learned to do one thing at a time, on the basketball court rehearsed plays became simply available steps that ten people, working in complex collusion, revised and rearranged in a continually changing performance. We were always putting together something new, but a thing made of familiar pieces, cut on less than a moment's notice to fit unique circumstances.

I grew late, nearly five inches during my senior year, too late to help my high school game. Even when I reached six feet, a magic number for boys in the 1950s, and my sleeve length stretched to thirty-five inches,

my hands remained those of a smaller man, and my ballhandling was
erratic. I had imagined myself first as Bob Cousey then, later and at my
most ambitious, Oscar Robertson. Pursuing these grand aspirations, I
tried during the summer following my sophomore season to force the
growth of my fingers, performing absurd exercises that I had read in
some sports magazine could lengthen bones, pulling with all my
strength on each finger for thirty seconds, squeezing a tennis ball until
my hands cramped, all to no avail. In time I modeled myself after more
limited players like K. C. Jones and though they, too, proved a standard
I could not meet, I developed a humbler game, one fit for intramurals
and industrial leagues, where the pleasure had to be found in modest
personal achievements and the grace team play allows—that of being
part of something better than myself, of contributing to accomplish-
ments beyond my own ability.

V.

Much as I loved the team game, it makes up only a small part of a
player's life. There is another, more enduring, game here, one that does
not eliminate the less talented, one to which we retreat, even when we
make the team, in moments of doubt or reflection. It is a game for the
long haul, one that persists after the appropriate age of retirement from
its more glorified relative. This is a personal game, the one with which
we began and the one that tracks our lives much as it did Rabbit
Angstrom's, measuring us from childhood to old age.

The pattern of our play is the trajectory that governs everything in
basketball; the arc of the shot as it rises on release until, after hanging
for the briefest and most wonderful of moments, it begins to descend.
The game starts with the childish lunges with which we push a too large
ball forward with the full force of our too small bodies. In these first
awkward efforts we do not so much go up as go forward, our game little more than a series of barely controlled falls that as often as not drops
us to our knees rather than lifts us off the ground. But even in those initial efforts we sense the possibilities and despite the humiliation of our
clumsy play, we keep at it, knowing that we will get closer to the basket

. . . . . . . . . .

in time. We grow into it, year by year getting taller, season by season feeling the increasing spring in young legs.

The play of kids, alone on blacktop or dirt or concrete, is about the future, a future that is only incidently a matter of teams and spectators. More than anything else, it is personal and private, a future to be felt in the muscles and the bones, culminating neither in championships nor bonus checks, but in reaching higher and with more grace than ever before. In our preparation the goal can be perfection, one in which there is only ascent, where we can hang forever, free and triumphant above the rim. That goal is what first drives us to the court, and the glory of adolescence is how easy it is to believe that this upward trajectory will prove limitless, if nowhere else in our lives, at least in the game.

We only recognize our highpoint as we descend. So accustomed to our upward progress, even at our zenith we expect to reach higher tomorrow, do better next year. But the game is long in the ascent, brief at the top, and longest in decline. Conventional wisdom says to stop when you recognize you are past your prime, to take up kinder, more earthbound activities like golf or tennis or bridge. But the true basketball player finds this impossible to do, knows it is not simply a matter of giving up one game for another. It would require giving up more, giving up too much.

I was in my early forties when I first admitted I was too old for basketball as a sport and in the decade since I have quit playing three times. Each time I gave up following some humiliation either of mind or of body. The first was the worst because it was a mental failure, suffered during a league game with college kids. Somehow I put in a rebound for the other team, not in some freak accidental tip-in, but with the ball fully in my control after I had gotten position and blocked out the younger players. In a sudden loss of concentration I went back up and scored at the wrong end of the court. We were ahead at the time, and I had played relatively well; some of my teammates thought it a joke, and one or two of our opponents suspected I was mocking them. I laughed hollowly and, offering no further explanation, removed myself from the game.

Two years later I made a one-game comeback, talked onto the

court for a contest between high school seniors and their fathers. They were physically better, but we knew how to win, beating them by taking our time, blocking out, and passing regularly to the youngest and most athletic among us. On the basis of that deluding success, I returned at forty-five to a league whose other players averaged less than half my age and substituted weight and cunning for long-gone grace and agility. This effort concluded midseason when after a tip-in I came down awkwardly and, too slow to catch my balance, fell on my elbow and broke it.

I have been in school nearly all of my life, which correctly suggests that, while a slow learner, I am educable. Again I quit, playing only in short sessions with a respectful son who, though taller and stronger, treated me with deference. Then my oldest daughter moved back to town, and I joined her on our driveway court as she practiced for the three-on-three tournaments she and her friends were entering in cities around the country. Encouraged by these judicious games of one-on-one, I relapsed and accepted her invitation to join in pickup games among her fellow law-school students. In one of these, I tried to break down court after intercepting a pass and tore a hamstring while making a move so routine no one realized anything had happened until I lay on the floor.

When we are very young, we play a game ruled by the future; we continue our absurd lunges, our clumsy dribbles because we know it will all get better. We accept the embarrassment in the conviction that we are headed in the right direction, toward greater strength and grace. Sometime in our thirties we begin to play from memory, ruled by the past. Each time I relinquished the team game, I did so not because I could not play with some degree of success or contribute to the larger effort, but because I could not wholly get the old game out of my head and forgot the limitations that come with time. The game in my mind became the one I could no longer play rather than the one in which I could still participate, and periodically it broke into my more controlled and modest real efforts and brought me back to earth.

The third phase of the private game is played in descent. After years of moving closer to the basket you watch it slip away. The hoop is always the standard of measurement, the thing even the child longs to touch. Teenagers work for the day when they can rise high enough to dunk, endlessly planning all the ways they will exercise this wondrous power when at last it comes to them. But in time we move in a different direction, and the basket slowly drifts beyond our reach. The weight of years holds us down just as in those anxiety dreams of our youth when, slowed by wooden legs, we move slowly, and with the greatest exertion. In those days, awakening to the relief that the experience was unreal, we rushed back to our exhilarating play. But in age that nighttime sluggishness becomes real, and the basket looms irrevocably beyond our grasp. Now we dream of lightness, in sleep we make the old plays, toying with the rim, hanging in the air far longer than we ever did in our youth. Even dreaming, we suspect this mockery, but awake to a renewed sense of loss, wishing it all back, closing our eyes in hopes of recovering some final fragment of the illusion.

In *Rabbit at Rest*, the final Rabbit novel, a now retired Harry Angstrom finds himself drawn from his Florida condo to a rundown playground with a netless hoop and, after popping a nitroglycerin pill, begins to play. "He is aware," Updike writes, "of his belly being slung up and down by the action and of a watery weariness entering into his knees, but adrenaline and nostalgia overrule." The kid with whom he shares the court pays Rabbit the only compliment left, the one old players dread: "You played once."

In old age the sport abandons us, moves us to the past tense, a time when those of us smarter—or prouder—than Rabbit give up competition, reluctantly abandon the leagues, and stay away from courts that will inevitably find us wanting and mercilessly judge our inadequacy. But, if we are lucky and not too greedy, the play—the singular play with which it all began—remains, a twilight game once more, played after work in the dim light of a backyard or in abandoned schoolyards or parks. At best it is done from the toes or balls of the feet, on legs that will take us no higher. It is bearable in part because it remains an act of imagination, one in which we no longer picture opponents, but younger selves. We remember more supple bodies, recall the stroke of an effortless shot. No one watches to note our slowness or the stiffness with which we retrieve the ball; no one contradicts the extra height we imagine in our slight leaps or the missing grace we picture in our hooks and layups.

The aunt I watched all those years ago has been so long dead I cannot clearly recall her face. I am now the same age as Rabbit Angstrom when he was tempted into the game that killed him, but I weigh less than he did, and my heart has gone this far without attacking me. And I am, I think, more prudent than he was, an academic rather than a salesman. Still, in one of my most frequent dreams I am leaping, feeling gravity's pull only to will myself higher—the way I used to account for Baylor's upward surge—in one last burst, rising to heights I took for granted thirty years ago. I awaken just as I release the ball above the rim, not in a defiant slam, but gently, softly, like letting go of a feather. Coming to myself I feel the weight of years and the hard consequences of my soft life. Nearly always in the days following this dream I go to some vacant court in the evenings and, after doing my best to loosen up, return to the old drill: shooting round the perimeter, driving the lane for little hooks and layups. Sometimes there is a momentary bounce in my step, an unexpected smoothness to a shot that brings the old play home once more, and the perfect rustle of a net rises from the dusk like a nearly forgotten song. Even in this diminished form I think basketball a wonderful game, one too good to ever wholly relinquish.

# Sacrifice

. . . . . . . . . .

*by*
LOÏC WACQUANT

> They are profane; they must change state. For this, rites are necessary
> which introduce them into the sacred world and engage them more or
> less deeply within it, depending on the role they will be called upon to
> play. This is what constitutes the entry into sacrifice.
> HENRI HUBERT AND MARCEL MAUSS,
> *Sacrifice: Its Nature and Function,* 1898

Every trade has its code of ethics, a set of rules and stipulations that define proper character, conduct, and intercourse to and amongst its members. In some occupations, this code is formalized, recited, even sworn to. In others, it is a loosely strung assemblage of norms and guidelines, learned and deployed in the very process of going about one's business. Thus medics take the Hippocratic oath and civil servants pledge allegiance to the public authority in the name of which they act, while new factory laborers receive casual yet pointed instructions from peers on how hard to work and when to renege on supervisors on the shop floor.

Prizefighting is no different. Boxers learn early on that, if they are to make it in the mannish craft of bruising, they must obey an occupational ethic that is no less abiding for being informally transmitted, no less stringent for being willfully embraced. Conveniently, the morality proper to professional fighters is encapsuled by a single solitary word: *sacrifice.* Sacrifice—the idea and the regulated practices it prescribes— seeps through and suffuses the lives of boxers in and out of the gym, from the bedroom to the ring, and everywhere in between. It is at once leitmotiv, motto, mantra, and magic formula believed to unlock the door of success and open the golden stairway to the "big time."

Boxers are incessantly reminded of the imperatives of sacrifice by attentive trainers, concerned managers, punctilious matchmakers, and other fight people around them. Sacrifice is at once means and goal, vital duty and prideful mission, practical exigency and ethological obsession. Sacrifice is, on the one side, engine of discrimination—it inexorably separates pugilistic wheat from chaff—and, on the other, instrument of conjunction—it binds into one great chivalrous brotherhood all those who submit themselves to it, from today's obscure "club fighter" to the celebrated "champ" of the game's storied past. And it bestows upon all those who adhere to its forbearing dictates the specific honor of the craft.

Any "pro" fighter worthy of the name knows that he ought to give himself over to his trade body and soul, *religiossime*.[1] His commitment cannot but be all-embracing and all-consuming. He must put his craft before everything else, be it his family and friends, his wife or lover(s), his job (when he has one), and all extant mundane concerns. His physical, mental, and emotional energies are to be conscientiously cultivated, preciously preserved for, and methodically channeled toward one purpose and one purpose only: maximizing fistic prowess and attaining peak performance in the ring. To this end, the wisdom of pugilistic tradition has laid down strict observances as regards three crucial domains of carnal existence: nutrition, social and family life, and sexual commerce. Together, these cultic conventions compose the holy trinity of the pugilistic faith.

I

Closing time at the Gary Police Gym on a damp September evening, a drab, vaultlike, room overdecorated with boxing posters on the edge of the I-94, where half a dozen pros toil under the tutelage of Sergeant Baylor, a local boxing figure renowned for his garrulousness and the facility with which he rents out the services of his charges so long as he pockets his "cut" of their purses. Dave "Too Sweet" Bulman, a surly black middleweight who recently turned pro, is finishing his daily workout under the watchful eye of big Zeke, his trainer (who holds two jobs round the clock at a local polymer factory), and his manager (a sleepy-eyed physician who heads his own sports-medicine outfit downtown). After a dozen rounds alternating "bag work" and shadowboxing, Zeke orders Dave to run thrice around the park at full speed. When the boxer returns a dozen minutes later, glistening with sweat, Zeke carefully towels his upper body dry and admonishes him on his culinary regimen, which has not been everything it should be lately:

> ZEKE:  Alright, stay off—no sodas, no sodas, a lil' Kool-Aid, you wanna just drink water, lotsa water, okay? Fresh fruits, try t'eat some broccoli an' stuff *raw*, if you can, salads fresh, stuff like that. Bake all your food, two steaks a week, y'know, you pick the days.
> DAVID:  [*Respectful*] Awright.

> ZEKE:  That's it for the steaks, [*Insistent*] *no* hamburgers, *no* French fries, *no* fried *nuthin'*, okay? That way when you get tired, you can, y'know, no greasy nuthin' in the way a-yo' breathin', y'understand? You wanna be [*Takes an exaggeratedly deep breath*] *wide open*, y'see what I'm sayin', be able to throw hard punches an' come back. Okay?
> DAVID:  [*Slightly reticent*] Awright.

> ZEKE:  An' you ain't got no weight to lose, really, y'know, it's fifty-eight right. They'll let you go with a pound. But you gotta, *you gotta stay ready, man.* Basic'ly now I want you to keep your diet straight—no sweets at all, okay?
> DAVID:  [*Growing more reluctant with every recommendation*] Okay.

> ZEKE:  No women, you stay away from 'em, just stay moved away from 'em. This is what you gotta do if you wanna win, if you don' wanna win . . .
> DAVID:  [*Interrupting his trainer with a firm voice*] Yeah, I *wanna* win.
> ZEKE:  . . . if you don' wanna win, you wastin' my time.

The first commandment of the pugilistic catechism is easily enunciated: Thou shalt not consume forbidden foods, foods that weigh the body down, excite its organs, and disrupt the delicately adjusted circuitry of its inward functioning and outward powers. But this commandment is not so easily obeyed, for it is not simply the nature and quantity of aliments that one must severely restrict and monitor. Rather, the fighter is to recast the totality of his relationship to eating as a physico-symbolic activity so as to embody through it the nexus of self and world conforming to his occupation.[2]

There is an obvious practical reason why nutrition is a haunting and ubiquitous concern in the pugilistic cosmos. Boxers compete in predefined weight classes and must typically reach a target "fight weight" set several pounds below their normal, "walking-around weight." Dieting is indispensable to shed all excess fat and, ideally, step into the squared circle with not an ounce of unneeded tissue on one's frame—a tensionful, martial, organization of flesh, nerves, and muscles aimed at another similarly configured human aggression machine. Check out whom a trainer cooks for, and you will know for sure who his favorite pupils are.

Once "in training" for a fight, to "make the weight" becomes the compulsive motif of the fighter's quotidian existence, the bout before the bout, over which he and his entourage worry and fuss continually. Yet pugs are rarely as disciplined at the table as they should be and dieting does not always do the job. Thus it is not uncommon for them to have to lose five to ten pounds in a couple of days of fanatic fasting and exercising on the eve of the fight so as to "weigh in" at the mark. Running and skipping rope with vinyl sweats on, shadowboxing beside a hot running shower, abstaining from drink, sucking on lemons to spit, taking turkish baths and even chemicals that speed up one's metabolism: A fighter will drop the weight by whatever means necessary.[3]

But, over and beyond their instrumental purpose, culinary observances, like their social and sexual counterparts, function as a ritual of separation from, and elevation above, the mundane world. They tear the prizefighter away from the earthly seductions that other members of society fall prey to. They communicate to self and other the depth of his engagement in the craft. And they inscribe within and onto his organism the visible marks of his commitment to its ethic.

My gym mate and sparring partner, Ashante, recently discovered just how bad McDonald's is for the body—rich in sugars and fat as well as horridly greasy. As a precautionary measure and to the dismay of his children, he has embargoed all fast food at his house until further notice. Cheese is another silent enemy he feels he must constantly guard against: "*Tha's bad for you, that make yo' stomach soft.* Tha's why I don't eat nona-that stuff when I'm in trainin'. But it's tough." Ashante is known to "blow up" between fights, putting on upwards of forty pounds on his stocky five-six frame. But through a murderous combination of dieting, running, and training, he somehow always manages to shed them in time for the bout. A matter of will, a test of occupational affiance and pride. Will he "make" 139 next month? He scoffs: "Ten pounds, that ain't nuthin'."

His girlfriend, Darlene, hastens to reveal that Ashante ballooned up to 180 pounds before his last fight in Cleveland: "His face was biiiig [*Cupping her open hands around her blown cheeks*], his neck was thiiick like that." Ashante pleads no contest — he was so bloated that his friends were wondering aloud if he had caught some kind of disease. Tonight's is his last ice cream (he will eat a gallon of it the day after his bout): "See, I wanna eat as much as I can now 'cuz I know Monday I'monna start back trainin'. Then when I start, I won't touch no ice cream till I fight. Once I'm in trainin', I don't touch no food tha's bad for me."

Ashante had taken the habit of gulping down raw eggs daily right out of bed before his morning "roadwork." An old-timer at the gym had assured that it would help him lose weight as well as gain strength. He did so begrudgingly: "I really didn' like the taste, y'know, it make you kinda sick. I tried to put a lil' bit a-honey in it to cut the taste but it didn' work." Eventually, he stopped "'cuz you know the side effects it has for men, Louie. So Darlene didn' want me to keep doin' it. Plus I *really* didn't like the taste, really." His girlfriend jumps in, tittering: "*You know raw eggs, they do a man what vitamin E do females.* You eat a lotta them and you be *hard as a brick*. Make you real-real hard, then you in big trouble." And just to make sure everyone understands what she means, she plants her elbow on the kitchen table and raises her forearm straight towards the ceiling, fist clenched, oscillating as if under tension. Ashante cuts in: "Sure make you hard as a rock, yeah you be cookin' man!" Darlene blurts out: "Like Big Daddy Kane say, [*Singing*] 'Get to work! Get down to bu-si-ness!'" We all explode in laughter. To compensate, Ashante now gobbles an assortment of vitamins, pills, and ginseng-based decoctions.

II

The second commandment of the prizefighter's catechism extends this abstemious principle from nutrition to sociability as follows: Thou shalt not lead a dissipated existence whereby your attention is scattered and your energies squandered. You shall minify the circle of people you deal with, curtail your transactions with them, rope off and stint whatever demands intimates press upon you, and give full priority to occupational requirements over all other intercourse. Most of all, you shall decisively refuse and repulse any and all activities that might tire, soften, or impair your body.

For Marty, who started boxing at age nine and has compiled twenty-four straight victories as a pro in only his twenty-second year, this is undeniably the most exacting claim the craft makes on its devotees. Growing up in lily white, working-class Hammond where he now holds a part-time job as purchaser for a metal recycling company, it was and is aggravating to turn away neighborhood buddies because you must rest, sleep, run, or train seemingly in perpetuity: "The hardest thing, really, I guess, givin' up like spendin' time with my friends sometimes you know or jus' *goofin' off in general.* 'Cause like three weeks before a fight, you know, I pretty much watch what I eat, I'm in at a decent hour, I'm up at a decent hour in the mornin' an' uh [*Firmly*] I don't have no sex two weeks before a fight usually. I go from my mother's house to the gym and from the gym straight to the house."

Detroit boxing guru Emanuel Steward has seen hundreds of talented kids fade and fall through the cracks because they could not let go of the joys of ordinary gregariousness or ended up getting "caught by the bright lights" of the city. They had the strength, the stamina, the skills, the style, but not the obstinacy required to become hermits of the ring. "When you train a kid at twelve or thirteen or fourteen, no matter how much talent he has, you can't tell if he's going to be a star because there are so many tests out there he's got to pass. It's like mines in a minefield. How many guys are going to get by all the mines? One guy goes to a party, gets the taste of alcohol, he can't get away. Another guy, a drug pusher gets him. Some guys, as soon as they're successful, if somebody says 'C'mon man, we got a big party to go to tonight,' they can't turn it down, they got to go to every party. Other guys, they can't say no to girls . . . That's another of those mines that can explode."[4]

Rising at dawn to do your "roadwork," clocking in at the gym every afternoon to put in your fifteen to twenty rounds of shadowboxing, hitting the bags, sparring, rope skipping, and calisthenics, heading straight home to bathe and rest, retiring early to get your mandatory eight hours of sleep so that your body may withstand the strain and punishment of training: The regimented life of the prizefighter is austere and dull. It leaves precious little room and time for girlfriends, homies, and family. Recreation and excitment are out, denial and Spartanism are in. Under such an eremitical regime, the web of everyday sociality shrivels and personal attachments tend to gravitate toward and accrete within the occupational milieu. No wonder boxers often liken their gym to "a second mother" and think of its members as their "other family."

The oral tradition of the trade gives pride of place to those fighters, big and small, who forfeit their personal life for the ring and, so the stories go, reap the just rewards of their dedication. Countless anecdotes vaunt their abnegation and the vigor with which they applied the principles of the ethic of sacrifice. In the manner of the "great ascetics" of the world religions, "the contempt they profess for all that ordinarily impassions men" might seem excessive. But "such extremes are necessary to maintain among the faithful a sufficient level of distate for easy living and mundane pleasures. An elite must set the goal too high so that the masses do not set it too low."[5]

"It wasn't so much the gymnasium workouts that Rocky did," adduces Marciano's trainer to explain the success of the only heavyweight champion in history to retire undefeated: "It's the way he lived. Every fighter pretty near trains the same, but all fighters don't live alike. If you were there looking at Rocky's training and the way he lived, it was hard to believe that a man could sacrifice so much of life and his family life and keep fightin'." Indeed, Marciano used to go into isolation and train for up to nine months at a stretch for a fight. His self-imposed seclusion was so total that the only times he encountered his wife were during brief platonic marches together, hand in hand, on the tarmac of the airport between planes and under the stern gaze of his manager. Legend has it that Rocky's single known weakness was to eat between meals in training camp: On occasion his trainer would find a couple of bananas hidden under his pillow after dinner and badger him about it.[6] No one is perfect, true; but everyone has a duty to strive to be.

The flipside of the drastic compression of social life demanded by pugilistic morality is the dilation and bolstering of the relationship of self to self. For sacrifice calls for an endlessly reiterated hermeneutic of one's own needs, desires, and capacities so as to regulate and reshape them, in short, a constant work of the boxer upon himself (as suggested by the etymology of asceticism, *askein*, to work). In his analysis of the "care of the self" in ancient Greece, Michel Foucault notes that there are "groups among which the relation of self to self is intensified and develops without for all that necessarily reinforcing the values of individualism and private life."[7] This is an apt description of the pugilistic care of self: For the expansion of the prizefighter's relationship to himself translates not in an elevation but a lowering of personal attitudes; not in an increase but a reduction of the independence of the individual from his occupational universe; not in a greater valorization of the private sphere but, on the contrary, a loosening of familial obligations and a lesser involvement in domestic activites as these become subordinated to pugilistic interests.

III

Back in Gary, while Dave showers, I get to ask Zeke what he thinks about "this woman thing" and how it interferes with the preparation and career of pro fighters. The trainer opines gravely and launches into a spirited harangue:

> It'll make you suffer, yeah. Y'know, if a woman says, "Hey, I, I, I wanna go to the show," an' uh, well you figger, you gotta have a full trainin' in, an' take her to the show too. Then your rest is important, y'know. An' then all d'time she squirmin' in her seat, 'cause she's

lookin' [*Wriggling his behind*] kinna *good an' hot*, y'know, an' lookin' at yo' beautiful body which you are *chiseling in d'gym*, y'know, an', an' then [*Raucous*] she gon' wanna do *som'thin'*, you know—*there you go!* she starts it, y'know.

An' you know yourself, after you done had *real good love* an' sex, man, what d'you do? Do you get up an' run aroun', or do you jus' lay down an' sleep? [*Triumphant*] What do *you do*? *Okay!* Y'see it makes you lazy, takes, takes somethin' outa you. You have to rest, you gotta get your nature back up, see.

So, there you go, you can make it to work. But can you make it to d'gym after you get offa work, y'know? An' then when you go home she's waitin' there, [*Whispering as if in shock*] *nothin' on under*, just a dress, pull the dress up, [*With an enticing, feminine falsetto*] "Hey baby," okay?

. . . Keep the right frame a mind, reverse the psychology, y'know what I'm sayin'? [*Sternly*] *Reverse everything.* Y'know, the woman's up there [*Again, in a sweet, mockingly seductive voice*] "Come on, baby, let's do dis, or let's do dat." [*In a kind but firm, placid, baritone*] "No, I'll take you to the movies, but after that we gotta come home an' you sleep in *that* room an' I'll sleep in *this* one. You hafta help me, you hafta help me make a, be sussessful at this. [*Almost whining*] You hafta *help me baby, pleeeze.*" Y'know, an' maybe she can understand better like that, if you talk to her like that. Say, [*Jovial*] "Hey, after the fight though, *I'm gon' break yo' back!*" y'know. An' she'll say, "*Really?* Break it now!" [*Firmly*] "No I'm not"—but you know what I'm sayin' . . .

The third commandment of the ethic of sacrifice is that which most clearly sets boxers apart from all other athletes, even those who compete in kindred "blood sports": Thou shalt not engage in sexual or amorous intercourse for weeks and weeks before the bout. During the phase of intensive training that eventually culminates in confrontation in the ring, all *aphrodisia* are strictly off limits. A fighter must abstain from any action or situation liable to arouse sexual emotions, divert his concentration away from his opponent, and thereby interfere with the methodical crescendo of his own *libido pugilistica*.

Trainers, managers, and boxers share in the belief, handed down by predecessors, that having sex drains the legs, shortens the breath, weakens the muscles, takes away aggression, disrupts balance and coordination, as well as blunts motivation. That weeks of training may be ruined by one single, brief sexual encounter, as Scottie, an old-timer from the Stoneland Boys Club, explained to me one evening as we sat watching the preliminaries of the Chicago Golden Gloves: "You can train for months, man, *if you fuck one time you're outa shape,* that's it." Why is that? I ingenuously asked. "*You be losing blood, man, when you fuck you lose blood.* You can't do it, I'm tellin' you. You're crazy if you doin' it." And he bent over toward me to whisper this ominous addendum: "You just can't afford to, man, don't fuck when you fight. You can't afford too: Boxin' is dangerous, *you can get killed in the ring.*" Ashante nodded somberly and voiced his agreement with Scottie on this all-important matter: "Even for sparrin'. You can't make love if you gonna spar, Louie: It take out all your aggressivity. If I'monna be sparrin', I gotta be aggressive, I gotta be fierce, I gotta have that edge, I gotta be in shape."

Theological debates rage in the gyms about the precise mechanism that makes sex such a deleterious activity for prizefighters. One school holds that the leakage of sperm and other bodily fluids—including "blood from the spine" said to escape via ejaculation in the heat of orgasm—debilitates the boxer by undermining the delicate inner workings of his organism. Others argue that it is not the sexual act itself that triggers a pathogenic dynamic so much as what one has to get through to get sex. My good friend Curtis, who recently fought his first tenrounder and hopes to break into the world rankings by year's end, is convinced that sexual intercourse causes such massive hemorrhaging of energy that there is no way one can recoup from it in time for the fight. "It weakens you. I don't care how much you been runnin' tha' day, you gonna feel weak after that, you gonna feel *exhausted.* [*In a sullen voice*] You not gonna keep your han's up. You not gonna be able to move d'way you normally woul' move. It's like, it's like bein' the day of the fight an' losin' nine-ten poun's before the fight: It takes a w*hole hell outa you,* you-know-what-I'm-sayin'?" His certainty stands on the bedrock of personal experience: "When I get intimate with a young lady, I'm *into it.* I put my back an' everythin' into it. I'm you know, aw shit! I'm jus' into it: I'm dreamin' my body right away, see-what-I'm-

. . . . . . . . . .

sayin'? It's like lettin' water out of a faucet [*He laughs and rocks back in his chair*]. It's like *takin' a cork out.*"

According to this interpretation, the prescription of sexual abstinence seeks to control what comes *out* of the body, just as the first, nutritional precept of the pugilistic ethic purports to monitor what enters *into* it. Not so, counter those who maintain that it is the social and emotional exertion required to obtain sex that wrecks the fragile architecture of training. Angelo Dundee, who worked the corner of two of boxing's brightest stars, Muhammad Ali and Sugar Ray Leonard, does not buy the hydraulic theory of sperm leakage: "I've had fighters who had to be locked up at night to keep them from chasing broads. Or had to have a sentry outside their room. And sometimes even that didn't help. One night I left my pal Lou Gross in charge of a fighter. Lou wandered away to have a drink and smoke a cigar, and when he got back, he looked in the room and found the fighter on top of a chick. Lou yelled, 'Don't come! Don't come!' I always tried to baptize my guys early: It ain't the sexual act. It's the chase. That's what wears you out."[8]

The two theories are not mutually incompatible and many are content to conjoin them. A veteran referee who campaigned for eight years in the middleweight division on both sides of the Atlantic provides this account of the cumulative effects of sexual pursuit and catch: "I think the way that it affects a fighter is that mostly it *softens you up*, it takes the edge away, you know, it makes you soft, you're just not as mean a fighter—*a fighter should go in the ring mean*, you know. If you don't have sex, you get a little mean. [*His voice softening for dramatic effect*] Sex makes you *mellow out*, um . . . also a fighter, when a young guy's having sex, *to get sex*, if he don't have his regular girl, he's going to be out *prowling*, losin' his sleep. And he might go in a bar and have a beer or something and sorta wear him out." More importantly, though, both schools concur that sex broadly defined tends to soften, weaken, pacify, in short, "feminize" the prizefighter's body. And for this reason it must be shunned like a plague. "I tried it," confesses Craig, a rugged, white light-heavyweight who joyfully returned to the ring after months of punishing rehabilitation to recover from a near-fatal motorcycle accident. "I just wasn't up to par. Wasn't fully the *man* I thought I'd be."

Again, fighters are continually reminded of the sexual sacrifices consented to by the legendary fighters of yore. This eloquent tirade on Sugar Ray Robinson by my venerable coach is typical of the genre: "He did like 'em women, yeah, but *he didn' mess wit'em, not too much* nohow. Not like some of the other guys. He like to have a lotta ladies 'round, enjoyed their company, for sure, but he left 'em alone when the time came for him to get down t'business. How d'you think he fought like he did for twenty-five years? Shiiit, Sugar Ray knew how t'take care of his self! All them old-timers, Sugar Ray an' Archie Moore an' Sonny Liston an' them, *they didn't last twenty, twenty-five years for nuttin': They wasn't messin' with d'ladies.* [*With a soft, rustling, voice*] They knew what they wanted." The message to the present generation is pellucid: If you want the glory, you have to withstand the agony. Be prepared to suffer. Enter into sacrifice.

## IV

He who ardently wishes to enter and rise in the pugilistic cosmos must strive to expatriate himself from the mundane world, disengage from its games, and grow indifferent to its seducements. He must be prepared to slaughter all of his profane interests on the altar of the ring. For only in and through the rigorous ascesis and occupational sequestration commanded by the ethic of sacrifice will he forge those qualities of toughness, abnegation, endurance, and disciplined rage needed to master the Sweet Science and to endure in the crafty trade of knocks.

If and when he does so, the boxer reaches a higher plane of existence. For sacrifice lifts him above his everyday station to thrust him into a special moral and sensual universe. A fighter becomes a greater man when he renounces those common things that common men cannot forego. For, as Emile Durkheim wrote in his celebrated analysis of *The Elementary Forms of Religious Life*, "[a]fter he has submitted himself to the prescribed prohibitions, man is not the same as he was. Before, he was an ordinary being. . . . After, he has moved closer to the sacred by the mere fact that he has distanced himself from the profane. He has purified and sanctified himself by the very fact of detaching himself from the lowly and trivial things that previously burdened his nature."[9] In sacrificing himself, he has engendered a new being out of the old.

## NOTES

1. It is not by happenstance that the expression "body and soul" is the title of numerous movies, novels, articles, and paintings about prizefighting (as well as about music, art, and religion), the most famous being the 1947 movie by Robert Rossen.

2. For an insightful account of this process in a different context, Anna S. Meigs, *Food, Sex, and Pollution: A New Guinea Religion* (New Brunswick, NJ: Rutgers University Press, 1984).

3. Joe Louis reportedly took regular sulphur baths to get from 238 down to 218 pounds when he came out of retirement to face Ezzard Charles in 1950. Thirty years later, Muhammad Ali ingested a thyroid medication that causes severe dehydration in his ill-advised attempt to return to the ring and earn a fourth heavyweight title long after his body had given out on him.

4. Cited in Dave Anderson, *In the Corner: Great Boxing Trainers Talk About Their Art* (New York: Morrow, 1991), 199.

5. Emile Durkheim, *Les formes élémentaires de la vie religieuse: le système totémique en Australie* (Paris: Presses Universitaires de France, 1912, reprint 1950), 452.

6. Ronald K. Fried, *Corner Men: Great Boxing Trainers* (New York: Four Walls Eight Windows, 1991), 186.

7. Michel Foucault, *Histoire de la sexualité*, vol. 3 *Le souci de soi*. (Paris: Editions du Seuil, 1984), 57.

8. Cited in Anderson, *In the Corner, op. cit.*, 80.

9. Durkheim, *Les formes élémentaires de la vie religieuse*, op. cit., 442.

# Grant Hall

. . . . . . . . . .

*by*
JAMES A. MCPHERSON

## OIKOUMENE

When I first settled into Iowa City, Iowa, which is close to the midpoint between the two coasts, athletics were of absolutely no interest to me. My chief concern was making a home for myself and getting on with my career as a teacher, which would, in turn, support my writing. For most of my life I had been on the move. I had spent my first seventeen years in Savannah, Georgia; then two years in Atlanta; then one year in Baltimore; then another year in Atlanta; then three years in Cambridge; then one year in Iowa City; then two years in Santa Cruz; then one year in Berkeley, part of which was spent commuting to Chicago; then one year in Cranston, Rhode Island; then two years in San Francisco; then another year in Baltimore; then two years in Charlottesville, Virginia; then one year in New Haven; then two more years in Charlottesville. Then, in 1981, I returned to Iowa.

Back in 1969, before I left Iowa City for Santa Cruz, I had lived for one year in an apartment on Brown Street. In June of 1981, when I returned to Iowa City, I rented an apartment on Gilbert Street, just around the corner from the Brown Street apartment. I considered this juxtaposition an act of fate, a sign that perhaps I was *meant* to be in Iowa City; or, again perhaps, there had been something I missed when I first lived here. I tried my best to settle in. During all those years on the road, I had believed that I had been building some *oikoumene* thing in the

Greek sense of the *oikoumene*, the places where there are homes. But friends of mine had been observing my movements in another light. One of them said, "Ever since we met you, Jim, you've been running. Why don't you settle in someplace and get some work done?" I have now lived in Iowa City for seventeen years, about as long as I lived in Savannah, Georgia. I have circled home.

When I lived in Iowa in 1968–1969, I was never really here. Officially, I was enrolled in the M.F.A. program in the Writers' Workshop, but unofficially I was already a writer. I took the required courses, taught undergraduates in the rhetoric program, might have attended some of the readings and a few of the parties; but each Friday afternoon, without fail, I took the bus into Chicago to spend the weekend with a Chicago street gang named, then, the Blackstone Rangers. I was writing a series of articles on this gang for the *Atlantic*. I returned to Iowa City Sunday evenings, or well after midnight, and if there was too much snow, or if it was too late to walk from the bus station to my apartment on Brown Street, I would go to my office in the old Rhetoric Building and sleep on the floor. I always kept a toothbrush and a washcloth there, so I could be presentable for my rhetoric class early on Monday mornings. I lived then, for some reason, a very Spartan kind of life. During that year, I learned very little about Iowa City, about the life of the campus and the communal life beyond it. Someplace, in the distant background of my memories of that time, there are the sounds of cheering fans, images of colorful floats parading through the downtown area, details of stories about athletes in the student paper. The woman whom I would eventually date, Maxine Thomas, was selected as the homecoming queen for 1968. I remember a picture of her, smiling benevolently and holding roses and waving, seated atop the rear seat of a convertible in a homecoming parade, the first black homecoming queen. She was also a first-year law student, and a mutual interest in the law became one of the bases of our bond. Her appeal had absolutely nothing to do with her tenuous connection with athletics. It would be accurate to say that, at the time, I harbored a profound distaste for athletes and their world. Since my early college years, I had ignored athletic games. I never attended them, never cared to watch them on television. I had never consciously established a friendship with a known athlete.

But in the fall of 1981, when I had a desperate need to fit into the community, a friend gave me some sage advice. "Now Mac," he told me, "you are living in a Teutonic community, and sports are a great part of this community's life. You should take an active interest in them." My friend was right. Beginning in late August, the mind of the entire community turned to football. Symbols of the Iowa Hawkeyes appeared everywhere. Sorority girls paraded before their sorority houses shaking black-and-gold pom-poms. And beginning in September, almost every Saturday, thousands of cars would sweep into Iowa City, from all the small towns, for the games in Kinnick Stadium. Long processions of people, most of them wearing black and gold, would walk almost the entire length of Burlington Street to crowd into the stadium. The Episcopal priest of the church I joined was also an announcer for the football games. He always gave me the soul handshake in the greeting line after his sermons.

A book that appeared during this time, *The Courting of Marcus Dupree* by Willie Morris, provided me with a telling insight. "In the East," Morris wrote, "college football is a cultural exercise. On the West Coast, it is a tourist attraction. In the Midwest, it is cannibalism. But in the South, it is a religion." I have kept this insight in mind for many years because I believe there is some truth in it. But the truth, I think, goes far deeper than football itself. Instead, on its deeper levels, Willie Morris's insight may say something profound about the differences between the *styles* of the various regions.

Iowa City was planned as a polis. Its model was Philadelphia, but also the style of Athens. According to one of the city's historians, Laurence Lafore, "Iowa City was planned as an exemplar of the decisive and pervasive influence of Greek and Roman ideals in American life; and in a way that would have been intelligible to people in the seventeenth century as the opposite of the word 'gothic'." Doric, Ionian, and Corinthian columns are still visible on University buildings and on some of the older houses. The Athens inhabited by Socrates and Aristotle and Plato was a polis in which everyone knew everyone else. It was a village with a cosmopolitan sense. Iowa City is such a village. It is not the antidemocratic polis of Socrates, who believed that everyone was good at some *one* thing and should be restricted to that labor. It is a

. . . . . . . . .

polis in which the president of a bank can be a former athlete, where the Episcopal priest sees no conflict between sermons and sports announcing. It is a city in which bus drivers and garbage collectors and clerks and postal workers almost always have advanced degrees. People delight in living here. Neighbors will shovel the snow off your sidewalk simply because they shovel in a straight line. Iowa City began as an attempt to reproduce the civil perfection of Athens in the American wilderness. Its subscription to democratic principles encouraged the same cosmopolitan sense that was in Athens, especially with respect to tolerance. Churches of every denomination have always coexisted in Iowa City. The only African Methodist Episcopal Church, Bethel A.M.E. Church at 411 South Governor Street, was built in 1868. Many of the homes in Iowa City were once stations on the Underground Railway. Runaway slaves were hidden in coal cellars and attics of homes I have visited. Someone has said that civilization rests on two very fragile bases—high culture and good top soil. Both are in abundance in Iowa City. But there is also a feeling of Greek civic virtue combined with Roman cosmopolitanism.

This was the thing I had returned to Iowa City to learn.

## POLIS

The first order of business, then, was for me to make connection with the world of sports. The most important connection emerged from its unusual blending of culture and democracy. A white male student from my first writing class here, in the summer of 1981, approached me that same fall for a favor. He explained that he was helping a black former athlete named Tyrone Dye (also known, from his days as a fullback on the Iowa team, as Rodan) to write his life story. He wanted me to meet Tyrone Dye and help with the book. I agreed to this meeting out of a somewhat paternalistic sense that I might be able to "do something" for a poor athlete. We met for lunch at Hamburg Inn No. 2, my favorite restaurant in Iowa City. The student entered with a very tall and very huge black man whose appearance immediately frightened me. He reminded me of something from which I had been running for most of my adult life. Like my return to Iowa City to live one half-block away from my old apartment, the image of Tyrone Dye also brought back memories, this time to my own college years in Atlanta, and to another huge black athlete named Tank. I had feared him.

But this present version of Tank was a gentle giant. There was something of a shy little boy in this seven-foot-tall, three-hundred-pound or more black man. Sitting, he filled the entire side of the table. His eyes moved quickly. He remained silent while the young writer told Tyrone Dye's story. He was born in Gary, Indiana sometime during the 1950s to a mother who did not want him. He knew very little about his father, and the other children teased him and called him Rodan. He claimed to be related to the family of Michael Jackson. A high school football coach took an interest in him, and he was trained to be a gladiator. His *lanista*, or his coach, must have trained him for the specific purpose of being recruited by some college. Indeed, he was recruited, by Iowa, during the early 1970s. He quickly became a star, Saturday's hero, and he learned that his job was to be ferocious on the playing field. His legend as a star began here. I saw pictures of him in football gear, in the sacred black and gold. He seemed to be straining to look ferocious. Because he was a star, a man of importance to the Iowa team, he was passed along in his classes. Things were made easy for him, as they were for other stars on the team. The goal of the team seemed to be winning, and to the extent that Tyrone Dye's presence guaranteed many wins, he remained a star, and was also cannibalized academically.

During his senior year he was recruited by a professional football team. After "graduation" from Iowa, Tyrone reported to the team's training camp. His expectations were high, and he trained with enthusiasm. But during summer practice he broke a leg. The *lanistae* of that team, trying to get rid of him, insisted that he should still report for farm team practice. Tyrone, a true Spartan partisan of *agogê*, the "rough upbringing" of the Spartan way of life, got up early each morning to walk with crutches to the farm camp. One morning he was given a ride by an elderly white couple. When they saw his situation, they invited him to live in their home. They were deeply religious people, and Tyrone began calling them "Mom" and "Dad." They wanted him to withdraw from the training camp, but Tyrone refused. Tyrone says that one day, in the office of a *lanista*, a gun was pulled on him and he was ordered to sign a release. I never learned whether or not he signed the release, but soon after this incident Tyrone Dye returned to Iowa City. By this time his fame had faded, his time as a star had passed. Tyrone slept on the streets of Iowa City, even during the winter months. A family of poor whites finally took him in. He began to do odd jobs. He could get no higher work because, according to test results, even with a college degree, he was illiterate.

Then a very beautiful thing, which involves the Athenian nature of Iowa City, took place. An old white woman named Miss Mary met Tyrone Dye in the Iowa Student Union, where he was sitting at a table trying to read a book. The two of them soon became a local legend. People began talking about the frail, elderly white woman and the huge black athlete meeting each morning at a table by the window in the dining room of the Iowa Student Union. They began with grade school books, and then moved up, grade level by grade level. Tyrone Dye began to read. A little white female had passed on to him, against the sage advice of Socrates, the belief that he could do something more than be a killer fullback on the football field. Tyrone began reading his way into a better understanding of the world around him. Also, he began to make contact with his mother's family in Arkansas. He began to visit "Big Momma," his mother's mother. He began to visit his family back in Gary. He began to take religion seriously. He became a Hawkeye again, and he began giving pep talks to the team. He was invited to travel with the team for games in other parts of the country. But just to ensure people that he was still the Rodan of playing-field fame, when some white policemen in Coralville, the next town from Iowa City, harassed him one night, Tyrone picked up one of them and threw him over the police car. But beyond this, he was still essentially a caring, gentle giant.

Now he wanted to write his story.

My heart went out to him, and I began to help him as best I could.

I began, then, to struggle with this new reality, to try to see deeper into the world that had produced Tyrone Dye. I met a track coach named Ted Wheeler, who had once won a gold medal at an Olympic event. He lived just around the corner from me, was from Georgia himself, and often invited me to his home for dinner. He grew collard greens in his backyard, and enjoyed cooking a pot of them for his friends and for the men on his team. Ted Wheeler is more than six feet tall, dresses elegantly, and is known to be a perfect gentleman. He also began to remind me of someone whom I had known before. There was an aristocratic manner about Ted Wheeler. He insisted that his runners excel in their academic work; he commanded them to violate Socrates' edict. He was always in deep trouble about this, but he always held his ground. Once, when an athlete was accused of raping a white female student in her dorm room, after everyone else was convinced of the athlete's guilt, it was Ted Wheeler who put up his home to support the athlete's bail and his legal fees. The rape occurred during the mid-1970s, but the athlete was not cleared of the charges until the mid-1980s. I began to admire Ted Wheeler.

I quickly learned that, since Iowa had always been a haven for black athletes, it was going to be assumed that I was also an athlete. There was at Iowa, during the early 1980s, a basketball coach named George Raveling. He seemed to be an eccentric, and his team began to lose games. In Hamburg Inn, during those years, I was almost certain to run into elderly people, coming into Iowa City from the country towns to attend games. They would be polite with me, even sitting at my table and sharing their newspapers. When the proper degree of "neighboring" had been established, one of them might look directly at me and whisper, "What's wrong with George?" My own strategy became, of course, one of "passing" as the most enthusiastic of fans. My password, especially during the Saturday Religious Ritual, when greeting someone on the street, was the incantation "How 'bout them Hawks?!!!" If I had to go into Seaton's Meat Market on a sports day, I was sure to find all the butchers watching a game on television. They had already assumed that I was an athlete because all the black males they noticed were athletes. I did not disappoint them. If I had to go into Seaton's on a Saturday, I always took my hammer along with me. I would look soberly at the game in progress on the television just to the right of the meat counter, and I would wave my hammer and shout

. . . . . . . . .

"Kill!!! Kill!!!" Such gestures eased my transition into the heart of the community.

But in those days I was only acting.

## HOMOIOI AND HELOTS

The stereotypes behind the real images I had of Tyrone Dye and Ted Wheeler came back to me as I watched the opening ceremonies of the Atlanta Olympics in the summer of 1996. I saw Muhammad Ali, with a stern dignity imposed by Parkinson's disease, bearing in a quivering hand the torch that would light the fire, which in turn would signal the official opening of the games. Muhammad Ali seemed much larger than life at that moment, and I dwelt on the irony of the moment. Peisistratos, an Athenian tyrant in mid-sixth century B.C.E., had established the first Pan Athenaic Procession in which all the people of Athens marched in a great procession to the Temple of Athena. This same Peisistratos the tyrant also sponsored the first written versions of the *Iliad* and the *Odyssey*. And he laid the basis for what, under Kleisthenes, his successor, would become the concept of *isonomia*—equality before the law—which, these many centuries later, would result in Muhammad Ali leading another great processional in Atlanta, a formerly segregated Southern town. There was an abundance of significant history in this event, and as I watched some of the sporting events, for the first time in my life, I began to remember the athletes of my own day in Atlanta, and I began to put them into context, inspired by the insight in Willie Morris's observation that "in the South football is a religion."

Willie Morris was talking about the style of ancient Sparta.

One requirement for all freshmen at Morris Brown College, which I attended for three years, was that they live with the athletes in Grant Hall. The first image these country boys saw, when they arrived by bus or by train or by car from the small towns of Georgia, Alabama, and South Carolina, was the image of an athlete. His nickname was Tank, and he seemed much, much larger than his honorific. He was deep, dark, purple black, with gaps between his front teeth. He sat naked on the steps of Grant Hall with a red head-rag on his head, weighing a thick paddle in his right hand, testing its heft against the palm of his left hand. There was the stuff of ritual here. Morris Brown College, a private, working-class institution founded and supported by the African American Episcopal Church, was in continual struggle to prove itself equal to the much more affluent Morehouse (called "the whorehouse") and Spelman. While the two elite colleges were supported by white philanthropy, Morris Brown was mostly supported by the collection plates of ministers in small towns in Georgia, Alabama, and South Carolina. Legend has it that the endowment of the college, in 1887, came from black washerwomen in the small towns, who collected Octagon Soap wrappers for their coupons, and who traded many thousands of them to the Octagon Soap Company for a certain amount of cash. On Founder's Day, while white Northern philanthropists visited the campuses of Morehouse and Spelman, gruff-speaking black ministers in shiny gabardine suits strolled across the Morris Brown campus, reaffirming its lower-class origins. Morris Brown made little pretense to academic excellence. Its chosen path to fame was through the number of athletes trained there who would graduate into the starting lines of professional teams; or the number of accountants or teachers who would go back into the small towns, settle in them, have children, and send more poor students back to the college. The college song promised as much:

> Alma Mater, Pride of Earth
> Gavest to me another birth,
> Haven for all hungry souls,
> Feeding them shall be our goal . . .

Tank's ritual purpose was to initiate the freshmen into this complex and ambiguous reality. While he had a sense of *his* role, the freshmen did not have a sense of their *own*. This is why they had to be instructed.

As in the Spartan martial utopia, athletes like Tank were of the *homoioi*—the peers. They had already proved their worth on football fields and basketball courts. Rough-and-tumble country boys themselves, they came to Morris Brown College already schooled in the norms of the *agogê*. Perhaps another word derived from Greek—helots, serfs bound to the land, belonging to the entire Spartan state—could be applied to the freshmen boys. Tank, "Bull" Thomas, and Ivory Jones dominated Grant Hall. The football coach, the resident *lanista*, a man named Coach Thomas, was the master of the dorm, lived in an apartment there with his family, and gave the athletes general license. It seemed to be their ritual obligation, to a structure much larger than themselves, to initiate the freshmen into the ways of the *homoioi* through random beatings. They had access to all the room keys in Grant Hall, and they used them religiously. Further proof of their power was their connection with a patron—a very rich black man, a homosexual— who lived close to the campus. They called him Pal. They were his clients in the Roman sense, his adopted sons. They told stories about visiting him in his home and watching television with him. Whenever a woman's face appeared on the screen, Pal would order, "*Get that bitch off!*" They laughed a great deal over the power of this refrain. They were served special meals in the cafeteria. Their brothers dominated all the fraternities. Their temples were the football field and the Joe Louis Gymnasium.

My roommate, a boy named Freddy Thomas, from a place called Eufaula, Alabama, was a very sensitive and gentle soul. He and I quickly formed a bond. To avoid the company of the athletes in the communal shower, Freddy and I got up each morning just before dawn. I can still hear his voice saying, "Let's go down, Room." Freddy helped me with math while I helped him with English. Through some luck, Freddy had an easy relationship with Tank. Tank liked Freddy. On those ritual occasions when the "peers" with their communal keys, raided the rooms of the helots, Freddy and I sometimes had luck. While we pushed against the pressure of the door pushing in on us, Freddy would shout, "Tank, Tank, *Tank!!!*" Once in a while, Tank's voice might be heard out in the hall. "*Y'all let Freddy alone!*" Freddy seemed to know the human side of Tank much better than I did.

Now I remember back to those days because, besides the resemblance in size between Tank and Tyrone Dye, I can see more clearly the outline of a certain code coming into focus. Grant Hall *was* a rough approximation of a Spartan village. The freshmen boys *were* rough approximations of helots. The athletes *were homoioi*. A group of country boys, some of them with intellectual ambitions, had been thrown into an institutional arrangement that had already settled on the athletes as elites. The athletes' job became one of democratic leveling, one of forcing the freshmen boys into accepting the preexisting arrangement. In Sparta the *homoioi* often arranged "secret missions" to kill helots who were too ambitious or too energetic, or who were getting too big for their settled status. Even the more enlightened Athenians, to protect their version of democracy, used secret ballots to ostracize, or to shun, those among them who had too much influence. Those chosen were sent into exile for years, and would be recalled only under special circumstances. This process of leveling down, with roots in the very origins of democracy, made the athletes of Grant Hall the enforcers of *isonomia* much more than they could ever imagine. They taught a life lesson that should have prepared anyone for the same rituals in the world outside Grant Hall.

They also made me into a kind of Spartan.

But I did not know this *then*. I did not know that such rituals helped to justify the expression of something deep in *human* nature. Even while I tested and toughened and trained, I felt deep anger toward the athletes of Grant Hall. I could not appreciate the gift they were giving me, and I just did not understand the more perverse aspects of the *isonomia*.

My uncle, Thomas McPherson, was the chaplain of Morris Brown College. A recent graduate, Thomas had enrolled as a graduate student at the Interdenominational Theological Seminary just next door to the college. He was chaplain of the college during both my years in Grant Hall. His first order of business was to make the attendance of vespers compulsory. Since many students, among them athletes, had other uses for the vespers hour, they cut it with an impunity that was religious. But Thomas retaliated by working with the dean to penalize this. A certain number of grade points were deducted if a certain number of vespers were missed. This enraged the athletes. They referred to him, privately, as Uncle Tom, among other things. Thomas had a habit of sitting on the vespers platform with his left knee crossed over his right leg at a distinctive angle. He became for the athletes just as potent an image as Tank, seated naked on the steps of Grant Hall, had become for me.

. . . . . . . . . .

One night the athletes came to my room and took me away from any help that Freddy might have given me. They blindfolded me and took me to a room in another dormitory. They also brought another freshman named Jerome Tudas. He was a very bright man who had already declared a major in physics. He was a mulatto, from New Jersey, and was extremely self-confident, if not cocky, depending on one's point of view. Both Tudas and I had been selected by the *homoioi* for one of their "secret missions."

"Is McPherson your uncle?" they asked me. I admitted this fact. They made me sit on a chair and ordered me to cross my left knee over my right leg. It took a few tries and some help from the athletes before my left leg was positioned at just the angle they considered right. Then they ordered me to hit Jerome Tudas. I refused. Then they ordered Jerome Tudas to hit me. Tudas complied. Then they asked me to hit Tudas. I refused. Then they asked Tudas to hit me. Tudas complied. This exchange went on until, in either anger or in frustration, Tudas, when his turn came around, hit me with such force that I lost consciousness. When I recovered, most of the athletes were gone. But Tudas was still there. He was deeply sorry, and could not understand why I had kept refusing to hit him.

I know now that my only athletic skill, back then, was running. In high school I had avoided athletics, in addition to most other group activities. I had arrived at college unable to even dance. But I could run with great speed, and I moved across the campus with such swiftness that my best friend, Edward Halman, began calling me The Flash. No one could see that I was juggling a great number of obligations. Besides the work required for my courses, I worked as a banquet waiter at the old Dinkler Plaza Hotel on Peachtree Street in downtown Atlanta. I could easily get to the Dinkler Plaza in fifteen minutes by running across the Hunter Street Bridge. I worked as a waiter at the Piedmount Driving Club in the Atlanta suburbs, and at Christmas break I worked as an extra in the post office. I worked part-time in the Morris Brown library. And I worked as a janitor in Grant Hall. I also worked as an assistant to Dean Robinson, the Dean of Men. It seems that I was always running, and this continued to be my only athletic skill. But to complete the required course in gym, I purchased a jockstrap and a sweat suit, and I reported to the Joe Louis Gymnasium on schedule each week and went through the required training of an athlete. I was always missing baskets, could not dribble worth a damn, and could not manage headstands. Still, I was enthusiastic in my efforts. The basketball coach, a tall mulatto man, was both patient and kind. He was always encouraging, no matter how badly I performed.

As an assistant to Dean Robinson, one of my jobs was to sit at night in his office in Grant Hall and handle any small matters that might come up. Another responsibility was to clean the bathrooms of Grant Hall with Mr. Murchison, the school janitor. In this way I came to know the personal habits of pampered athletes. Dean Robinson always went home at the end of the day, and responsibility for Grant Hall then resided with Mr. Thomas, the resident *lanista*, the football coach who lived with his family in a private apartment just behind Dean Robinson's office. My immediate supervisor was an older man, a graduate student at the Interdenominational Theological Center. He was a former athlete, was muscled narcissistically, and was a member of Alpha Phi Alpha fraternity. I wanted very badly to pledge Alpha, but Dean Robinson, a cigar-chewing Phi Beta Sigma, had already hinted heavily that he expected me to pledge Sigma. The Alpha men were considered the intellectual and physical elites ("O, when an Alpha Man walks down the street,/He looks one hundred per from head to feet . . ."). Edward Halman had already pledged Alpha, and he was trying to bring me into the club. The older man in Dean Robinson's office, then, was my potential big brother. When I finally did buck Dean Robinson and pledged Alpha instead of Phi Beta Sigma, I delivered my soul into the small hands of this big brother.

I was soon required to take over his office hours, for which time he still collected pay. I was required to "make a run," at any time of night he named, down Hunter Street to Pascal's to get for him a fried chicken sandwich. I became his private helot. I was required to write love letters to girls on campus who had attracted his attention. Whenever I objected or refused, his reply was always, "Then I'll see you at the Pledge Club meeting!" They beat you at Pledge Club meetings. Big brothers from all the colleges in the Atlanta University Center, many of them former athletes, would turn up at these meetings in multi-

·   ·   ·   ·   ·   ·   ·   ·   ·   ·

tudes. They were smug, wore the Alpha colors, and caressed thick, carefully polished wooden paddles, also showing the Alpha colors. The pledges were required to "give up some skin" to any big brother who asked for it. The required technique was to bend over, holding one's balls with one hand and bracing one's self on the floor with the other. Then the big brothers would go to work. I never cried. Some of them were particularly hard on me because of their memories of compulsory vespers. Others suspected that I was a homosexual because I had never had a date or had even been seen with a girl. I can still remember this interrogation:

"Pledge McPherson, are you a punk?"

"No, big brother."

"When was the last time you had you some pussy?"

"Last week, big brother."

"On campus?"

"No, big brother. She lives in the city."

"What's her name and address?"

I gave the only Atlanta address I knew. It was my grandmother's address, my father's mother, who lived over a funeral parlor on a street many, many miles away from campus.

"Pledge McPherson, you better get yourself some pussy!"

I could take the beatings. But I could not take the constant orders, which I knew were calculated to degrade me. This was why I had refused to hit Jerome Tudas. One evening, during the pledge season, the big brother in Dean Robinson's office, ordered me to "make a run" up Hunter Street to Pascal's to get him a fried chicken sandwich. Something in me had had enough. I said, "No. Get it yourself!" I even said, "No, *motherfucker*!" This was the first time, I think, that I had ever used this word in anger. Some nights later, at a basketball game in Joe Louis Gym, this same big brother shouted to me from his bench on the other side of the basketball court, "Pledge McPherson, run down to Pascal's and get a fried chicken sandwich for my girlfriend!" I ignored him. He shouted again above the noise of the crowd: "You go and get that chicken sandwich or I'll burn your ass at Pledge Club meeting!"

Then I shouted back: "I'm not *going* to any more Pledge Club meetings. I *quit* the frat!"

Now, here in Iowa, these many years later, I still wonder what mysteries might have resided on the other side of true brotherhood inside the
frat. I have read that those who survived the Spartan *agogê*, the rough
upbringing, moved into eating clubs, and from these a select few were
elevated to the *homoioi* who enjoyed complete equality and who had
complete dedication to the Spartan state. Restriction was the key to all
of Spartan life. At the height of Sparta's power, I have learned, there
were only a thousand Spartans with pure citizenship. The others,
though they far outnumbered the *homoioi*, had no such rights. I know
now that restrictive access is the key to all elite groupings. But the athletes in Grant Hall were the first to raise for me a certain question:
What if the quality of the *agogê*—sleeping on beds made of bulrushes,
taking cold baths, wearing a single garment, eating gruel made of pig's
blood, hiding foxes under one's garment, and remaining stoical while
the famished fox eats away at your own famished intestines—is *defi-
cient* in comparison with the quality of the tests you have set for *yourself*? What if what resides within the mystery of full acceptance by the
"peers" proves to be not worth the price that has already been paid?
Over every stage of my life since Grant Hall, in areas far, far
removed from black American life, the voice of the big brother in the
Joe Louis Gymnasium has come back to me, again and again and
again. It always begins with your own eagerness to commit to something, to "pledge the frat." One moves as far as one can with pure
enthusiasm. Then a point is always reached when something is asked
which, if done, would betray some part of one's self. This, I know now,
is the way of the world, the way of all greedy institutions. Even street
gangs, those now sophisticated enough to imitate the rituals and norms
of the "higher" levels of society, require their pledges to take drugs, to
vandalize cars, to prostitute themselves, even to kill other people. This
has *always* been the way of the world. Some infection of the soul dis-
eased enough to breed a degree of amorality that becomes *normative*,
but most especially an unwavering and fixed *loyalty*, must be the price
of admission to almost all elite groups, whether *homoioi* or the athletes

. . . . . . . . . .

of Grant Hall. These rough-and-tumble men taught me something essential, something that I have always kept in mind ever since. There is a point, which *always* comes, when a certain trade-off is required for continued advancement. One must watch carefully for this point, with the practiced eye of a quarterback. One must *not* look for the ball being thrown but rather for *any* patch of clear blue or green space. Then one must *run* toward it, and *away* from catching the ball and scoring the winning point and riding on the shoulders, briefly, of one's peers. One must run like a helot from Grant Hall toward the Hunter Street Bridge and Peachtree Street. One must run like the wind, and not look back, no matter *what* it is that one is leaving behind. A certain amount of *self-esteem* resides in the quality of such a run. One must run like a fox, like an Athenian Greek, in one's own private Olympiad.

## DEME

The Spartans were said to be like hedgehogs because they were slow, cautious, austere. They knew only one trick, but they knew it well. The Athenians, in contrast, were said to be like foxes. They were adaptable, clever, able to suffer defeats and then regroup and reverse those defeats. In Socrates' view of democracy, a person was good for only one thing. He might have been describing the Spartans rather than his fellow Athenians. Or he might have been describing the athletes of Grant Hall. I remember that, late one night, during my second year in Grant Hall, a white policeman holding a gun brought one of the athletes into the lobby. He stood behind the athlete just outside Dean Robinson's office. The athlete had been arrested for either buying stolen property or for receiving stolen property. He looked humble and afraid. The handcuffs on him, I believe now, had been calculated by the policeman to send a certain message to the other athletes. The handcuffs symbolized the prerogatives of the structure of white supremacy to invade, and even to dominate, the stronghold of the *homoioi*. An awareness of this prerogative was in the cold face and manner of the officer. The cuffed athlete had implicated others of his peers in the crime, the policeman said, and he was there to search the rooms of all the men named by this one humbled athlete. He had not bothered to get an official search warrant. I felt unequal to this problem, so I woke up Coach Thomas in his apartment behind Dean Robinson's office. Coach Thomas was a big man, a huge man, but he seemed to swell even larger when he confronted the smirking white policeman. But after he had listened to the allegations, he kept his attention, and his rage, focused on the athlete in handcuffs. "Did you receive stolen property?" he shouted at the athlete. The athlete began to moan and whine and whimper, like one of Richard Pryor's characters. "Aw, man, I didn't do nothin' . . ." "Did you receive any stolen property, and did you sell or give any to anybody here?" his *lanista* shouted. By this time all the athletes had come out of their rooms, as had the freshmen boys, their helots, and had crowded into the lobby of Grant Hall. The white policeman, with his gun, seemed to be dominating all of us, except Coach Thomas. The athlete finally admitted to Coach Thomas that he had received some stolen property and had sold some of it to some of the other athletes. The coach required him to name all the men in the presence of the policeman. Then Coach Thomas shouted with absolute rage in his voice to all the assembled athletes: "I want you to go to your rooms and get every item that you got. I want you to bring it all down here." The athletes scattered, while the *lanista* looked at the policeman with a silent, studied fury. When the athletes had returned with their booty, Coach Thomas ordered them to give every item to the officer. Then he said to the policeman, "There it all is. You can take it. Now, don't you ever, ever, ever, *ever* come into this dorm again without a search warrant! *Do you hear me?* Don't you *ever* try to raid this dorm again on a *bullshit tip*!" The coach towered over the officer, almost unable to keep himself from attacking the little man in the blue uniform. In that moment I, and all the other helots, saw the deep country-boy fear drain out of faces of the athletes, and we saw their renewed confidence, or manliness, returning. The *lanista* was leading his team again, and now they seemed ready to charge. The policeman saw it, too. There is a kind of self-hypnotic gaze that comes into the eyes of white people when they know they have power over black people. The sleepy, glazed eyes say that they have faded out of their individual selves and have merged with something much larger. This knowledge seems to be beneath the shallowness of their smiles. They seem unconsciously engaged with

. . .   .   .   .   .   .   .   .

some mentoring voice suggesting, *"Exterminate all the brutes!"* This same unconscious sense of self had been behind the policeman's power-smile from the moment he had entered Grant Hall. But after Coach Thomas's words, the race-glaze faded into only the pale face of one individual white man facing a football team under the discipline of their coach. He gathered up the stolen items and hurried out the door of Grant Hall. "Now," Coach Thomas said, "I want all of you to go to your rooms and don't come out again!" They shuffled away like the hedgehogs they were, moaning and whining.

This was my sophomore year, and I began to respect Coach Thomas as a different kind of person from his athletes. When I worked at night in Dean Robinson's office, I would share my papers with him. Coach Thomas was a private, kindly man, one who was just trying to do his job and take care of his family. To me he became a role model of something larger than the Spartan code, the *agogê*, of Grant Hall. I wrote a paper on the life and death of Sir Walter Raleigh for a literature class and asked him to read it. He liked it, but could not understand why I chose to end the paper with Sir Walter's noble words on the scaffold. I think that Coach Thomas was much more interested in the practical matter of winning one's way through life than he was in noble statements at the point of death. Football must have meant almost everything to him, but he still maintained the urbanity to endure the impracticalities of this world. I liked him.

During this time the Atlanta Public Library had just been integrated, and on Saturdays I would dress in my one suit and walk across the Hunter Street Bridge to Peachtree Street. I would turn left onto Peachtree and walk past Rich's, past the railroad station, past the Dinkler Plaza Hotel, and walk on to a place named Five Points. In this place five streets came together. On one corner there was an old Loew's theater featuring a permanent display of scenes from *Gone with the Wind*. On the Peachtree Street corner was the majestic Atlanta Public Library. I had never had any unrestricted social access to white people, and so I thought it proper to be at my best. This is why I wore my suit to the library. I just did not know the "white" customs of the country. Very few black people went into that library in those days immediately after its official desegregation, but I was almost always there on Saturday mornings. The library allowed people to check out books, records, and paintings. I always borrowed as many as my library card allowed. The attendants were always gracious to me. I always returned the borrowed items on time.

During one trip home from the library, in my suit and with some borrowed paintings under my arm, a white man came up behind me on Peachtree Street. He moved quickly to my side, and with his right elbow he knocked me in the side as hard as he could. He said, "*Get on the other side of the street, goddamn nigger!*" Then he hurried on down Peachtree Street in his business suit. I gathered up the paintings, much more angry than hurt. Then I remembered Coach Thomas facing down the arrogant white policeman in the lobby of Grant Hall, and decided that I would not take this insult. I followed the man all the way down Peachtree Street, until we reached the area of the train station. Then he crossed the street and went into a bar. I followed him as far as the door, looked in, and saw him seated on a stool at the bar in a crowd of white men. A black woman was at the end of the bar washing glasses. I crossed Peachtree Street again and went up to a white policeman, who was directing traffic at the station. I said to him, "I want to report someone for assault and battery. He's now in that bar across the street." The policeman said he could not leave his post but would put in a call for someone else to hear my complaint. I crossed Peachtree Street again and waited outside the bar. I waited for almost an hour. Finally, a squad car pulled up, driven by a young white officer. I told him that the man I was charging with assault and battery was inside the bar. The officer looked intently at me, but he did walk with me to the bar door. I pointed to the white man in the business suit. The young officer looked puzzled, but he went into the bar, from which I was happily segregated, and brought out the man. He was drunk, and must have been drunk when he elbowed me. I repeated my facts to the officer and to him. "Did you hit him and call him a nigger?" the young officer asked. The middle-aged man denied it. "Why," he said, "I happen to *love* nigras." He went back into the bar and soon came back out with the black woman, the dishwasher. "She knows me," he told the officer. "Tell him how much I like the cullids," he ordered the black

JAMES A. MCPHERSON     79

woman. "Yassuh," she replied. "I know him," she said to the officer. "He likes the cullids. *Yassuh*." The officer called me aside. "If you complain," he told me, "you'll have to go downtown to sign some papers." "Let's go," I told him. He went back over to the man in the suit and the black dishwasher. "*Yassuh*," she kept insisting. "I knows him and he likes the cullids." The officer said that the three of us would have to go in his car to the police station. Then he took us to his car, and we sat there, the officer behind the wheel and the drunk white man and I in the back seat. We sat there, equally arrested.

All of my life I had been passive. I was quiet and withdrawn. I did what my family expected of me. I seldom talked. I tried only to protect those few things that were of great importance to me. People called me shy, strange, a doormat, stoical, a person who could take it. I was all of these things, but I thought of myself as something more. In my private view, some things were of greater importance than others: not hitting Jerome Tudas upon someone else's order; refusing to return to the Pledge Club because this action would turn my life back over to the athletes who would become my tormentors again. I had already seen through the athletes. I had seen that they were Socrates' ideal citizens with a single skill. They were hedgehogs with only one way to exhibit their prowess. I did not want to be a hedgehog. Nor was it a matter of civil rights, which was then the new religion in the air. There were always group activities based on theatrical demonstrations calculated to attract the attention of the media. I wanted to do something for *myself*, outside of any group involvement, something private but also *right* according to my own scale of values. And so we continued sitting in that police car, across Peachtree Street from the train station, while the Old Atlanta and the Becoming Atlanta—the white middle-aged man in the business suit and the young white policeman—silently anguished over the issue of what Atlanta would become.

The officer would not start the police car. He seemed intent on lecturing me on the byzantine procedures that awaited me once I filed my complaint. I would need a lawyer, bonds, fees, witnesses, court dates. The list went on and on. Most likely, he viewed me as an agitator, or as someone linked to a protest group who had set up this incident for purposes of publicity. He was torn between his legal duty to help me and his fear that he was being drawn into something beyond his own powers to perceive or even to control. As for my assailant, he was then proving himself an unworthy antagonist, and even an unworthy white man. He put his hand on my shoulder, he patted me, he moaned. He straightened my tie, he apologized, he offered up a lifetime of heartfelt acts toward the cullid. The young white officer hated him—this was reflected by his face in the rearview mirror. While his sympathies were with his white compatriot and with the structure of white supremacy they shared, he was being forced, more and more, to sympathize with what was becoming for him a tragic distortion of what was supposed to be the best genetic expression of the human race. *Never allow a white man to cry in front of you. Afterward he will hate you for seeing this show of weakness and will seek to do you harm.*

And so we sat there—the young officer listing the legal difficulties ahead of me, the drunk man fawning, and I torn between the two— while the car did not move. And then it came to me that I was degrading this drunk white man in the same way that he and his ancestors had degraded me and my ancestors, the way the athletes in Grant Hall had tried to degrade me. It came to me—not then, but afterward—that the institution of racism was itself a kind of *homoioi*, that the individuals were advanced from one level to another within the mind-set, simultaneously giving up the most human parts of themselves, until they reached the level of peers. This level was the point at which nothing else mattered except complete dedication to the race, or to the frat, or to the team. This was the only *good* left to contemplate.

I never knew whether or not the young officer ever understood the nature of the *human* issues his parked car raised, but his manner told me that, for an instant, he hated our fawning white companion much more than he hated me. As for me, I saw, for the first time in my life, the fear of a white man, and it made him *human*, not superior. I began to understand, then, that I should never get into the habit of oppressing anyone, because I could easily become like this empty, fawning white man.

I got out of the stalled police car and allowed the officer to have the victory he had tried so hard to plan. He could not see that my own

. . . . . . . . . . .

victory, under such circumstances, would have been a Pyrrhic one. I walked away. When I got back to Grant Hall with my paintings and my story, Coach Thomas told me that I still had grounds for a civil rights suit against both the drunk white man and the police officer. I told Coach Thomas that I did not have the time and the energy and the money to follow through with the complaint. But privately, I did not want to become a hedgehog, knowing only one way to fight.

I wanted to get out of Grant Hall, and out of Atlanta. I wanted to find something worthy of defending by myself. I think I wanted to learn to improvise, to become an Athenian fox, instead of a race-bound Spartan hedgehog. I wanted to become anti-Socratesian in my actions, and work against the fate of a fixed purpose settled by single-mindedness. I wanted to run like the wind, toward something *new* and fresh and green.

### OIKOUMENE

Ted Wheeler, the Iowa track coach, reminds me of the basketball coach at Morris Brown, a kindly man who gave me an A in gymnastics. I now find myself imposing on this nameless man an ethic that Ted Wheeler once explained to me: "Winning is not everything. When you win, somebody else loses, and you must feel human sympathy for that person." Ted Wheeler is an Athenian *lanista*, as was the Morris Brown *lanista* who gave me an A for mere effort.

It happened in this way: During the examination period of my first year at Morris Brown, I was still juggling responsibilities. I was still working with Mr. Murchinson, doing janitorial duties in and around Grant Hall. The morning of my final examination in gym, during which I was expected to perform all the tumbles and headstands that had been practiced for a full year, I made my usual rounds of the bathrooms and staircases in Grant Hall. I scrubbed the toilets and collected the trash. Then I took the rubbish out of Grant Hall to a garbage collection unit. While I was dumping the trash, I misstepped, and my left leg slipped between the gratings covering an underground sewer. My leg went through the grating all the way to my left kneecap, where my fall was stopped abruptly and where my left kneecap took the full weight of the stop. The kneecap was badly damaged. I washed and bandaged the wound as best I could before putting on my jockstrap and my shorts and heading to the Joe Louis Gymnasium for my final exam. There I stood in line while the others demonstrated their mastery of the techniques. I remember that a man named Maddox was exceptionally good. When it was my turn I tumbled as best I could, did backrolls as best I could, did the assigned headstands. I did them no better and no worse than I had ever done them, except that blood began seeping through the bandages on my left knee and I was in tremendous pain. The basketball coach, who was scoring our performances, watched me favor my left leg and saw the bloody bandage. He advised me to go immediately to the infirmary.

The A that came in the mail that summer taught me something about the old Athenian idea of athletics. It taught me that the discipline imposed on the body was intended to discipline the mind and the *spirit*.

Except for my grade in English, this was the most prized grade during my freshman year at Morris Brown.

A grade much higher than this one was awarded three years later, the day of my graduation from Morris Brown College. It happened this way: During my three years at Morris Brown College, I had never had a girlfriend. There were some girls whom I liked, and one whom I loved, but none of them ever responded to me. I had spent my junior year at Morgan State College in Baltimore, and I fell in love with a girl there; but after my year at Morgan was over, I had to go back to Morris Brown, and the girl in Baltimore withdrew from me. From my freshman year on at Morris Brown, I had held onto a fantasy of sitting with a special girl on a certain cement bench located under some trees on the lawn of the campus. During three years of running back and forth across the campus, I had envied the men who sat with their girlfriends on that bench. I believe that this slab of broken concrete represented for me the height of romantic love. It was superior to all my desires for sex and for love-tinged telephone calls in the night. I had had none of these things during my years at Morris Brown, but there was always the visible promise represented by the concrete bench.

There was a girl I had come to like, a warm, mature, older girl who had already graduated from Spelman College and who had ambitions to become a professional singer. But she was the girlfriend of Jerome Tudas. It happened that, during my senior year, I became editor of the yearbook as well as coeditor of the school newspaper. My office was on the ground-floor room on the left side of Grant Hall. Jerome Tudas, who was then a teaching assistant in the physics department, had an office just across the courtyard from me. His girlfriend, Jean Waymer, used to cook food for him in her sister's home and take it to him in the evenings. She often stopped by my office on her way back home to talk with me. She was a very pretty, very warm, and refined young woman. She was always smiling. She listened to what I had to say, and she made me feel that I did indeed have something to say.

The day before the graduation ceremony, Jerome Tudas and I had dinner at Pascal's. He bragged about the hot date he had for graduation night. He mentioned that a certain girl had had her hand under his black robe during graduation practice. He was confident in his belief that the next night his passion would be consummated. I asked Tudas if he would be taking out Jean Waymer after the graduation ceremonies. Tudas said that he had no plans for her. I then excused myself, went straight to a telephone, and called her up. I told her that Tudas had said they would not be going out together after graduation. I asked if she would be willing to have dinner with me. Jean said yes.

After dinner at Pascal's on graduation night, Jean and I walked up Hunter Street and back to the Morris Brown campus. We walked slowly in the sweet, warm, early June Atlanta evening. Jean Waymer always giggled at the slightest thing. She always smiled. We walked back to the almost deserted campus, and when we were on its lawn I asked Jean if she would do me a favor before I took her back to her sister's house. I pointed to the concrete bench under the trees on the lawn almost across from Grant Hall. I asked if she would sit on it with me. She laughed. But then she did walk with me across the lawn and sit with me on that bench, that love seat. We sat there for a long time in the bird-filled, sweet-leaves-smelling Atlanta evening. We sat there. Looking forward from that bench you could see Fountain Hall, the main teaching building. To the left of Fountain Hall was the other teaching building, Grant Hall. Most of its windows were dark. The freshmen boys had already left, and the only people in were Coach Thomas and his family and those athletes who had no place to go. I remembered back to the Christmas vacation of my freshman year, when I worked as an extra in the Atlanta post office and also as a waiter at the Dinkler Plaza Hotel. In the late evening hours I would walk across the Hunter Street Bridge and back to my room in a dark Grant Hall. The place was dark and quiet and foreboding, the way it looked from the perspective of the concrete bench.

I tried to kiss Jean Waymer, but knew nothing about seduction. I had never thought beyond getting someone to sit with me on the bench. Jean Waymer giggled. Then she laughed. She kissed me for all of the days I had spent learning to be Spartan inside Grant Hall.

# The Natural

.   .   .   .   .   .   .   .   .   .

*by*
TERI BOSTIAN

When I was a kid, morning kickball at Willetts Elementary was the rite of passage into more organized sports, and most if not all nine-, ten- and eleven-year-old boys raced to the school yard before homeroom to claim positions in the lineups of our only two teams. Our field was no field at all, but blacktop, gravelly and sometimes sticky on hot days. And I stood at the very center, on the pitcher's mound, the painted circle that is the hub of playground baseball diamonds everywhere. One morning my team had picked up two outs, and we were itching to kick again before the bell rang. As I turned from passing the ball around the infield, Marty Britt stepped into the kicker's box.

Marty's family lived across from ours, on Route 34 outside Monmouth, Illinois. He and his perverted brother, Lonnie, used to come over at dusk in the summer and fall to play hide-and-seek. Lonnie hid with my older stepsister, Lorie, claiming later how he'd felt her up behind our barn or under the smelly rabbit hutches. Marty and I hid together too, but we were too giggly and afraid of getting caught to try what Lonnie talked so much about.

Marty was my boyfriend then—though, at ten, to put such a definitive term to a muddle so pleasing and yet so mortifying, and ultimately so fickle, would have been premature. He used to leave baskets of butterscotch disks and dandelions by my front door on May Day, and after school he gave me rides home on the back of his banana-

85

seated bike, stopping by deserted softball diamonds on the long way home to see if this was the day I'd say yes to a kiss. I said yes only once, and Marty's moist lips left a mark so wet on my mouth it felt the same as when my stepbrothers held me down, spit on my face, and then blew on it. I liked Marty mostly because he liked me.

In the kicker's box, though, he was out of place. I watched him take a couple practice kicks—to get his steps and timing right—and I tried to remember if I'd ever seen him playing before. One or two of his friends played, and though they might have been more athletic than Marty, playing kickball with the rest of us, they were pretty mediocre. Maybe Marty had played on my team—just further down in the kicking order. Or maybe he was pinch-kicking this time for a regular player who was sick. Maybe he'd never paid any attention to kickball, and was just as surprised to see me as I was him. Whatever, there we were, and I knew after a minute of thinking about it that it was either him or me.

Kickball was for those of us still too young to play Little League. We usually played nine or ten to a side, and, because we had no adults around as coaches or umps, we followed devoutly the rules of baseball. The one exception was a base runner had to be touched by the ball to be called out. A defensive player could either hold the ball and tag the runner on his way past, or he could, and usually did, hurl the ball at him and send him flying. It wasn't as easy as it sounds—most of us, being nine or ten, couldn't consistently throw the heavy vinyl soccer ball and hit what we aimed for. All in all, it was a good balance, offense to defense. Every so often, though, the older boys would chunk the ball at our heads, beaning one of us so unexpectedly that we would flop like cartoon characters onto the blacktop, fattening red welts on our small heads, skinning knees, and bloodying clothes that would have to be explained to our mothers. Mrs. Nolan, our purse-lipped school nurse (who frowned especially on the cuts and bruises I showed off proudly), usually patched up one or two of us every morning before the bell.

My own abilities were pretty solid, if not always outstanding—I imagined myself as a Pete Rose sort of player. Charlie Hustle, my dad would say. Consistency, he'd say, doesn't wear you out as fast as fame.

.   .   .   .   .   .   .   .   .   .   .

I could be counted on to kick over second and snag at least a single, a double if the outfielder bobbled the ball—an error not so crazy for grade school fielders. On a good day, I'd boot it out over third base and might, once in a while, if I lucked out and caught the left fielder sleeping, end up with a homer. This outfield couldn't be suckered in, though, like they'd been once or twice at the beginning of the school year, figuring on a bunt or a short pop fly because I was a girl—I'd punted it over enough heads to keep them in their places.

On defense, I pitched. I liked being at the center of the game. On the mound, I had to bowl the ball as fast as I could over the plate without bouncing it on the blacktop. Then, when the ball was kicked, my job was to cover the short infield; to grab bunts, near-fouls, and miskicks quickly; and to sock the runner with the ball. Having a hand in every play pressured me to take the game more seriously than I would have out in left field; that pressure and constant practice improved my skills—my hand-eye coordination, my speed and aim, and my ability to think fast—making me a better pitcher than anyone out there.

My dad had taught me how to throw correctly—I never ever tossed the slow, soft trajectories my mother did, with the limp wrist and too much elbow. We practiced at home with his old glove and a grass-stained baseball; I stood on my imaginary hump of a mound, while he crouched behind a pretend home plate. With no paint or plate to guide me, I aimed for the almost padless mitt opened like a clam at his squat-high chest. I learned quickly to feel the beginnings of the pitch from my legs, hips, back, then through my shoulders and from my arm. I felt like a spring, the spiral uncoiling until the ball shot out from me like a bullet. Dad said I was a natural.

"Your arm—and then your hand and fingers—are mostly for guiding the ball," he would say, throwing it back slowly to demonstrate, then settling down again onto the balls of his feet. Growing up in Sandusky, Ohio, he had caught for summer baseball league teams, then, later, for the Farrell Cheek plant fast-pitch softball team. He'd also tutored and warmed up my uncle Kevin, his youngest brother, who (family legend has it) was once offered contracts with the Detroit Tigers and the Cleveland Indians. (Uncle Kevin was said to have turned them down to marry his high school sweetheart, something my dad snorted at privately, as if Kevin had believed girls and baseball didn't mix.) Throwing like a girl, for Dad, was less a signifier of sex than it was a statement of character.

"You just listen to me," he said, plopping the clam on top of my head like a hat. "Your old dad'll teach you everything he knows. One of these days, you'll be good as him. Maybe better."

Throwing a kickball was not throwing a baseball, but it was a start.

I blinked to make sure, but it was Marty all right. He liked those earthy colors like tan and brown, and was given to wearing corduroys. His Buster Brown bangs lay flat and long on his high forehead, and I thought, for a split second, he needed it cut. And I noticed again, as when we had huddled close in the summer, hiding in the cubbyhole of my basement entryway, that the flesh of his cheeks was so thin, so pale and translucent I could see the network of purple veins underneath. Suddenly, he seemed so vulnerable.

What a girl thing to think, I thought, and I looked around the field to see if anybody else had noticed. Brian Swanson and Mark MacKenzie hadn't seemed to. They were my best friends, and the three of us were the fastest runners in all three homerooms. At our age, running fast in p.e. class stood as the prerequisite trait of an athlete—until we got bigger and stronger and could prove ourselves otherwise. The girls who tagged along with us during school, and who stood on the other side of the fence behind home plate while we played—they were the ones always clucking about clothes and hair, about which boys were dogs, who was cute and who was sensitive. I had never thought about that sort of stuff before; my friends and I talked about Monday Night Football. It's not that I didn't think I was a girl—of course, I knew that. But I'd always been able to do what I wanted, so what I was really didn't matter. I guess I just didn't think about it much one way or the other.

I wondered, looking at Marty, if he had told any of his friends about us. That would be trouble, and I knew it. If you're girly enough to have a boyfriend, you're too girly to play against him at any kind of sport. No one really thought of me as "girlish," I don't think, and I was in on some of the ways boys thought because of it. It was a sin for a guy to play like a girl—not to know how to kick or throw right, and never concentrating on learning. The only thing worse was letting a girl beat you. But while boys will forgive other boys almost anything, a girl who beats you is unforgivable. She's taken advantage when someone is down, like a stranger in town shooting the hero in the back. If everyone found out I was girl enough to go with Marty, they'd think I was too much a girl to play kickball at all. I didn't know this so exactly then, but standing on the mound I had the gut feeling I was the one who was vulnerable.

Marty wasn't much of a go-getter—not in the particular ways most fourth grade boys like to think they are or could be, especially in sports. I remember thinking of him during school only when the whole class played Smarty, the old grade school trivia game; the inevitable rhyming nickname we offered up each time seemed to slide right by him like a perfectly good pitch. His swing wasn't slow—it just wasn't sure.

He went through the motions of a player at bat, pretending to dig up dirt in the box, running through his kicks, trying to be manly and athletic like everyone else on the field. I could see in his face, as I hoped the others could not, the flashes of mixed emotions—his fear, worry, anger, and, mostly, confusion; each was as recognizably distinct to me as the knowledge that I could easily be the one to fall in this duel. We weren't used to showdowns with each other. When we played in the summer, either hide-and-seek or war—where each side threw rocks from its driveway at the other until one side was pelted into bloody, welted submission—Marty's eyes or mine knowingly slid over wherever the other of us hid. If we were caught, the penalty was small: Those were family games, and we were among the youngest and least skilled of the players.

Marty stood still in the box, finally, and I started up: "Hey batta, batta, batta," a chant I'd picked up, no doubt, from the older boys who played on Little League teams. Usually, after I'd had a chance to size up a kicker, I would get more to the point. If a kicker was younger, for instance, or too fat to race the throw to first base, or someone who always miskicked or kicked short, it was my duty to tell the field: "Easy out!" probably the nicest observation I ever made. I can't, of course, recall having said anything mean; as far as I was concerned, I called them like I saw them, the same as Sparky Anderson or Johnny Bench or any of my other sports heroes would—informing your teammates was just part of the game. And everyone knew that the pitcher had to try to rattle those opponents who could be. On the playground, children intuitively understand the psychology of power and weakness, and they will exploit it ruthlessly. Even against those who, in any other situation, they would try to protect.

Before school had started up that fall, my favorite cousin, Keith, came for a visit, along with his mom and dad—my dad's oldest sister, Barb, and her husband, Cliff—and Keith's older brother, Mike. Mike, pretty creepy himself, made friends with Lonnie Britt right off, and for two weeks each had a sadistic sidekick for terrorizing farm cats and small children. What I remember of Mike to this day is mostly limited to the first part of their visit when he had my youngest sister, Marie, and I dance barefoot, singing snatches of Abba's "Take a Chance on Me," while he threw a pocketknife at our toes. We finked to Dad, who obligingly clapped Mike a good one upside the head. The episode outraged Aunt Barb and Uncle Cliff—not because they didn't believe in striking a child, but because Mike was theirs to smack, and, besides, they wanted us punished as tattletales. This was one reason the Orshoskis went home a week early that August.

The other reason started when Keith, who had always been my best friend on family visits—going fishing with me, and hiding from the pest officially known as my little sister—suddenly said he was a better baseball player than I was, better at all sports. (He had started Little League in his hometown of Bay View, Ohio, and he knew as well as I did that, as a girl, I wouldn't get to, though I was convinced then, and still am, that I would have been plenty good enough.) He wanted to prove it, so right away he challenged me to a race down our quarter-mile driveway. And he won. No big deal, I thought—I'd been right up on him. Later, we had a rock-throwing contest, for aim and distance, and I won. And, finally, I punted the Nerf football further and turned straighter cartwheels. These were big deals to Keith, and he couldn't take losing. He pestered me at every turn, making a contest of everything—who could drink Kool-Aid the fastest, who could drink more, who could shoot the Dixie cup into the trash all the way from the refrigerator. After aggravating me for days, Keith finally spit it out: "You can't beat me—you're nothing but a goddamned girl!" His voice cracked on the last word, making it seem like both fact and question, as in "You are, aren't you?"

It seemed to me as if he wanted me to be a girl, the kind of girl who acts scared of dirt and grass stains, the kind who doesn't care who runs faster—just as long as she gets some attention when they're finished. Keith had never talked to me like that before—before, we hadn't given much thought to who was a boy and who wasn't. But he was different that year. He walked with that slow, bow-legged Neanderthal shuffle boys get when they move up to Little League, and, I think now, he was expecting me to like him for this newfound boyness; like as in *like*—you know, that kind of like some first cousins flirt with for far too long. He was making me uncomfortable, confusing me: I couldn't be a girl and be best friends with him at the same time, and I didn't want to have to act differently just because he'd bugged out. Finally, I just slugged him one in the gut and told him to leave me alone.

I told Dad, too, the next morning after breakfast, when everyone else had gone out to play. Dad never treated me like a girl—never pretended I couldn't mow the lawn or go hunting with him to scare up the rabbits from the raspberry brambles near the railroad tracks behind the farmhouse we rented. If I didn't want to wear the dress Mom set out for me in the morning, he would wait for me in the car while I snuck pants and a shirt into my satchel—unless it was picture day or some other special occasion, like the spelling bee.

"He makes me so mad, Dad," I said, drying the dishes as he washed them. "I want to knock his block off."

"You think you can?" he asked without pausing to look at me.

I was surprised by his sudden seriousness. When Dad told stories about his fighting days in those years after he quit high school and went into the army, before getting married and having children, his tone was at once wistful and dreamy, and vivid with the drama of jaw-smashing fistfights and blackened eyes. I expected him to play along with my bravado, to let me talk for a while like he did.

"Yes," I answered, certain I could, but unsure if that was reason enough. I'd never seen a real fistfight, nor the circumstances leading up to one, where what was at stake was clear.

Dad held a plate up to the light from the back porch window, inspecting it for stubborn egg blotches. "Sure as shit," he said. There was a slight lilt in the phrase, a question yes, but an affirmation too.

I knew then if I balked I would become the kind of girl Keith had accused me of being—and though Keith might not know it this visit, I would. And Dad would.

Dad wouldn't look at me. He waited for an answer. The right answer. Dad never backed down from a fight. Not if he'd been insulted. Not with pride at stake.

I turned to him, waiting for him to see me, for that moment of understanding that takes place between a man and his son the way it does in old movies, and when he let the plate fit into the rack and glanced down directly into my eyes, I said, "Sure as shit, Dad."

That afternoon, before supper, Dad positioned Keith and me at the bottom of the big hill in our side yard, where the ground leveled off but still left enough space to keep us from falling onto the gravel driveway. I saw him motion over Aunt Barb and Uncle Cliff, and he built up the story with barks and gestures he might have used to tell a story of his own. And though I overheard him say that we were both going to have to learn, I knew he was really sticking up for me.

Keith and I waited a long minute or two before one of us threw a fist; we knew we had to, but neither wanted to do it first. At the top of the steep hill stood the adults and all our brothers and sisters and cousins. Marie clung to Dad's pant leg, waving the hem of her short dress in the air the way she did when she was nervous or scared. Mike, on the other side of his dad, threw a right uppercut into the guts of the air, his mouth snarling, his eyes narrowed. Keith looked back at me, a little panicked, and threw a wide first punch that glanced off my left arm and collarbone.

I stood shocked, my feelings hurt more than my arm. He really hit me, I thought. I rubbed my arm and looked at it, checking for blood or

. . . . . . . . . .

at least swelling. My face reddened as I realized they were all waiting for me to retaliate—but where? I'd never considered the placement of punches before. In my anger and embarrassment, I pistoned my right arm forward and up and thwacked him squarely on the forehead. He stumbled back a step or two into our lilac bush, where the small purple pistils stank and rotted and fell away from the brown stems.

It didn't feel good, his skull under my knuckles—what a dumb place to hit him, I thought. But I felt relieved, anyway. I'd done it. I hadn't chickened out. As Keith furiously brushed mushy petals off his pants, I stole a glance at Dad. He wore loose shorts and a stretched white T-shirt, and he stood at the top of our hill with his arms crossed over his big belly and chest like a reigning Mr. Universe whose muscles bulged too roundly for his grip on them to relax entirely. He nodded once, then lifted his cleft chin, returning me to the fight. I was ready, my small fists wadded up tight and bloodless. I crossed my thumbs over my first three fingers, and stepped toward Keith again.

He was mad. He hauled off and belted me on the nose, squashing it and making it bleed. I could feel the warm ooze cover my upper lip, and when I pinched it off Keith backed away like I would smear it on him. I wiped it in a comma on the hem of my shorts, thinking dimly of how, later, I'd have to wash it out myself.

The murderous red spread everywhere. Keith would punch me, and I'd whack him a good one back. The faster our fists flew, the less we cared where and how, until we came closer and closer together, and the punches became eye-gouges and biting, and the tears and sweat and snot mixed, and the blood stuck to my fists and his fists, and to my face and his face, until it looked as if we had beaten each other to pulp.

Keith had his arm around my neck in a headlock, and as I twisted and struggled to slip out, he reached down and yanked at my bangs. I exploded.

"Don't pull my hair! No fair hair pulling—only *pussies* pull hair!"

I kicked him hard in the shin, and as he bent to cover the hurt I ran at him and pushed him over backward onto the upward slope of the newly mown lawn. My whole body lay sprawled on his, my hands holding his down, my knees grinding his to the ground. He couldn't hit me, but I couldn't hit him either. So I bit his cheek, and when he screamed I spit a big gob between his eyes. He tried to spit back, but I just laid my head at the side of his like I was resting and smelling the grass. He bucked and bucked to throw me off, and it must have been a sight for my mother, but I hung on until Dad's voice in my ear said that was enough, and he pried me off Keith from my waist and set me down a few feet back.

Dad pulled Keith from the ground and brushed off his backside. The meaty hand patting hard on Keith's shoulders and back and the seat of his pants made Keith hold on to my dad, his eleven-year-old arms around my dad's big, curly head and burly shoulder. I was hurt for a second, but Dad turned around, still holding onto Keith, and said, "C'mere." He dropped to his knees and pulled us in to him, Keith on his left, me on his right, and we cried and wiped our noses on the sleeves covering his warm and strong arms. Dad held us there in private communion until our chests stopped heaving for air and comfort. When his grip relaxed, and we stood before him again, he put a formal, almost ceremonial end to what had happened.

"Give me your hands," he said, and he laid his in the air palm up. We overlapped them on his like teammates do before a tough game, and he topped them with his other large one.

I sniffed back my runny nose, and noticed with some satisfaction that Keith's sniffles matched mine. I snuck a glance from our hands to Dad, but this time he didn't acknowledge me.

"Are you done fighting?" he asked.

We nodded our heads yes.

"Well, that's good, because neither one of you's better than the other—isn't that right?"

We knew the right answer.

"Are you still cousins?" he asked, leading us.

Yes, we nodded.

"Still friends?"

"I'm not the one who didn't wanna be friends," I blurted, heaving, ready to cry again full force, but Dad shook our pile of hands, saying, "Shh, shh, c'mon, c'mon." It was almost over.

"Friends?"

.    .    .    .    .    .    .    .    .    .

I hesitated, waiting for his answer first. He peeked at me shyly, embarrassed, then at the ground, then at Dad. I watched Keith's eyes search Dad's face. Could he trust him? Was this for real? Keith's brown eyes widened so they looked as they must have when he was newly born—with a belief and innocence so pure it made me blink and look away.

"Yes," he whispered. And Dad pulled us close again, briefly, murmuring that he loved us, and that we had nothing to be ashamed of in front of anybody else.

"Okay?"

"Okay," Keith and I answered in unison.

"All right. Now, why don't you both get on up to the house and wash up. Just march right past your mothers—I'll take care of them. If we're lucky, they might let us have some dinner. You hungry?"

"Yes," "Uh-huh," we each answered.

"Well, then go on, get up there." And he opened his arms and let us race each other up the hill.

I've unlaced my running shoes and am about to undress for the sauna, but men's voices at the entrance of the women's locker room seem close enough to be inside. The woman on the bench down from mine buttons her shirt quickly and stands.

"Are they coming in?" she asks me.

"I don't know. I don't think there's any work scheduled for today."

It's after two in the afternoon, when the lunch crowd of women who work out in the Field House at the University of Iowa have showered up and returned to work. This woman and I often meet here at the same time; she's getting ready to run, and I'm just finishing. If we speak, it's not more than a hello, how are you—the quiet here is essential for our own warm-up and cooldown.

"Goddamned men," she snaps. "They can't leave us alone, can they?"

She's a small and plain middle-aged woman, and her sudden hostility jars me. The men's voices grow louder. She slips on her shoes with purpose and walks to the door. No one comes in, and after a moment she sees they are coming out of their own locker room and shouting to someone still inside. She comes back to the bench and begins again to undress.

"If they only knew we come here to get away from them . . ." Her voice trails off.

Up until a few short years ago I would not have understood the underlying defensiveness in her voice. Though officially segregated from the male athletes in middle school in the late 1970s, I always imagined a certain secret kinship with them I never felt toward most of the girls with whom I played volleyball, basketball, and outdoor track. I wanted to play with the boys, even if they were by then physically stronger and more agile—boys tested my skills and mental alertness, and I felt a sense of comfort with them.

With the girls I felt only discomfort, as with a new baseball glove that chafes and inflames and seems impossible to break in. They were resistant to everything I'd learned about sports: teamwork, respect for one's coach, practice, playing well, winning. Rather than firing up the enthusiasm of the bench, better players seemed only to inspire resentments, then accusations of favoritism and unfairness. Many of my high school games were lost as a result of a coach—browbeaten by players and their parents—attempting to rectify his or her seeming inequities.

To be fair, my high school was a small one where athletics drew all the girls who were or who wanted to be thought of as popular. Some played passably well; others did not. Invariably, though, most had had no experience with sports before junior high and high school—neither watching them and discussing them, nor playing them. These were the same girls who stood behind the fence while I played kickball, acting as if they didn't want to play because they weren't allowed to or because they were afraid or because they had somehow learned that's not how girls are.

After high school, I found pickup volleyball games at the local YMCA; the only game up to my skill level then was the men's games two nights a week. Most of the men liked me well enough and appreciated that I had good training and played well—nothing annoys male athletes more than a novice who slows the game down.

.    .    .    .    .    .    .    .    .    .

I remember two or three men, though, who thoroughly disliked me, and who told me over and over "this is the *men's* night," and that I "should play on coed nights." (And I did once in a while, but only to encourage my mother who was, along with most of the others on coed night, just learning how to play.) If I happened to play on their team, I could anticipate a frustrating night of not getting set, of being pushed out of position when blocking, and of feeling shut out of any sense of team they may have shared with the other (male) players.

Though I have encountered this kind of man everywhere I have played since, whether at the YMCA, on beaches or sandlots, in college intramurals or physical education classes, or in the pickup games and city-sponsored leagues I've played in since I started grad school here in Iowa City, I always believed there was a solution to their antipathy. If I played better and harder, I thought, or if I became a more encouraging player, they would come to accept me, to respect my know-how and skills. I wanted the high fives, the joking around and easy laughs, the pats on the back (without condescension) that they so readily gave each other. I wanted them to acknowledge the place I had earned among them. Instead, they ignored me—the variety of ignoring that's indifferent when I've done well and spitefully self-satisfied when I haven't, as if that's all that could be expected of me anyway.

I have thought about quitting volleyball, about taking my running more seriously maybe, or about buying a pass to the Fitness Loft where women with Walkmans ride lifecyclers and stairsteppers or take low-impact aerobics. But volleyball is what I love, what I have worked long and hard to be good at, and separating myself out from the men in self-proclaimed segregation only seems like sanctuary. What it really is is throwing in the towel—exactly what they would expect of a woman.

Instead, I keep playing. I play pickup with the guys three or four times a week, but I also volunteer in university physical education classes, where I encourage interested students (male as well as female) to get in on local pickup games. In the fall, I attend university women's games where I get to know the players, their coaches, and the enthusiasts sitting beside me in the stands—all of whom have introduced me to other women athletes like myself, who I have since played with on women's city league teams, intramural teams, and teams in the USA Volleyball, the governing body that hosts regional and national tournaments year-round. In the spring and summer, I'm on duty as an "experienced player" for a local high school club team whose coaches want their players to have challenging scrimmages. And once a year I spend four days at an adult development camp to sharpen my physical and mental skills and to play with competitive yet friendly men and women from all over the Midwest.

The solution is not fighting against those men as I have so often done in the past, nor accepting their status quo, nor escaping it by giving up. The secret, I think, is understanding that there's something bigger at stake than individual feelings, something bigger than whatever game and group of people I am playing with at any given time, bigger perhaps than the sport of volleyball itself.

The woman on the bench down from me is dressed now in a long T-shirt over compression shorts; she snaps her cassette player closed when she's ready to go. She seems cranked still from the men's voices pushing into our space. She'll work it off, I think.

"Hey," I say before she leaves, "see you tomorrow."

She smiles slightly, and waves back.

I grab the towel out of my locker and fill a bottle with water to pour on the sauna's dry, hot rocks. Inside the steam-filled, darkened room, I sit erect on the pine bench, naked and already sweating.

"Hey, batta, batta, batta, batta . . ." The infield chanted right along, most of them bent over, their hands balanced on their knees.

The tops of my ears burned red, full of blood and potential shame. I raised my right arm back in the classic pro bowler underhand scoop, and swung it hard to the plate. Marty approached the ball quickly—too quickly—so that he arrived before the ball, forcing him to skitter his steps to catch the timing.

"Swing!" cried the chorus of the infield. Somewhere in the back of my head, along with all the conflicting thoughts and feelings of aloneness, I felt some relief at not being the lone hawker.

Marty swept his foot toward the ball, but too late, lifting it limply out of bounds between home and first. Against his pale skin, his embarrassment stood out like a birthmark, his wet lips glaring purple. He pushed aside his fallen bangs and walked back behind the plate.

We were one out from the bottom of the inning, and I had visions of a thousand plays in the few short minutes Marty stood in front of me. And though I'd decided on how to play him—the same way I would play anybody else—I couldn't stop feeling sorry for him, feeling hysterically like I was doing something I needed somehow to justify.

I wanted to ask Dad if I was doing the right thing: Should I give him an easy pitch, like we do the littler kids? But that would shame him, and me.

Should I see if somebody else wants to pitch (for the inning? for the whole game?)—or would they think I was wussing out and never let me pitch again? Will I have to explain myself later, when Marty takes me home? Will he take me home? Should he? Will I have to kiss him then?

No Dad. And no coach to give me hand signals. No Mr. "P.E." Daly to egg me on the way he did in gym class every day.

"Come on, batta! Come on, batta! Right here, batta—kick it right here!"

If I hadn't slung the ball right then, my voice would have taken on a stranger pitch, something very much like a scream.

Again, Marty started for it early. Stride—stride—stride. The ball closed in. Skitter-step, skitter-step. Marty swung his foot and caught the ball on a rock bounce, lifting it straight up between home plate and the pitcher's mound.

He didn't run, I couldn't help but notice as the catcher and I converged on the falling bomb, and it added to my shame for him. My teammate and I looked at each other quickly before I waved him off. It crossed by mind to miss, but Marty hadn't moved at all, and I would've had to bust him one with the ball for the out anyway.

I cupped my arms for the catch, and it landed there with a dull whump. With the ball then safely hugged to my chest, I eyed Marty the way my dad might have eyed me in the same situation. I wanted him to get it, but I also wanted him to see on my silent face what I was dying to say out loud: *Please, Marty, I'm so sorry—please don't be mad at me—I did the right thing, didn't I?* But of course he didn't get it; looking at him that way must have seemed like I was rubbing it in. And as our teams traded sides, in the rush to and from the field, I caught sight of Marty making his way slowly, unnoticed, to the far side of the playground, with his hands in his front pockets and his narrow shoulders slumped with cold. I dropped the ball, leaving it for the opposing pitcher, and stepped outside the circle.

# A Spectator's Notebook

. . . . . . . . . .

*by*
KRIS VERVAECKE

When I was a girl, I played brutish softball on hot summer days in a cow pasture with the other girls in the neighborhood, a neighborhood which was actually a scattering of a few houses outside the city limits of Omaha. These were homes inhabited almost solely by females: There was the widow Edgerton and her daughter, the Hellerman twin girls, the Kosinsky girl, two Martin girls, and three Vervaecke girls, of which I was the oldest. The Hellerman, Kosinsky, Martin, and Vervaecke fathers were gone all day and most evenings, some not returning even at night, except for Mr. Hellerman, who created a kind of father emergency for the rest of us by rolling into their driveway Monday though Friday evenings at 5:30 sharp. (Nancy Kosinsky's father did sometimes drink at home instead of out, which created another sort of father emergency, because he'd dress up in his Shriner's outfit and ride roughshod over everyone's lawns in his little Shriner's jeep, shearing through my mother's canna bed, sending up humiliations of red petals.) We envied the Hellerman girls, but the other mothers said that Mr. Hellerman was a very *nice* man, but not a *man's* man — a distinction I found confusing, along with the implication that a *real* woman would want a *man's man*.

No mother or father or brother ever came down to the pasture to coach or referee our games, so we girls were left to our own devices. Mary Hellerman and I were always the captains of opposing teams; no one challenged this arrangement because it was understood that the whole point of the game was to build tension between Mary and me until we had no choice but to lay down our bats and balls and injure each other.

The pretense for our fights was an alleged infraction of the rules, which were crudely drawn, like the diamond, in the rising dust. Mary would accuse me, or I'd accuse her, and our shouts ("You cheater! You fat, ugly liar!") would bring us close enough to smell each other. The Herefords would lift their heads in mild interest; the other girls would draw near. Then we'd sharpen our taunts until one of us landed the first slap. I still remember the satisfaction of smacking Mary's bony, sun-burned arm. And the coarseness of her long brown hair, coated with sweat and dust, sticking to my fingers as I pulled it. She was several inches taller than I, which allowed me to punch her stomach. Her mother never seemed to make her cut her fingernails, so Mary left long furrows down my arms. Blood! What a thrill and relief it was to see it bubbling up through our sultry sleep of resignation and resentment.

Later some boys moved into the neighborhood, and most of the girls retreated inside to talk about them on the telephone. I played baseball and football with the boys: They were stuck halfway out of nowhere, too, and so they needed me and sometimes even weeny-armed Mary, to play. These games were also primitive, tackle-and-roll-in-the cow-dirt affairs. Then, one January afternoon during my eighth-grade year, running laps around the gymnasium for seventh-period coed gym class, I broke out in a sweat. Perspiration spread under the sleeves of my prison blue uniform like twin maps of Texas, and, quite abruptly, it mattered to me that my corporeality was revealing itself so grossly in the presence of boys. In panic and humiliation, I plastered my arms to my sides, slowed down to a trot, and became a girl.

It would be years before it dawned on me that a game might be more than a prelude to a fight, more than a release from preadolescent bore-dom. Through the eyes of my daughter and sons, who play in school and community league sports, I began to see a game as a sustaining drama dreamed up by the will and the scarcely imaginable possibilities of the body. And although I see that *the game* claims vital parts of their imaginations, I can never experience it in the same way.

Driving home from work, I catch part of a radio quiz show:

GAME SHOW HOST: Question number one. Who won the 1991
  Super Bowl?
BUZZ!
MALE CONTESTANT: The New York Giants!
HOST: Sorry. I'm afraid that's not the right answer.
MALE CONTESTANT: But it is! The Giants beat the Buffalo Bills,
  20–19, in Tampa Stadium!
HOST: Sorry! Who won the 1991 Super Bowl?
BUZZ!
FEMALE CONTESTANT: I don't know, and I don't care!
HOST (also female): Yes!!! That's correct!!! [BELLS RING AND
  WHISTLES SOUND.] Yeah!!! Congratulations!!!

I'd be a whiz on that show. Although I grew up in the Nebraska vortex
of Big Red football and *should* be capable of being swept up by my nation's preoccupation, even as a kid, I was too *embarrassed*. I hated it
when everybody was supposed to dress in red, gather around the television set, and feel excited. Or maybe it is closer to the truth to say that
I was embarrassed to find that it was over watching a football game
that the passions of others were aroused, while *I*, who was usually the
one to go around *feeling* things, could not manufacture even a fleeting
rivalrous impulse toward the state of Oklahoma, a wind-worn, sun-
dulled place much like the place I lived.

Years later, after living on the West Coast, I returned to Nebraska,
showing up one autumn Saturday to do some research at the university
library. In my characteristically oblivious way, I had failed to find out
whether there was a home game, and so it took two hours to make my
way through the traffic in Lincoln, and, finally parked, through the
throngs of hoarse, red-polyester-suited people to the library door.

Where I found the door locked and library closed, because it was a
Big Red Saturday.

Fortunately for me and my prejudices, my kids—Ben, Emily, and
Andrew—were never interested in playing football. Basketball's their
game, and sometimes soccer, or tennis. They run track and practice
martial arts. When Ben went through a Dan Quayle phase when he

was fifteen—deciding that when he was grown he would abandon the income bracket to which his mother belongs and possibly even vote Republican—he took up golf, practiced every day for an entire summer, and won the city championship for his age division. For a few moments, he was a kind of celebrity, at least to some sweet old men we ran into at the grocery store. I was proud of him, but he was already discarding the polo shirts he'd begun wearing and letting his golf clubs gather dust. He started paying more attention to politics and environmental policy and thinking about what he wanted to do with his life. I suspected it was closely listening to Republicans that soured him on golf, but I can't say for sure, because I wanted only to listen and observe, not pry. Sports has been one of the ways he's defined and differentiated himself, stretched far beyond and past his mother, surprising her with the slam dunk.

■ ■ ■

For me, the experience of raising children has no equivalent in terror and love. For long stretches of years as a single parent, I've watched as *the game* dreamed up my sons and daughter, giving them things I could not, letting them shed, for the game's duration, grief, rage, loneliness, or boredom, and allowing them to take on skill and cunning, filling them with inspiration and determination, sometimes awe.

December 1987. At ten years old, a stubby little blond boy, Ben sits in rapt attention during any game, understanding it intuitively, committing himself wholly. At a Kansas Jayhawks basketball game, I take him down to the court so he can watch his team jog into the locker room. We are so close to their immense, shining bodies that, as Milt Newton trots past (he'd scored eighteen points and accomplished several steals), Ben is able to scoop up, into his cupped palm, a few drops of Newton's sweat. For a moment, Ben holds his breath, staring down at his glistening palm. Then he straightens and begins carefully applying the sweat to his own skin, up and down his arms, patting it into his very pores.

August 1992. Over speed bumps so pronounced you need a forty-thousand-dollar vehicle to get to the other side with your teeth intact, I

. . . . . . . . . .

wind up the narrow road to the country club, to which we don't belong, to pick up Ben after his eighteen holes. He is nowhere to be seen. It's 105 degrees, and so I get out of the car, with my book, and settle myself under the stingy shade of an ornamental tree next to the parking lot.

"Mom!" I hear Ben say. "What are you doing?"

"Well, I'm just waiting for you," I say, bewildered.

"Get up! Get up!" he says.

After we're settled in the car, I ask what's wrong.

He struggles, not wanting to hurt my feelings. Wiping sweat from his forehead, he then passes his hand over his eyes.

"Sitting in the grass?" he finally reproaches, a bit incredulous I don't get it. "Mom, my God, you looked like a hippie!"

August 1995. Everything has been loaded into the car: clothes, photos of the family members and the dogs; Ben's iguana ("Jay") is resting securely among the rocks in his aquarium, wedged, in the backseat, between the lifting equipment and the reference books I insist he take. We've hugged and cried and said everything there is to say about his going off to college. He does not want me to drive to the university with him, not this time; we've already done this for parent orientation and his enrollment in the honors program. He says he'll look like a baby if his mom helps him move into the dorm.

"One more thing before I leave," he says. "Mom, will you watch this with me?"

He slides Michael Jordan's "Air Time" into the VCR, and, sitting together on the couch, we endure the strains of the background music massacred by the worn-out sound track on our VCR. As we watch Jordan's volitant performance, his pure, vibrant grace and athleticism, the way, under pressure, his quotient of joy increases—he fakes, spins, and drives through, dunking over the head of somebody who's at least seven feet tall—Ben says, "I get chills, Mom, I really do."

Unsophisticated? My son, whose father died, as Jordan's did a few years ago, a senseless, violent death: What spiritual toll does that exact on a child? What does he understand the body to mean, knowing his father's body was robbed of life?

I remember his martial arts phase, which followed the Republican golf phase, all the demonstrations I attended of Filipino, Korean, and Chinese stylized fighting: Ben whirling nunchuks, throwing and catching knives, breaking the requisite boards and bricks. At home, when his sister or brother or the dog came up behind him, he'd leap up and chop the air, spinning off an instantaneous dramatization of his charged, secure masculinity. Then he'd get down on the floor to reassure the startled dog. "It's okay, baby," he'd croon. "Benny would never hurt you."

He doesn't need a role model, exactly, isn't interested in the personal or moral failures of athletes, isn't drawn to their celebrity. Instead he needs the example of pure jubilation in the body, the triumph of spirit, strength, determination, and talent.

■ ■ ■

I teach at a small liberal arts college thirty miles from where I live, a Division III school with an active athletic program. While the college cannot offer athletic scholarships, many of the students are there primarily to play sports, and it is their athletic not scholastic achievement that inspires the college to find sufficient financial aid for them to attend. These are mostly white kids from farms, or towns such as Beebeetown, Mechanicsville, Altoona, Correctionville, or What Cheer, Iowa. (I listen closely as my students tell me the names of their towns, hoping for an ironic inflection, but I'm always disappointed.) Some of the students are fairly bright, but, because they were stars of their high school classes—football, wrestling, basketball, track, or golf—they haven't read any books.

I don't mean that they haven't read many books, or that they haven't read the great books. I mean that, except for comic books, they haven't read even one book, that is, you know, sitting down, opening a book, and reading it, beginning sentence to the next, sentence by sentence, paragraph by paragraph, all the way to the end. They've simply been passed from one class to the next without doing the work.

"Do we really have to read the whole thing?" they ask me plaintively, as we begin the first book on the syllabus.

Because my children and I live in a university community that insists on higher educational standards than most (although, believe me, these standards are nothing to boast about), by the time my children were in fifth grade they could read and write better than most of my college freshmen. Because my children attend a public school where, although there are drugs and skirmishes and occasionally weapons, there is a reasonable expectation of safety and order and the opportunity to be educated, they will be able to compete with their academic achievements, not a reverse layup or three-point shot. They are fortunate because games are play for them. On the other hand, because my children are not particularly gifted athletes, they've not had the playing time or attention from coaches that their more talented or parent-coached peers have had. All three of them need those things, not because they will bring glory to their schools, but because we all need joy in our physicality. When I travel to a school in Altoona or someplace like it to attend one of my daughter's basketball games, at first I'm distracted by my awareness that this town is one of countless others where we're failing to sufficiently educate some, if not many, of the children. Then I pick a spot in the bleachers several rows behind where her team will sit and wait for my daughter to come jogging in.

As Emily bounces onto the floor in her green-and-gold uniform, her eyes scan the crowd to meet mine. She's always happy before a game, and now, a few minutes before the whistle, she's luminous with excitement. The girls warm up, shoot, huddle, then go to the bench. Emily's one of the shorter girls, but she moves fast. I take inordinate pride in the fact that it wouldn't occur to her to go out for cheerleading. Sometimes when I pick her up after practice, ready with food she can stuff into her mouth, she cannot contain her exuberance: "Mom, I swear to God! We worked so hard, it was the most fun I've had in my entire life!" Sometimes, watching them practice, I think back to our cow-pasture softball and wish, well, that Mary and I had learned to play the game.

The girls are on the sidelines, waiting for the game to begin. I look at Emily's golden brown head among all the other bright heads with their French and cornrow braids (the girls braid each others' hair as they ride the bus to the game). The whistle blows, the ball's in play; the air is filled with shouts and squeaking shoes and the bouncing of the ball. Each time there is a substitution of players I watch my daughter's slender back lift with hope then go slack with disappointment. Unlike most of the other parents, I do not give a damn whether West High's teams win State or anything else; I want all the kids to have their playing time. The game wears on; West High is once again kicking butt. Not until the last minute or two of the game, when her team has maintained a twenty-point lead over the second half, do Emily and several other girls get to play.

She maintains her composure until we get in the car, then crumples in humiliation. Once we're on the highway, forty miles to home, freezing rain coats our windows, but I can't see well enough to find a safe place to pull off. I drive with trepidation over the slippery road, through the foggy darkness, while Emily cries so hard it sounds as though she will break apart. "Mommy, I'm such a failure!" she weeps. At first my attempts to comfort her only increase her misery, so I shut up. I'm left to listen and worry about the road and think my resentful thoughts. I remember all the years in elementary school when she was "benched" in the classroom—left to do bulletin boards for the teacher—because she'd already mastered what was being taught. I think about the studies that suggest that girls who compete in athletics are far less likely to drink or take drugs or become pregnant.

To make myself feel better, I remember her thirteenth birthday, when she was the high scorer on her team with nineteen points. I can still see her dribbling the ball down the court, passing, rebounding, shooting, so far from any self-consciousness about her body it was as though the game had dreamed her up, supplying her with a body that moved as though sure of itself and its momentary grace.

■ ■ ■

One of Ben's names for his younger brother, Andrew, is "Trancer." Years ago, when Andrew played outfield in Little League, he often faced *away* from the batter in deep contemplation, and it was only with difficulty that his coach or I would pull his attention away from his thoughts and redirect it toward the real danger he might be smacked in the back of the skull by the ball.

.     .     .     .     .     .     .     .     .     .

"Andrew, get your head in the game!" the coach would holler, but Andrew never actually did. It worked out better when he went out for track. Long-distance running gave him plenty of time to think. Until recently, I thought the last thing he'd ever want to be was a jock.

July 1996. A Saturday morning, the window open while I work at home, bringing in the breeze fragrant with freshly cut grass and the steady thump thump thump of the basketball on the driveway. Andrew, who has just turned fourteen, bounces a ball in order to think. Two hours might pass in bouncing and shooting hoops before he appears in the office, as if from a dream, to tell me what's on his mind.

He wanders in wearing a wrinkled T-shirt and shorts, barefoot, his dark hair mussed. I'm surprised again by how graceful and muscular he is, how tall—five-foot-ten last time I measured him—but it seems possible that he's grown another inch since I fed him breakfast.

He plops down on a chair next to mine. Up close there's a little acne and a few whiskers, new this year, and the chickenpox scar on his cheek from when he was three.

"Hi, Mom." Here's something familiar: It's obvious he hasn't gotten around to brushing his teeth. He's lost in thought. "I love you, Mom," he says absently.

"I love you," I say, patting his rather huge and hairy knee, adding, "You look like a derelict."

He registers this and looks pleased.

Then he wakes up, turns toward me, says in a voice heavy with portent, "Tomorrow."

"Tomorrow," I say cheerfully, because this is my role: to refute the objections he'll make because he's scared to go to the two-week writing scholarship workshop that begins the next day.

"It's going to suck! They'll treat us like babies, probably make us go to bed at ten o'clock!"

This will be the first time he's been away from home for two weeks, one of the few times he's ever been away, even to stay with family. Three summers ago, when he stayed at my mother's, he got so homesick he went on a hunger strike so that he could come home. Since that time, he's grown a foot, his voice has dropped an octave, and his shin bones are as thick as the beef bones we buy for the puppy to chew.

"Oh, I doubt it," I say. "They chose you based on your manuscripts and test scores, so they know you're not babies."

"Yeah," he says. "But I bet everybody will already know each other except for me."

"They come from all over the state, so I don't know how they'd already know each other."

"Yeah, well, I don't care," he says, sounding satisfied. "They're probably all a bunch of nerds, anyway."

"Probably."

"What do you think?" he asks, pushing up the sleeve of his T-shirt, revealing what I can genuinely describe to him as an amazingly well-developed biceps.

"Wow," I say, trying to take in the irony—or anti-irony—that all that grunting and weight lifting in the basement had been in preparation for a smart kids' workshop.

The next day I drive him to the university where the workshop will be held; after the three-hour orientation, I am to return to drive him to the dorm. At the appointed time, I pull into the parking lot. There is a cluster of girls at the shelter, surreptitiously watching the boys playing basketball. I scan the crowd of boys as they jump and shoot, and four times I think spot my son, but from this distance and with the sun in my eyes, I can't discern Andrew from the others. As I step out of the car to go look for him, he opens the passenger door.

"Mom!" he says. "Get in the car!"

His face is flushed, jaw set. Someone might see me, confirming the rumor he has a mother.

"How was it?" I ask, backing out.

"It sucks," he says. "We're on such a short leash. WE HAVE TO GO TO BED AT TEN O'CLOCK! And the boys are like all into role-playing games, though some of them are pretending to be intellectuals. It sucks so bad you wouldn't believe it. The books they go around recommending to each other are like science-fiction stuff they think is great literature."

"That's too bad," I say.

.     .     .     .     .     .     .     .     .

"It might be okay, though," he says. "Some of the kids are pretty cool."

"That's good," I say, noticing the lovely cumulus between us and the enormous sky.

"One kid asked me what kind of game system I have, and I said 'Game system?' And he said, 'You know like Sega or Super Nintendo,' and I said, 'Game system? I don't play game systems.'"

"You really shut him off," I say.

"Well, I didn't really shut him off," he says, hedging.

Trailing him down the hall of the dorm where he'll live for the next two weeks, I watch as he nods to the other boys. As he unlocks the door to his room, he whispers, "Nobody I couldn't take if I had to," and grins before giving me the briefest and most furtive of hugs good-bye.

Over the next two weeks, he phones only once, and, in a breezy tone, tells me he's having, definitely, the best time of his life. My friend who lives across the street from the dorm and has promised to spy on my child, reports that every evening Andrew's out shooting hoops with the R.A. and a couple of the other scholarship guys.

In the remarks at the closing ceremony, Andrew's muscles emerge as a kind of theme, and, in the final ritual of parting, each kid autographs my son's manly biceps.

■ ■ ■

When I mention to Ben that I'm writing an essay about sports, he looks stricken. "I don't think that's a good idea, Mom," he says, honesty overriding tact. "I mean it's not something you can read about and understand in that way. You have to have a feel for it, an intuition. You have to *love* it."

"I'm not pretending to love it," I say a bit defensively.

Is there anything about sports I love?

Closing my eyes, I remember swinging my bat and solidly hitting the ball, the shudder of the connection a physical exultation traveling down my arm. I remember tossing the bat aside, and, as though suddenly released into the wild, racing through the shimmering heat, toeing each dried cow pie base and sliding into home.

I remember running hard, free of ambivalence, of pity. I remember the powdery dirt and the minty smell of the weeds and the unreasonable beauty of the sky.

"Mom," someone is calling. "*Mom!*"

I open my eyes.

"You're as bad as Andrew," Emily informs me. "Why are you just sitting here?"

"I was remembering when I was a kid, playing softball."

"Oh, my gosh," she says, mildly exasperated, "playing in the dirt with your friends doesn't count, Mom. I thought you were going to write about when I was the high scorer on my basketball team with nineteen points. On my thirteenth birthday, remember?"

"When did I say I was going to write about that?"

"You didn't, but I told you you should. It was so awesome. We were playing Southeast, the gym was packed, and everybody from Northwest was yelling my name. I kept throwing the ball up there, and it kept going in. My team was pounding the floor, yelling 'Em-i-ly!' Then I did a layup, and it won the game. Don't you remember?"

"Of course, I remember."

"Well, all right then," she says, satisfied. "*That's* the story to tell."

# Leaving Home

. . . . . . . . . .

*by*
GERALD EARLY

> This is the story of America. Everybody's doing what they think
> they're supposed to do.
>    JACK KEROUAC, *On the Road*

## PART I: NO LONGER MAKING THE THROW EASY;
## NO LONGER MAKING IT HARD.

In the spring of 1977, about four months before I left Philadelphia for
good, I began to ride my girlfriend's bicycle every day. I am not sure,
even now, why I started to do this. Maybe it was a physical-fitness
craze. I was running a lot in those days, practicing yoga, hanging
around boxing gyms, doing a hundred push-ups a day, a hundred sit-
ups a day. I was a vegetarian, although I found being one to be slightly
absurd. I didn't stop eating meat because of any moral concern about
killing animals. I was indifferent to that, thinking that it was not a sign
of the depth of one's humanity how much one could recoil from the ex-
pressiveness of one's own brutality and its bloody needs and deeds.
There were black boys I grew up with, boys whose roots were Southern
and agrarian and who often, when elementary school age, went South
for the summer to spend time with relatives on farms, who worked in
poultry shops and meat-packing plants when they were teenagers,
wearing aprons smeared with animal entrails, their arms dyed in blood,

their processed hair capped in hair nets adorned with chicken feathers; they slaughtered animals for a living. When I visited them on their jobs, puddles of blood everywhere, I looked upon their work with utter indifference. Back in 1965, when I was thirteen, a friend of mine once tried to get me a job at a poultry store called Giordano's, located at the corner of Ninth Street and Washington Avenue in the heart of the Italian Market. If I worked Friday afternoons and evenings and all day Saturday, from six in the morning until six in the evening, I could earn twenty-five dollars. I didn't take the job because I didn't want to slaughter chickens all day. I hated the smell. But my friends who did this were paid well, twenty-five dollars was no inconsiderable sum for a teenaged boy in 1965, and they needed the money or thought they needed the money and no one, no one I knew, stopped eating meat because one could see quite vividly animals dying messy, cruel deaths. There were the two laws of life as most fatalistic working-class people believed: first, eat or be eaten; second, which followed from the first, all life is equally precious and equally expendable, depending on where you are in the food chain. Thus, it is good to be like the mariner who gave the whale his throat after the whale swallowed him in Kipling's *Just So Stories* tale: a man of infinite resource and sagacity. And an irritant to those who would eat you.

I suppose I became a vegetarian out of some sense of the political but not in the way that that might be most commonly conceived. I thought food was political in the sense that, internationally, some people got a lot of it and a lot of people got a little of it. And the poorest people I knew got the worst food and paid the most money for it. My mother always used to go to a fancy Jewish meat market and buy very expensive cuts of meat. We could hardly afford them but I ate better than any black kid in my neighborhood. My mother told me that the food sold to black people in their own neighborhoods was slop. "I'm not a slave, so I'm not eating slop," she said. I stopped eating meat because in 1970, while in San Francisco, I read a book by Jethro Kloss called *Back to Eden,* vegetarianism at its most radical, at its most ludicrous. I was also hanging around a lot of black Muslims then, and food was a big political deal with them. There was something about the astringency of strict vegetarianism, the sheer discipline and will,

. . . . . . . . . . .

that made it attractive to me. But it meant something to me as well to say to the world that a black man refuses to eat just anything that is given to him. I was also reading *The Rule of St. Benedict* at this time, a couple of pages every day, and the spirituality of denial was strong, too, the search for simplicity, stripping to the essence as boxers, my favorite athletes, do. Becoming vegetarian was something like, in the spirit of *The Rule,* doing a prolonged Lent. I never became a vegetarian because I thought of my body as some holy temple. I was very self-conscious of my body as a repository of shit. I was very aware of my functions of elimination. But I thought of my body in this way for another reason. When I was boy I was friendly with two Italian brothers, C. and A., who lived around the corner from me. They were a few years younger and for a time looked up to me. They were fascinated by my skin color. At first, they thought I was black because I drank a lot of chocolate milk all the time. "Drink white milk and you'll be white like us," they told me. Then, one day in the summer of 1964, when I was twelve, the year of the race riot in North Philadelphia, C. got mad at me because I wouldn't lend him some comic books, so he said to me: "Do you know why white people don't like colored people? 'Cause your skin's the color of shit. Colored people are full of shit." And then he ran away. That made me aware of my body in a new, and I suppose, tragically profound way that I never forgot.

My preoccupation with my body during my last months in Philadelphia, with the physical, had to be, in thinking back on it, something like a response to the paralyzing implications of boredom and restlessness. I was still trying to learn to be an adult, to shake off my adolescence. I needed to get away from Philadelphia. I had been there through high school, through college. It seemed repressive, uncouth, confining, and dirty. People new to the city often described it as "tough" and I was told by more than a few that Philadelphia Negroes, myself included, had, what other black folk called, "an attitude." Philadelphia was and is a tough place, lots of tough ethnics, tough Italians, tough Irish Catholics, tough Jews, tough Hispanics, tough blacks. And they all seemed to be fighting each other in a war of all against all. I went through the city thinking all the time I had to be on my guard. I kept thinking someone, somewhere, would jump me unawares. Now, the

city was making me sick, literally sick, filling me with the venom of my
own psychic bile, and so the vegetarianism, the fixation on body, was a
way to find a cure. I was slowly taking on the regimen of an athlete as
if it were a form of penance and redemption. I was twenty-four years
old, in the best physical condition of my life, and thoroughly hated my
existence and its circumstances.

One evening in 1977, I and my girlfriend, Ida, who was to become
my wife, were driving in her car, a Nova, which I had had the misfortune
of driving when it was rear-ended a few weeks earlier by a man who had
no brakes and no insurance. The trunk was ruined, smashed, although
the car still drove well enough, despite a bent frame. Before the accident,
despite the fact that I was a black man in my twenties, and despite the
fact that I lived in Philadelphia where the police acted a great deal as if
they rather thought the location a unique combination of Vorster's
South Africa, Stalin's Soviet Union, and Hitler's Germany, I had been
stopped by the police only once in my life. The oppressive police presence was not the imaginative projection of an overly sensitive, somewhat paranoid, minority male mind, although I naturally exaggerate
somewhat for effect. By 1980, three years after my departure from
Philadelphia, the city had more cops per square mile than every city in
the country except two. Philadelphia had 4.3 officers per one thousand
residents, more than any other city in the country, far more than much
bigger cities like Chicago, Los Angeles, or New York. Here was a city
that lost 3.3 percent of its population in the 1950s, 3.7 percent in the
1960s, and 13.4 percent in the 1970s. Between 1972 and 1980, the city
lost ninety thousand jobs. But our police force kept growing. Frank
Rizzo, the tough Italian cop who rose to police commissioner, and eventually mayor, set the tone for law enforcement, especially in the part of
the city where I lived. Rizzo, known as the Cisco Kid for his tough demeanor and derring-do, worked out of the Twelfth and Pine police station for a time, just ten blocks from my home. I heard about him all the
time. He was surely the most famous cop in the history of Philadelphia
and arguably the most famous cop in the country, aside from J. Edgar
Hoover. He was solely responsible for the city's law and order atmosphere. Naturally, there was always in the air the aura of police brutality,
at least, in the air that black people breathed. As I was growing up, the

black newspapers were always filled with stories about police brutality. I had heard that many white policemen thought of whipping and shooting blacks as a kind of sport. During the spring of 1964, there was a police brutality case that affected me deeply. A twelve-year-old black boy was shot to death by a police officer in front of his home at Twelfth and South Streets, about seven blocks from my home. He had been sitting on his front steps playing cards with his friends when a patrol car pulled up, and the cops started searching the boys. One of the boys refused to be searched and ran around a parked car. The cop ran after him, but could not catch him, which made the boy laugh; the other cop finally jumped the kid from behind. There was a scuffle and the boy was killed. No one is sure why the boy refused to be searched. He had nothing on him but a pen knife and a pack of cigarettes. Only the importation of several hundred police officers prevented a riot in the neighborhood when news got around Christian, Catherine, Carpenter, Fitzwater, Bainbridge, and South Streets about what had happened. At a subsequent hearing about the incident, the cops were exonerated. As captain, as police inspector, as deputy police commissioner, as police commissioner, and as mayor, Rizzo said he would support the police whether they were right or wrong. He was true to his word. When I read about the boy's death in the paper the following day, I thought about how much time I spent playing coon-can, tonk, pitty-pat, and knuckles on the steps with my black friends. "It could have been me!" I kept thinking hysterically. "It could have been me!" That was the summer I stopped playing cards. I only played forms of baseball.

So, I can only attribute my avoidance, my evasion of the police as sheer luck; some of it can be explained by the fact that I rarely drove a car. The one time I was stopped by the police was as a pedestrian. (I used to walk all the time all over the city, despite being mugged several times. The cops were of no help in those instances and so I stopped reporting the incidents as long as I survived them with my life and my clothes.) The most common way for the police to stop people is by requesting that they pull their cars over. Of course, the police did stop gangs of pedestrian teenaged boys, especially black boys, but I always walked alone. As Ida had a car, she would insist that we use it whenever we went out. She lent it to me while she was out of town, which was how it got wrecked. Once the Nova was wrecked in this accident, I was stopped virtually every time I was in the car. The combination of an out-of-state license plate (Texas) and a smashed-in rear end was simply too rich for the police to pass up. I was told by a cop that a car with a messed-up trunk signals all sorts of possibilities to the police.

This particular evening Ida had picked me up from work and we were going somewhere to eat. I was driving when the police flashed us to pull over. I was in a bad mood. The cop went through the usual business of wanting to see my license, the car's registration, wanting to know what happened to the car, if the accident had been reported and the like. Then, the cop, a gum-chewing white guy, before going back to his car to call in my license number to see if I had any outstanding traffic violations or arrest warrants, said, with something of a smirk, to Ida, who was dressed in white, "Hey, are you a nurse?" Somehow, this question, the way it was asked, made me nearly explode. "It's none of your god—" I started to say, when Ida, in a loud voice to drown out mine, said simply, "No, officer, I'm not a nurse." "You gonna say something, buddy?" the cop said to me, eyeing me intently, curiously, not necessarily maliciously. This was certainly a moment of truth if there ever was one. Ida gripped my arm, pressing it tightly. "She's not a nurse, that's all I was going to say," I responded quietly. I had thought that vegetarianism might save my life. After this incident, I was sure that leaving Philadelphia was about the only way I could do that.

Better now, I thought when I gave up vegetarianism, which I did when I no longer lived in Philadelphia, to be concerned with how to live in a messy democracy than in the excessive self-absorption of keeping your bourgeois ass alive in all its bourgeois sanctity. At this time also, I worked with a bunch of black guys, many of whom rode bikes all the time. Most of them were obsessed by some form of physical culture. Perhaps this influenced me. I wanted to fit in with them. I never did, not entirely. But I was never outside, either. I was, after all, black, and among any group of black folk that is bound to mean something. It's bound to mean that you have some idea, if not exactly what it means to be black, then certainly what it means not to be white. That counts for a great deal when white people aren't around. In any case, I

live, in relation to them, a kind of half-life, like a carbon isotope awaiting decay, like a deformed fetus struggling to be born.

Something odd had happened to me by stages since I graduated
from high school. I stopped following baseball. I don't exactly know
why but it happened gradually, almost imperceptibly. From the time I
was about eight years old until I left high school, I loved baseball pas-
sionately, madly, thought about it every day during the season and a
good many days during the off-season. In 1964, when the Phillies had
a six-game lead with twelve games left in the season and seemed a lock
to win the pennant, I acutely remember the agony of seeing them lose
ten games straight. They wound up finishing not even second but third.
It was the year Richie (Dick) Allen, the team's first black superstar, won
the Rookie of the Year Award. Allen was famous in the black press in
1960 when he signed with the Phillies for ninety thousand dollars, the
biggest bonus ever paid a black player. It shocked most black folk in
Philadelphia that the Phillies paid it. Most of us considered the Phillies
to be a fairly racist team; I had been told those horror stories of how
Ben Chapman, manager of the Phillies back in the 1940s, baited Jackie
Robinson by calling him everything but a child of God. It was so terrible that Chapman was forced to make a public apology to Robinson.
My mother never forgot that. "You can put me in my grave and it
won't be said I ever rooted for the Phillies," she said. Allen was the
principal reason I became interested in Philadelphia. He muscularly
swung one of the heaviest bats in the majors and hit mammoth home
runs. There was an immediate problem when he arrived because he did
not wish to be called Richie but Dick. The white sportswriters did not
take to him or at least they did not take to *that*. In February of that year,
Cassius Clay had beaten Sonny Liston for the heavyweight, announcing immediately after the fight that he was a member of the Nation of
Islam and was adopting the name of Muhammad Ali. For a good long
time, for many publications well into the 1970s, Ali was referred to by
his "God-given" name of Clay. Allen seemed to some white sportswriters, perhaps, another of these overly assertive black athletes who
wanted to make a big deal about his name. It was not lost on me, even
then, that a black person wanting to call himself something, even in the
most minor way, was a political act. The other important black Phillie

at the time was Wes Covington, a powerful, left-handed hitting, part-time outfielder, who was considered an Uncle Tom in some quarters, al-though Claude E. Harrison, Jr., sportswriter for the *Philadelphia Tribune,* the city's black newspaper, usually wrote supportive columns about the enterprising Covington, who was always hustling jobs in the off-season. (This was before the average professional ballplayer made enough money not to have to worry about work in the winter.)

I followed Allen's career with great avidity from 1963 to 1969, when he was traded to the St. Louis Cardinals for Curt Flood who never came to Philadelphia, opting, instead, to sue baseball for the right to go wherever he wanted. He lost the suit but baseball was never quite the same for me. (It was certainly never the same for itself as Flood ushered in the age of free agency.) Baseball seemed irrelevant in the age of the politicized black athlete. I also felt something deeply akin to shame that a black ballplayer would quit the game rather than play in Philadel-phia. As a result of this, I went through college and never gave baseball a thought, never read the sports section of a newspaper except for sto-ries about boxing. I don't know what happened to me. All I ever thought about was getting out of Philadelphia, and boxing. It was odd because in 1977 the Phillies were a very good team. They had a very good team the year before (Allen had returned after playing in St. Louis and Chicago and the white press was very willing to call him Dick) when they won over a hundred games but lost three straight in the play-offs to the Cincinnati Reds, the Big Red Machine, as they were called. The Phillies won over a hundred games in the summer of 1977 with a team that included Hall of Fame third baseman, Mike Schmidt, and Hall of Fame pitcher, Steve Carlton (who, in 1972, when the Phillies won only fifty-nine games, won twenty-seven of them himself). There was Garry Maddox, a great defensive center fielder ("Two-thirds of the world is covered by water, and the rest is covered by Garry Maddox," the Phillies announcer would say), and Larry Bowa at shortstop, and "Shake and Bake" McBride in right field. The guys at the office where I worked talked about the Phillies all the time. They were certainly talking about them when I left in the middle of August. I seemed all the more the oddball that I never took an interest in the games or in their conversations about them. Ironically, I knew more about baseball, certainly about its history, than anyone in the office. I loved the game when the team was terrible, I thought. That counts for something. Maybe riding the bike was compensating for the loss of my beloved baseball. When I was twelve, that summer, the summer of the Phillies' splendor and collapse, when I was playing stickball, or soft-ball, or half-ball, or real baseball, I spent hours throwing a ball against a wall, playing whole games, indeed, whole seasons, in my mind in such splendid renditions of play and glory that I often entirely forgot where I was or who I was. But it comes back to you as you grow older, as you always knew it would, that you were just a lonely kid throwing a ball against the side of a warehouse building, and you realize how tough it is to keep an interest in this sort of thing, in this act of throw-ing for the sake of throwing, when there is no one there to throw the ball back.

I did not start riding Ida's bike because I liked bicycles or bicycle riding. When I was seven or eight, my mother bought me a bicycle for Christmas, twenty-three inches with training wheels, a Schwinn, a very good bike. My mother was poor, very poor, but she always be-lieved in buying quality. She hated cheap things. I guess cheap stuff re-minded her of being poor. But a well-made thing gave you dignity and you wouldn't have to spend your life rebuying it, was what she always said. I don't think she bought me the bike because I asked for it. I think she thought I should have one. All the kids, especially the boys, were riding bikes and I guess she felt I should be one of their number. She never bought bikes for my sisters. So, I not only had a bike, but I had a bike that was the envy of my friends. I tried to learn to ride it but was always deathly afraid of falling; the bike seemed so high off the ground. The training wheels seemed no help at all. I could never con-trol the bike. It wobbled dangerously every time I was on it. I hated bike riding, even before I got the bike, and was a bit disappointed that my mother bought it. I must have asked for something else. But my mother bought me things like football uniforms and army fatigues and toy guns. I don't think I ever asked for any of this stuff. But of all the things to help with the formation of my masculine identity, not an un-toward concern for my mother who found herself, as a widow, rearing a boy in a house of women, why a bike? My aunts always expressed to her a great concern that I would grow up a sissy. When I was a very small boy my uncles would sometimes come by on a Friday night and watch the fights on television. They would have me sit on their laps and watch with them and sip their beer a little. I hated the fights at that age and the beer as well. I did like sitting close to them, a sure sign of homoeroticism, I guess! At any rate, I suppose their exposure all worked in the end because I like prizefights and beer today and am not interested in cuddling up to men. In any case, of all the masculine toys my mother bought for me, some of which I did request, I hated the bike most of all. It was common for bigger kids in the neighborhood to take the smaller kids bike riding by placing them on the handlebars of the bikes or on the bike seats while the big kids, the riders, rode the bikes standing up. I endured my share of this, hating it all the while. I hated the feeling of being up in the air, which is how bike riding felt to me as a kid. I would get panicky and squirm a lot, thus making the bike hard to steer. Bigger kids were glad when I got my own bike because I was never a good passenger. Neighborhood friends tried to teach me to ride it after my sisters failed. I was told all the tricks of balancing and steering; my mind and psyche was greased like a chute with all the rhetoric of confidence-building to such an extent that the bike riding should have happened with ease. I did not lack determination. I hated the bike but I did want to learn to ride it, if only to be accepted by the other kids, if only to show my sisters, who rode the bike around the playground and in the street with poise, even verve. When a certain level and type of teaching failed, instruction grew progressively more peremptory. Finally, there was masculine ridicule.

"You just a little punk, if you scared to ride a bike," I was told.

"Jerry is a baby! Jerry is a baby! Jerry is a baby! He's scared to ride a bike! He's a little faggot!" the kids chanted.

One day, when riding alone, I fell from the bike and scraped my knee pretty severely. In fact, I came close to knocking my teeth out as I scarcely missed hitting my head against a curb. I was not going very fast. But suddenly, as the bike wobbled and swayed, I simply pitched headlong over the handlebars and fell off the bike. There was certainly something about the accident that was horrifying to me, unbelievably frightening because it was so violent and unexpected, but there was something as I thought about it that seemed funny, too. I must look like a fool on a bike, I thought to myself. And at that point my pride dictated that I would never get on one again. Was it worth it? I thought. And that was it. I limped home with my trouser leg pulled up, my knee bleeding, pretending I had suffered some sort of war wound, that I had a kind of badge of courage, a little trickle of blood running down my shin. I left the bike where the accident happened. My mother bandaged my knee and then angrily sent me back to get the bike before someone stole it or before a car ran over it. I was half-hoping for one of the those alternatives. But it was where I left it, bright red-and-white chrome, the tires still gleaming black and new, lemon yellow streamers dangling from the handlebars. I never rode the bike again. At first, various neighborhood kids used the bike until one of them rode it over some glass and the tire went flat. The tire was never repaired, so the bike just sat in our alley, a narrow storage cove next to our house, for many months. Eventually, the good tire went flat as well. Dust snowed upon it; the chrome showed small signs of rust from being exposed to dampness. Finally, in another year or so I gave it to one of my cousins. That was the end of the beginning of my life as a bicyclist.

I began riding my girlfriend's bike, a five-speed racer, very sleek, I cannot remember the maker, in March or April. I remember the spring of 1977 was especially warm in Philadelphia. Thursday, 26 May, the day junior-lightweight boxer Tyrone Everett was fatally shot, it was probably over ninety degrees. It was the same five days later for his funeral. The service took place at the Beulah Baptist Church at 1701 Bainbridge Street, just one block from my own church, St. Mary's Episcopal Church. Those are a few odd blocks there, in South Philadelphia. There must be four or five churches within a two-block area, all black, and all different denominations. It is odd to think that black people have lived in this neighborhood in Philadelphia since the eighteenth century, and presumably no better off then than they are now. At Everett's funeral, it was impossible to get within a block of the church. The crush of people made the sweltering weather even more unbearable. Everett was a popular fighter. Even Mayor Frank Rizzo paid his last respects. I could see him, big and sweating, yet remarkably impressive, as the crowd parted with great respect, even awe, as his bodyguards pushed their way through the throng. He was truly a man with presence, a combination of a padrone and a cowboy, his was a magnetic, palpable throb of power and assurance. There was, at that time, a serious effort to have him recalled. It was the talk of the city. I didn't sign the recall petition, ostensibly because I was a city worker, and I was afraid I would lose my job if I did. But looking at him there before the crowd, I realized that I liked him a great deal, liked him in spite of myself and perhaps in spite of himself as well. I understood the nature of his incredible and boisterous ambition, of his monstrous ego, of his good-natured paternalism, of his need to be the utter and complete personification of his city, and the bottomless, energetic, omnipresent source of its redemption. The sheer force with which he believed that his own dynamism was inextricably connected to the dynamism of the city made many of us Philadelphians, even us black folk, believe the city was some magnificence awaiting the awakening kiss of this, our "dago" prince. Rizzo embodied a kind of masculine cool in his own square, conventional way, simply because he seemed like a man who would brook absolutely no nonsense from anyone. He expressed his ideas, such as they were, in very simple, blunt terms, with no sense of anguish and no sense of doubt. He seemed in control of himself, yet there was nothing about him that seemed puritanical or stoic; this was something of a contradiction as he was a heavy smoker, a man who could become easily tongue-tied, and a very stiff campaigner who, when he had to make speeches on the stump, would sweat through five or six shirts a day. Yet he was the greatest man to come from my neighborhood in South Philadelphia, and that fact, at that shimmering, heat-soaked, bitter moment in May, drenched in a snowy sea of pollen and willow buds and burdened by the sorrow of young male death, meant something to me. Yes, odd weather like that makes an event stand out in your mind, gives it a resonance and meaning because the absurdity of it, the sheer unreality of it, seems all the more remarkable, all the more intensified.

Ida, my girlfriend, never rode the bike. Her father had given it to her for Christmas and I think she thought she would pedal it around the city for exercise. But she did not like bicycle riding, and she was not much inclined to exercise, in any case. I asked her one day if I might use it as it was sitting next to her refrigerator in her efficiency apartment, gathering dust. It bothered me that the bike was just sitting there. It was a boy's bike, as it was the rage at the time for women to ride men's bikes. I think, though, I would have ridden it had it been a girl's bike. That would have made it just a bit eccentric, nonconformist. Another reason I began to ride the bike was because the workers for the public transportation system of Philadelphia went on strike. SEPTA (South-Eastern Pennsylvania Transportation Authority) stayed on strike for forty-two days. The city was a virtual parking lot of traffic as everyone started driving to and from work. A bike worked better in all that madness. Ida, who normally took public transportation as she thought Philadelphia was an impossible city to drive in, drove her car and had to get to work an hour earlier and leave about two hours later than normal. After the strike was over, I just kept riding the bike.

The first day I used the bike I pedaled over fifty blocks. I wobbled all over the place, was nearly run over by irate motorists, went the wrong way on several streets (I hated having traffic to my back), and at times stopped the bike so violently and suddenly that I nearly threw myself from it. That night in bed every muscle was sore, especially my thighs, as if someone had beaten me with a stick. I was an inveterate walker, a runner, in tremendous condition, so I was astonished that bike riding would make me feel that bad. By the end of the week, I felt much better. I kept riding, and yet, oddly, my ability as a bicyclist did not improve, just my capacity to endure long bouts of it. I could pedal for hours without getting tired.

I worked as communications supervisor (a glorified dispatcher) at the Crisis Intervention Network in downtown Philadelphia, a gang-control agency started by, or should I say under, Frank Rizzo, the mayor of Philadelphia through most of the 1970s, in fact, the first cop to become mayor of a major city. Most of the guys who worked there were from the streets, the majority had been street-gang members. As a black guy with a degree from the University of Pennsylvania (in something as quaint and irrelevant as English), I stood out in this particular setting. The other supervisors were also black guys with degrees from the University of Pennsylvania. (I had no idea, at first, that I was part of an old boys' network. But once I realized it, I felt rather "connected" and proud of it.) The executive director, Bennie Swans, who was eventually fired for theft, was not a Penn guy. He knew the streets, too, but like an Irishman of the nineteenth century was hoping to parlay his connections in both the streets and the inner sanctums of local power into a political career. The gang problem in Philadelphia had reached its peak in the early 1970s. In these years as many as forty-five boys a year were being killed in street-gang wars. The approach of the Crisis Intervention Network, essentially run by former gang members, was something novel, taking the gang-control enterprise out of the hands of the police and the social workers. By the time I joined this organization, there were very few gang killings, although poor black folk continued to be murdered in significant numbers. That is to say, that black folk continued to kill black folk, particularly black men continued to kill other black men, like a kind of sport, an open season of despair washed in blood. There was a group in Philadelphia then called the Black Mafia, an extortion, drug-pushing, and loan-sharking group with rumored connections to the one of the local Nation of Islam mosques. Everyone feared them and they were largely responsible for a good deal of the violence in the black communities of Philadelphia at that time. No one's life, I mean to say, no one's black life, seemed worth very much and there wasn't much that the Crisis Intervention Network could do about that. Most of the street guys rode bikes, were, in fact, intensely engaged in varieties of physical culture, including sex, and when I hitched my bike to the post with the rest, I felt as if I belonged a bit more than I had before. Whenever I walked up to the Crisis Intervention office, there was a sense of entering a kind of club, an inner sanctum. At times, a line from a Sly & The Family Stone song would run through my head about all the squares going home. It was not a place that outsiders could easily penetrate, and a certain hipness attached to me because I worked there. During my thirteen months there, I rarely saw a white person, had absolutely no social interaction with whites. It was a world where, I

. . . . . . . . . .

suppose, I was likely to find out, as Ralph Ellison put it, my black possibilities or my male possibilities. I never felt so isolated and confined in my life, like an athlete in training. But for what? I felt rather like a man amongst men.

## PART 2: TO PRODUCE PURPOSE AS THE FITTER BREED . . .

> It would be in contradiction to the conservative nature of the instincts if the goal of life were a state of things which had never yet been attained. On the contrary, it must be an *old* state of things, an initial state from which the living entity has at one time or other departed and to which it is striving to return by the circuitous paths along which its development leads. If we are to take it as a truth that knows no exception that everything living dies for *internal* reasons — becomes inorganic once again — then we shall be compelled to say that '*the aim of all life is death*'. . .
> SIGMUND FREUD, *Beyond the Pleasure Principle*

After my sixteen-year-old cousin was murdered in a street-gang war in 1973, it was pretty easy for me to think about death and dying. I kept thinking that that could happen to me if I didn't get out of the city, although I never fought for a street gang, knew little about them. Being a young black man always made people ruthlessly assume things about you: The cops assumed you were a criminal and the gangs assumed you were a member of some other gang. Your life seemed there for the taking because no one who would think to kill you thought that, after all, your life was worth much; that anything significant was, finally, being taken. I found it frustrating and horrifying to live among people who didn't think your life was worth anything. I thought, at first, that working for the Crisis Intervention Network would save my life by making me part of a bureaucracy whose purpose was to prevent black men from killing each other. But things never turn out as you think they will.

M.S., one of the dispatchers who worked with me, wanted very much to become a gang worker and get out of the office. He was a street guy who had been demoted, and, I guess, it was the intention of the bosses never to let him back on the street. He lived with his wife and family in the Richard Allen Housing Projects in North Philadelphia, a very tough place, and he told me once, very casually, matter-of-factly, that he watched television every night with a shotgun on his lap. "A lot of bad things go on in the hallways where I live," he said. "People be wanting to break into your joint while you sitting there, so I have to be ready for that." I asked him if that didn't bother him, make him tense. "It's not the best way to live, but it's all right," he said, almost in a deadpan. "Everybody got some shit they got to deal with. Life goes on. I ain't no more tense than anybody else. I figure I got to move when I get some money, but it's not so bad living there. You just got to be prepared to jack somebody else up before they jack you up."

We talked boxing all the time. I guess it was a way to talk about death without really talking about it. There is so much, symbolically, about boxing that seemed very much like death, leaving aside, for the moment, the possibility of actually dying from the punishment taken in a prizefight or in a number of them over a period of years. Boxing, like the violence in the streets, was about male expendability. But boxing also seemed to me to be about returning to some earlier state of life, an affirmation of that, not something more primitive, something more truly ironic, more truly ambiguous about the human condition. Is it noble, in the end, or only degrading? Is there real pleasure in the body, in the end, or only greater sources of illusion and unhappiness? That was and is boxing for me.

During the 1976 Olympics, which produced one of the finest crop of boxers in American amateur history, including Sugar Ray Leonard, John Tate, Howard Davis Jr., Leon and Michael Spinks, M.S. said to me one day, "Shit, you know Sugar Ray Leonard could beat Roberto Duran right now." Duran was lightweight champion and, with the exception of Muhammad Ali, was the most talked-about boxer around. He was very good in those days, with incredible power, a killer's instinct, a proficiency to cut off the ring, an intense dexterity. No one fought with his rage, as perfectly mannered and polished and deliberate as an artifice, to win. "Leonard's good," I said, "but he's not that good. He can't beat Duran yet." M.S. shrugged, "He'll kick Duran's ass." They were good conversations, as I remember. It felt good to talk about boxing with these fellows because they really loved the sport.

In high school, I went with a Jewish friend to a boxing match at the Arena on Forty-sixth and Market Streets. That fired my passion for boxing to a fever's heat. A local fighter named Sammy Goss lost to another local fighter whose name I can't remember. That was the top of the card. It was a good fight, evenly contested, and the decision could have gone either way. The fighter who won was white and I thought that perhaps that was why he got the decision. I used to follow very closely the career of Joey Giardello, a tough fighter from Brooklyn who wound up in Philadelphia. He got one shot at the title in 1960 against Gene Fullmer. It was a draw. He didn't get another shot at the middleweight title until he was thirty-three, in 1963, when he beat Nigerian fighter, Dick Tiger. I always thought Giardello got the nod in that decision because he was white and because he was fighting in Atlantic City, a stone's throw from Philly, and he would naturally benefit from what is called a "hometown" decision. I don't know why I thought this as the two men fought each other twice in 1959 in very closely contested affairs. To Giardello's credit he fought everybody including Sugar Ray Robinson, Fullmer, Hurricane Carter, George Benton. I loved following his fights and I think my first conversations with this Jewish kid at my high school were about Giardello. I was much more drawn to boxers like Giardello and Sammy Goss and another local named Stanley "Kitten" Heyward, a welterweight and middleweight, than I was to Muhammad Ali, although, of course, I admired Ali tremendously. But for me, Ali was not really boxing. Boxing was these local guys, pretty good, highly skilled craftsmen, who were on the verge of championship fights, better than bums but not truly Hall of Fame fighters. The biggest fight of my boyhood was not any Ali fight but rather when local middleweight Bennie Briscoe fought Heyward in 1965. "Watch a good lower weight with fast hands and a bit of heart," my Jewish schoolmate told me, "They always give the best account of themselves in the ring." He liked talking like Freddie Brown or Anglo Dundee or Cus D'Amato, someone like that, some old prizefight head, cynical but wise. We were always striving to be wise aficionados so that the old guys on fight night would take us for more than a couple of school boys. But the Jewish kid knew his stuff. He introduced me to *The Ring* magazine, which I started to read religiously. He liked going to the gym to watch the fighters train, and I started tagging with him. This was not the beginning. This was the middle. My interaction with the guys at the Crisis Intervention Network was extending the middle.

One of the street guys at Crisis, R. J., was running a little school where kids came to learn to box. He talked boxing all the time and even invited me to come to North Philadelphia to see his little school of peewee gladiators. Some of his kids were in the Golden Gloves and the PAL (Police Athletic League) boxing tournaments. Sometimes a party of the guys went to the Blue Horizon, at Broad and Master Streets, the temple of professional boxing in Philadelphia, to see a card. Often, someone knew at least one or two of the local guys on the card. I was going to the Blue Horizon a lot in those days to see matches. There were some good middleweights in Philly then: Bad Bad Bennie Briscoe, Willie "The Worm" Monroe (whom I saw beat Marvelous Marvin Hagler in 1976), Bobby Watts (who also beat Hagler), Eugene "Cyclone" Hart (whom Hagler beat in 1976 at another fight card I saw). Of course, heavyweight Joe Frazier was the most famous fighter in town (although after two losses to Ali and a brutal beating at the hands of George Foreman, he was considered, in 1977, shot, over the hill), but Philadelphia was a good fight town, a lot of aggressive, well-schooled black fighters who probably learned the rudiments of the craft on the streets and the schoolyards having "fair ones" against war lords of various street gangs and playing slap-to-the-head with guys to improve their speed and hand-eye coordination. I once saw two teenage boys, with good, fast hands, play a game of slap to the head with the rhythm and movement of a kind of ballet. Ida was not surprised by the production line of Philadelphia fighters, saying, "You Philadelphia Negroes with your uncouth, tough attitude act like you're at war with the world." Yes, I guess it was a kind of war but I never knew what anyone was fighting for and how one joined a particular side. It means a great deal to be on a side. Once, in the office, a bunch of the guys were standing around talking, the radio was blaring, and it always was during working hours, on one soul music station or another, when, suddenly, Martha Reeves and the Vandellas' 1964 hit, "Dancing in the Street," came through the tiny, shallow-sounding speakers. The effect was electric and communal. The room became absolutely silent, and we each seemed linked to each other in

. . . . . . . . . . .

some magical way because we all thought the same way about the song, about what it meant, especially in 1964, a year that everyone in the room remembered when sides were very clear, if foolishly and destructively so. There was a joy in that song that black people had become so accustomed to reading out as the celebration of a black nation. This is what home is, at last: when you understand a place exactly the way those with whom you must live understand that place.

I saw R. J.'s kids once or twice at his little school, pipe-stem-armed youngsters, flailing away at each other, trying not to cry when they had been hurt. I remember once when I was nine playing a game of slap-to-the-head with a kid, a little squirt who imagined himself a tough guy. He slapped me silly, slapped me until my ears rang, until my ears were swollen, until the tears ran down my face. It is no mean experience to have the living shit slapped out of you. I never quit though, so despite my being no match for this boy, I earned the respect of the other boys just because I stood there, in a tight square of maybe twenty or thirty feet, and took a fairly substantial beating. Most of R. J.'s kids were not going to become fighters even on an amateur level; it was too hard and one had to sacrifice so much, take so much punishment, in order to even become a good boxer on that level; maybe one or two would become professional fighters. R.J. was very proud of his school. "I teach these boys how to live in the world," he said to me once. I thought they were being taught precisely how not to live in this world but to aspire to live in some other better world that did not exist. The ethics of sports romanticized male life by giving sacrifice, discipline, the very sense of tragedy embedded in masculinity a kind of transcendence and charisma. Maybe that is why we talked about sports so much at the Crisis Intervention Network, as a way of masking why we were all there in the first place.

At the time I was working at the Crisis Intervention Network, the most popular fighter in Philadelphia was a junior lightweight with fast hands and slick moves named Tyrone Everett. He grew up in South Philadelphia, "the city's dumping," as one writer put it, "the place for vast, unwanted projects such as the ugly concrete structures that house the Philadelphia Phillies, Flyers, and 76ers, along with giant oil tanks, incinerators, and huge industrial parks." He honed his craft on these streets where there were a lot of housing projects as well, something the white ethnics down there hated as they felt, and rightly so, such buildings would not be placed in white *middle-class* communities. Everett became an amateur, then a professional, and had enough success to buy himself a tavern and his mother a house. He had a string of girlfriends, as one might expect, and was the father of three children. In November 1976 he fought for the junior-lightweight title against champion Alfredo Escalera, quick hands, quick feet, what they call in boxing circles, "a cutsey," though with a tendency to backhand and rabbit-punch his opponents. The fight took place in Philadelphia at the Spectrum, one of those "vast, unwanted projects" in South Philadelphia, and I think everyone who worked for the Crisis Intervention Network, except me, went. There was a great deal of expectancy and palpable excitement as Everett was heavily favored to win. I am not sure why I didn't go. Maybe I thought I would bring Everett bad luck. Maybe I felt a premonition that he wouldn't win. But how could he lose when he was fighting in his hometown? All he had to do was stay on his feet. Even if he didn't fight well, he would get the benefit of the doubt in a hometown decision. There were plenty of tickets floating around the office, so it was not for a lack of opportunity that I didn't go. Guys were so confident of an Everett victory that they were talking about Everett fighting Duran in a year for the lightweight title, "if Duran don't eat his ass out of the lightweight division," as one of the guys put it. Everett was well known in the office; some guys knew him personally. Many of us had seen him fight on several occasions and had even gone to see him train. The knowing coves thought Everett had the potential to be a truly great fighter and so did I, although I didn't think he could beat Duran. Everett beat Escalera rather easily over fifteen rounds, convincingly, punishingly, but he lost the decision. Everett was one of the few boxers in history to lose a decision in his own hometown. Two of three judges were Latins, and this may have tilted the judgment to Escalera. In any case, Everett was bitter about the loss and bitter about Philadelphia fight promoters not arranging that the judges were going to favor him in a fight where he was clearly the favorite and that he clearly won. "If you a black man in Philadelphia," one of the crisis guys said the next day after the fight.

· · · · · · · · ·

"You always fighting a goddamn war to get what everybody else gets without a struggle."

On Thursday, 26 May, after having signed a few weeks earlier to fight Escalera again, Everett was shot to death at the home of Carolyn McKendrick at 2710 Federal Street in South Philadelphia. One bullet to the head. Everett was twenty-four years old. He was found in her bedroom. Ms. McKendrick was a drug pusher. In her home, along with Everett's body, was found, on the dining-room table, fourteen pink pills, thirty-nine glassine bags of heroin, and several bags of marijuana. McKendrick was eventually tried and convicted of killing Everett, although why remains unclear. The main witness at her trial was Tyrone Price, who was in the house at the time of the murder. Price's appearance caused a stir at the trial; the *Philadelphia Tribune,* described him as "wearing a woman's long-sleeved, see-through, pink flower-print blouse with a tan sweater tied across his shoulders, tight-fitting red slacks that reveal the outline of bikini-type panties underneath, and a processed-fluffed hairstyle.

"Spectators were further aghast at Price's well-developed breasts and buttocks that resembled the pronounced physical features of a female. Both [Defense Attorney] Serota and [District Attorney] King at one point referred to the witness as 'she.' " Price apparently aided McKendrick in her drug business.

Price never admitted to having an affair with Everett but testified that McKendrick caught them both in the bedroom and the bed was mussed. Apparently, she shot Everett when he gave her dismissive answers about the condition of the bed. The public naturally assumed that she killed him because she had virtually caught him in the act of homosexual lovemaking. That Everett made love to Price is almost certainly true despite Price's denial. Yet why McKendrick killed him remains unclear. She knew he had other women; indeed, he lived, from time to time, with another woman whom he said in the papers was his fiancée. Why didn't she kill him over this if she was jealous or deeply anxious about his infidelity? If she killed him because she was particularly disgusted about his being unfaithful with another man, why didn't she kill them both? Indeed, witnesses reported that both she and Price left the house together after the shooting. If she was a woman who could coolly operate a drug business, know deeply and intimately the hard side of life and the denizens of the underworld, why would she suddenly go haywire at the thought that Everett was bisexual? It seems more likely she would have laughed in his face and called him a fool. On the other hand, pride on the streets is a very sensitive matter, and black people kill other black people, as is generally true among the poor, for, what amounts to, trivia. Alas, these questions were never answered at the trial. Such questions at most trials almost never are.

At the time of the Everett murder and trial, Crisis Intervention Network seemed as if it was about to close down. We had gone several weeks without being paid, and there were rumors that we were going to be shut down at any moment because we could not get our federal grant renewed and Rizzo could not afford to pick up the tab. In order to win reelection in 1975, Rizzo gave the unionized, nonuniformed city workers, most of whom were black garbage collectors and laborers, the biggest contract in history: a 12.8 percent raise, a new paid holiday—Martin Luther King Jr.'s birthday—free life insurance, and 100 percent Blue Cross/Blue Shield coverage. In order to pay for this contract, Rizzo had no choice but to raise taxes after the election. He raised the city wage tax from 3.2 percent to 4.3 percent. There were howls of resentment from Rizzo's army of white ethnic supporters. Moreover, he refused to lay off any city workers, something that could have been easily accomplished as he had bloated the city payroll and horribly abused his patronage privilege. It was this tax hike that precipitated the recall petition. I don't think anyone at Crisis signed the recall petition. We all wanted our jobs.

Meanwhile, my stomach was tied in knots all the time. There was screaming and cursing in the office, an eerie sense of impending violence, especially on the days we were supposed to be paid and nothing materialized. Secret meetings of management, to which I was never invited, about how Crisis was to deal with *this* crisis, were held but never resolved anything. I wanted to get married, and I wasn't even sure if I could pay my rent, let alone kick in my share to support a household. I was sponging off Ida and feeling appropriately unmanly in the process. Perhaps I felt unmanly as well because I hadn't signed the recall petition, even though I believed that Rizzo should be recalled, not that he was a bad man but that he was not a good mayor. All because I wanted my lousy job. No, there was another reason for not signing the recall petition: Rizzo symbolized something to me about my own life, about my own ethnic origins, about the nature of my own ambitions, about my city, both good and bad, reprehensible and virtuous, that could not be dealt with by a simple recall. Perhaps you cannot say yes to what you are but you cannot say no to it either, so simply, so definitively. Perhaps I could not live in a city led by Frank Rizzo, but I could not deny that the city that made Rizzo made me and the city that Frank Rizzo made, made me possible and spun out my possibilities like pennies scattered across a pavement. Rizzo was a product of the liberal revolt against corrupt Philadelphia politics that resulted in the 1951 election victories of reformist patricians, Joe Clark as mayor and Richardson Dilworth as district attorney, changing the antiquated city charter and destroying the entrenched Republican machine that ran the city for decades. Rizzo was a rising young police officer, known for being rough and enforcing the law with a certain macho recklessness. The liberals needed Rizzo in the 1950s. They needed his connection to the ethnics and to the white working class that was so valuable to Democratic reform politics. So, while many complained about Rizzo's excesses, the liberals who ran the city in the 1950s ignored them. Indeed, they helped to aggrandize Rizzo's image as a head-busting, no-nonsense cop. By the 1960s, it was clear that Rizzo had become such a dominant figure in local politics by seeming to transcend politics itself that it was inevitable that he would become mayor. Rizzo was the culmination of liberal reform, the most expressive populist, the penetrating political presence the city ever produced. He was the voice of the little people, the forgotten, abused white ethnics, the man in the street, a blue-collar guy who worked his way up through the police department. Frank Rizzo was so powerful as an entity all to himself that, by the time he ran for mayor in 1971, he transcended the machine politics and both parties of the city. As an ethnic kid from the same working-class neighborhood, I loved that about Rizzo, loved that feature of his aspiration: to transcend the institution that you wished to rule. Rizzo never had to give up being an ethnic, never had to cross over, to run the city. He had only to be himself. This was his extraordinary triumph. It is the triumphant fantasy of every ethnic, and I think the triumphant fantasy of every black.

There is a certain obvious irony about Rizzo in that Italian Americans were usually associated with lawlessness in America. In the late 1950s and early 1960s, as Rizzo was becoming a major force in Philadelphia not only in police affairs but as a civic persona of extravagant rectitude, Italian Americans were protesting a television show called *The Untouchables* that they felt depicted them in a terrible light, as bootleggers, murderers, loan sharks, and gangsters. Rizzo had to be one of the few, if not the only, Italian American law enforcement officials to testify before the Senate Investigations Subcommittee on Vice, which he did in June 1962. As a symbol of law and order who was also an Italian American, and not an Italian American who was seen as a sellout by his own people, Rizzo *had* to be of immense worth to liberals in 1960s. This was precisely what made him valuable to conservatives and the right wing as well, being a disaffected white ethnic who achieved a form of success that other white ethnics could understand and appreciate because it was so inextricably bound to the exercise of real power at the expense of the very Ivy League-educated liberals who scorned white ethnics but who made Rizzo's rise possible. And all the white ethnics voted for him: the Irish Catholics of Frankford, the Italians of South Philadelphia, even the Jews of the far Northeast. The only ethnic minority that didn't vote for Rizzo in great numbers or any numbers at all were the blacks; they were alone in the belly of this particular beast. When Rizzo learned when he first won election as mayor in 1971 that he had not won a single black ward in the city, he felt genuine bewilderment and pain. He couldn't understand why blacks wouldn't vote for him. "I am not a racist," he would say repeatedly, an assertion so cunning and so complicated in both its affirmation and denial of the truth that it could only have resulted from a unique mixture of a flinty innocence and a childish egoism. Rizzo was never personally a racist, but he was, ironically, when one considers that he was a creature of the tradition of American political reform, the most charismatic manifestation of the white urban backlash against the Civil Rights movement. So, the liberals must ask themselves, was it worth it? Was Rizzo, the duty-bound, white ethnic knight hacking through the pestilential growth of our crime-ridden streets, worth the divisiveness, the anguish, the money he cost? How much should a culture be willing to pay for its legends, its mythical figures, which Rizzo so clearly was? Or how much did it cost our city for the white elite to use the white ethnics as the wedge against the changing urban demographics that were producing, in the 1950s, 1960s, and 1970s, an increasingly black city, but a city that had so little to offer blacks? But Frank Rizzo's reign was not the end of anything in Philadelphia; it was the middle that eventually produced the end the liberals perhaps, and the blacks, certainly, had been waiting for: a black mayor.

"Those niggers are crazy," I shouted at Ida one evening. "I gotta get outta there before I attack somebody or somebody attacks me. Life with black people is like being at war. I'm getting battle fatigue." In my most fevered moments, I realized that working at the Crisis Intervention Network was something like being on a slave ship, a contraption meant to take you to a new place of vistas and possibilities called the New World and to a new religion called progress, all the young males snatched and manacled together, doubtless an irritant to the thing that swallowed them but at the cost of being an even more virulent irritant to themselves and each other. On Monday, 30 May 1977, the *Philadelphia Inquirer* ran this story: "Anti-Gang Program in Turmoil":

> The controversy, which has been simmering for months, appears to have been touched off by the following:
> Recent firings by [Bennie] Swans of two CIN workers assigned to West Philadelphia who were well-known and apparent[ly] highly respected by gang leaders in the Mantua area.
> Suspicion that in addition to routine gang-control activities, CIN workers have been ordered to "spy" on gang members who associate with organized-crime figures and to report such activity to the police.
> Growing resentment among these gang leaders that Swans is using them and CIN as a stepping-stone to a political career.

Everything in the paper was true but *that* truth, such as it was, was not even the point. During the entire thirteen months or so I worked at the Crisis Intervention Network, there was always tension between Swans and the street guys, and between the street guys and the other supervisors. Once, a street guy threatened Swans with two guns, while brandishing alternately a copy of Marx's *Das Kapital,* a situation that required very delicate crisis management as the guy was nearly insane with anger. There was a great deal of stress in the office. Some of the street guys seemed particularly on the edge and were not to be fooled around with. I handled them with kid gloves and stayed out of their way. But with the other supervisors, there was always a sense of machismo, of making the street guys respect you, especially because they never thought any of the supervisors could actually get out in the street and work with the gangs. I had no desire to prove them wrong. On at least three occasions, supervisors got into fist fights with street guys. I remember one of the street guys coming in one day and saying to me, "You Penn niggers are full of shit. Educated niggers always making it on the backs of the people in the trenches. Just using black folk to get fancy jobs and fancy titles." I simply shrugged at this outburst and said, "Excuse me for living." Another street guy, M., always liked to say, "Niggers and flies. Niggers and flies. The more I see niggers, the better I like flies. Niggers get on my last fucking nerve. And the niggers in this office get on my nerves more than any other niggers on the planet." There they were, glittering like stilettos, resonant like curses against God, all my black possibilities, darkened and coarsened by my own helplessness and the frustration of the men around me. The Crisis Intervention Network was a story of how a type of black masculinity is a rather tragic community, self-consciously tragic. After all, we all knew we were together as a working group to stop black men from killing other black men and there was something comic, absurd, ironic, stressful, and despairing about that whenever we thought about it, which was often. The conjunction of the death of Everett, the recall drive against Frank Rizzo, and the unraveling of the Crisis Intervention Network convinced me beyond doubt that I had to get out of Philadelphia, as if this place, alas, were falling apart in the rubble and rumble of the internecine racial conflict that makes being black and male in America so ineffably hard in subtle ways, and so impossible to romanticize. I wanted to save my life before I became as convinced as the people around me that it wasn't much worth saving.

. . . . . . . . .

## PART 3: WHO HAS GATHERED THE WIND IN HIS FISTS?

. . . my taste was me . . .
> GERARD MANLEY HOPKINS, "I Wake and Feel the Fell of Dark"

I am all at once what Christ is, since he was what I am, and
This Jack, joke, poor potsherd, patch, matchwood, immortal
diamond;
   Is immortal diamond.
> GERARD MANLEY HOPKINS, "That Nature is a Heraclitean Fire
> and of the Comfort of the Resurrection"

"You see, there was this game," I said. Ida looked up, mildly surprised
that I had suddenly broken the silence. I was driving a big U-Haul
truck, one of the biggest you can rent, and in it were all our worldly belongings. We had just gotten married, and now we were on our way to
Ithaca, where I was to start graduate school at Cornell. Four days before we were married, the city commissioners, by a vote of two to one,
voted against the recall petition by claiming that more than half of the
211,000 signatures were invalid. Frank Rizzo would remain mayor.
Everyone at Crisis Intervention Network kept his job. Rizzo maintained his obstinacy about not laying off workers. I was not sure which
was the biggest anticlimax of my life: Rizzo beating the recall, Crisis Intervention Network managing to keep its doors open, or my departure
from the city. The recall of Rizzo was the end, I thought. His triumph
over that was the end of the end. Ida and I were moving on what felt
like the hottest day in August. I was sweating so heavily that even my
trousers were drenched. I had spent the entire night before loading the
truck with two friends, two fellow supervisors, two fellow Penn
alumni, from the Crisis Intervention Network. We hadn't done a very
good job, downright inept, although I could lift and fetch tirelessly,
endlessly shifting stuff but to no advantage. Finally, we three just sat
down on the curb and drank Cokes and laughed about my dilemma.
"The truck's not big enough," they said. "You better rent another
one." "I can't," I said. "I don't have any more money, and, besides, I'm
not even sure I can drive this one." Next morning found me, alone now,
still trying to find room for half of our belongings and furniture and no

place to put them. So poorly had the truck been loaded. But my mother stopped by that morning with her friend, C., and he rearranged everything and helped to load the rest on the truck. "This truck's plenty big," he said, "if you know how to pack it." We would never have been able to leave Philadelphia without his help, but finally we did. Ida's bike was the very last thing that went in the truck. C. drove our car behind the truck and my mother drove their car.

C. had joined the police force in the 1950s, and when one considers the nasty internal politics of any big city police department and the extraordinary pressures, both from their white colleagues and from the black and white publics, that black policemen must endure, I rather thought that his retirement twenty-odd years later was something of a heroic achievement. I certainly admired him enormously. Oddly, I never had one real comfortable conversation with him, because he loathed sports. I discovered, particularly so on this day of my departure, how difficult it was for me to talk to any man with whom I had little in common, if he was not interested in sports. As I watched him load the truck, I remember that Frank Rizzo also hated sports. When he first ran for mayor in 1971, Rizzo was invited, that August, to participate in a celebrity home-run-hitting contest at Veterans' Stadium against his blue-blooded opponent, Thatcher Longstreth. Rizzo, a high school dropout, had never played a sport in his life. Longstreth had been a star football player at Princeton. Rizzo was a much bigger man, but he had no idea how to swing a baseball bat. He gripped it as if he wanted to grind it into sawdust, and he swung with all his strength. He struck out every time. Longstreth, gripping the bat lightly and with a controlled swing, hit several over the boards and easily won the contest. Rizzo was booed, and I felt embarrassed for him. I was never sure, when I spoke to C., if I felt embarrassed for him or for myself that he did not like sports, but I always felt embarrassed.

"This game," I continued, "this game was called Dead Box and we used to play it in the schoolyard all the time on autumn and spring days. Numbers were painted on a four-square block of smooth concrete from one to fourteen on the perimeter of the square. In the center were the last two numbers, and in the exact middle was the Dead Box with a skull and crossbones. Well, see, at first, my sister taught me this game. We used to use a soda top or a bleach-bottle top for our playing pieces, and we would kind of fling the pieces from square to square, because, you see, the object of the game was to get your piece in every number and finally land in the Dead Box square and become a killer. If you could hit someone else's piece as you were going around the course, you could skip a number. If you hit someone into Dead Box, you could advance two squares, and if you hit that person out of Dead Box, you could advance five squares. The object was to become a killer and kill the other tops before they killed you. Then, you would go around and kill everyone's piece by hitting it with your own. It was a swell game. But we had problems, my sister and me, playing the game, because our tops were too light and the wind would blow them off the square. Then, it took a long time to play, because we flung the caps. We could hardly guide them where we wanted them to go.

"Then, you know," I said. Ida was nodding slightly, looking a little quizzical, "One day, I started to play with these boys, and they taught me to use a bigger top, like the cap from a gallon of orange juice or something like that, and to fill it with clay so that it would not be driven off course by the wind. Finally, they taught me how to shoot the thing, like a marble. And then, you know what, that game turned into a true thing of beauty. Those kids were so skilled at this, it was like watching someone play pool or something. It was like negotiating the geography of a boxing ring. There was this one boy, R., who could shoot his top with such accuracy that it was actually something joyful to behold. I could never beat him. He could hit your top at different angles and knock you from here to yonder and then, then, well, then, it was like golf and you had to, as they say, 'Play the ball where it lays.' And he always became a killer first and killed everyone else. Little R., who was still sucking his thumb at the age of nine and ten and watched *The Three Stooges* all the time. We all did that, watched the Stooges, watched *Popeye* cartoons, read comic books. For a long time, I didn't want anything other than that, and then when I finally wanted something else, it seemed as though I was spun through the air to a distant star and could never reach anything in my past anymore. It was all taken from me, and I, lighter than air, just hovered like a ghost over everything. Did you ever feel that way? One day, I came so close to beating him. We had, what we called, our World Series of Dead Box, our championship, the ultimate game to decide who was the best. It was a fair one, one-on-one, him and me. So you see, I was a killer and so was he, and he killed me before I could kill him, and I just stretched out on the concrete bodily and screamed, 'I'm dead. I'm dead. O, the agony, the agony.' It was funny but the games were so tense, so closely contested that I had to do something silly like that to relieve the pressure. It was awful to die like that in that game. It was so real that I thought I was really dead, I mean, really dead, as if the whole world had stopped moving. But R. stood over me and grinned, and finally I opened my eyes and grinned, too. 'Get up off that ground,' he said, 'Before somebody really kill you.' 'If somebody killed me now,' I said back to him, 'I wouldn't have far to fall.' What a wonderful game that was, Dead Box. And we used to call R., all of us kids, called R. the King of Dead Box. He was the best player, the best shooter. If you had seen this kid play, you would have thought it was like a kind of dance or something like that."

I was a silent for a long time, thinking about Dead Box and those days of playing. And it occurred to me, as clear as anything and at last, that I was leaving Philadelphia, and I had vowed that I would never return to live there, never return to that life. I kept remembering the song the Delfonics used to sing, the Philly boys with the Philly sound of Gamble and Huff, a song about a guy who kept trying to leave some girl but couldn't, then finally one day he does it.

"Didn't . . . Didn't . . ." I stammered suddenly. I could feel Ida looking up again. "Didn't I, I, I bl-blow your mind th-this time," I said triumphantly. I turned and grinned at Ida. In order to live life cleanly, you had to know where the end was, matter-of-factly. The end was not Frank Rizzo, because the end always comes long before the end that you think is the end. And the end for me was December 1965 when Stanley "Kitten" Heyward, bloodied and battered though he was, beat Bennie Briscoe and became, for a few moments, the best middleweight in Philadelphia. The Kitten was my favorite fighter. I followed his career with the passion of a groupie. I lived for his fights. I wanted him so much to beat Briscoe, and he had, in that the judges gave him the decision. But I could not believe he had a won a fight where he had been so

. . . . . . . . . . .

badly beaten. I wanted to cry. What's the end of winning something that you really didn't win? Was it worth it? And if you have to ask that question, if you even think it, then that's the end, whether you want it to be the end or not. That was end of everything for me, that fight. The end of boxing, the end of sports, the end of Philadelphia, the end of a life as I knew it. And it, the end, was not in the beginning but in the middle, and I never recognized it. You have to know the end, the true end, or otherwise you waste so many years thinking that you're wait-ing for an ending that you've already had. "Yes," I said, driving the U-Haul, "you have to know the end." Ida looked at me, a wry smile on her face, as if she couldn't figure out what I was talking about. All that time, she thought that I had been talking to her.

# *Hamburger*

.   .   .   .   .   .   .   .   .   .

*by*
ANTHONY WALTON

Most of my adolescence was spent wondering—worrying, really—if I was ever going to be able to measure up to the considerable challenge, as I perceived it, of "being a man." My worry didn't have much to do with the typical concerns about women and sex—how to impress the former in pursuit of the latter—though that was a small part of it. It had to do rather with something both more innocent and much darker: I would lie awake nights at the age of eleven or twelve wondering how a man went to work every day, how he paid a mortgage, how he kept control of the complex and crazy variables that came with a wife and children. I didn't see how it could be done.

I don't know why I worried about these things. It was odd, to say the least. I think it may have been because my father worked his way up from nothing; because in that peculiar way of children I was aware of more things than I could consciously *know,* and sensed beneath the placid surface of suburban life the fragility of what we had.

In any case, my fretting set me apart a little from the rest of my peers. I don't think they wasted too much time worrying about the distant and unforeseeable future, a future several of them, I'm sorry to say, would not live to see. I don't, of course, know for certain that they didn't worry; this was not the sort of topic discussed by boys of that age in that time and place. But I felt lonely, and deeply insecure. How could I ever know for sure that I could handle the everyday pressures of being a man? What I decided to do, living there in the Midwest in

. . . . . . . . . .

the mid-seventies, was to prove myself (*to* myself) in the way that boys and young men seemed to do then—I decided to play football.

There was more to it than this, of course, and some of it a good deal more innocent. In one sense, I simply wanted to be a part of the unself-conscious and uncynical spectacle that was sports at that time. The mid-sixties through the mid-seventies were a theater of many dark dramas in the country's life, but that time was also a golden age for the sport of football, an age when the spectacle of twenty-two men wrestling and thrusting for turf on a fall afternoon still had a feel of dignified authenticity, of enormous integrity. This was before the entertainment aspect had overrun the game; even the professionals then seemed to be playing for pride and honor.

The teams and heroes of that era, the Green Bay Packers, the Baltimore Colts, the Kansas City Chiefs, the Pittsburgh Steelers, the Oakland Raiders, the Dick Butkuses, the John Mackeys, the Larry Csonkas, the Walter Paytons, seemed real, seemed closer to the ground. Football seemed to be something that men *did,* not just a marketing vehicle for caps and jackets, not just a way for loudmouths and reprobates to become multimillionaires. I wanted to be a part of it. I wanted to be like them.

I first played tackle football in the seventh grade, suffering a serious knee injury when I was clipped (blocked from behind and below the waist, an illegal move) in the last game of the season. Short, slow, and fat, I played noseguard that year, my chief responsibility to clog up the middle so that other boys could remain unblocked and make tackles. My injury was severe enough that I missed several weeks of school, limped through the winter, and was tentative and handicapped as a player the next year. But I enjoyed the attention, the solicitude of the coaches and other kids, and the status I seemed magically to possess as the survivor of such a calamity. I can still remember the pleasure of having girls who would not otherwise have known I existed signing my cast and helping with my cane and books.

Football was a serious affair where I grew up, in the Fox River Valley of northern Illinois; if not quite the life-and-death cosmic undertaking that was basketball, then a very close second. The valley is lined with

towns and cities—Elgin, St. Charles, Geneva, Batavia, Aurora—that
are now considered suburbs of Chicago; but at that time, twenty years
ago, they were principally prairie towns whose inhabitants tended to
work in the factories and foundries of the two largest municipalities:
Elgin, home of Elgin watches and Borden's Dairy, and Aurora, which
boasted Caterpillar Tractor, Lyon Metal, Richards-Wilcox, and my
father's plant, All-Steel, among many others. Most of these plants have
since closed, leaving behind demoralization and economic dislocation.

There was a good chance if you were a young man living in the valley that your father did something to earn his family's way that was
physically demanding, if not dangerous—another reason why it was so
important to be "tough" in those towns, why a little boy might spend
hours wondering if he measured up. Those factories were places where
men lost fingers and arms and eyes, and in one particularly horrific
accident, a man had been crushed and burned to death by molten steel
in a foundry. I used to listen to my father get ready for work every
morning and wonder how he found the strength.

My own football life became fixed—something I could no longer
turn away from—my freshman year in high school. I was attending, for
academic and avoidance-of-trouble reasons, Aurora Central Catholic,
a medium-sized diocesan high school. Catholic's Chargers were the
most consistently successful team in that part of the state, due largely
to the genius of head coach Michael Dunn. Coach Dunn—handsome,
black-haired, stocky, and willful—saw the entire field at once, whole,
rather than in segments, and had a gift for talking, cheering, and flog-
ging pre-MTV adolescents into decisively accomplishing tasks they
might not otherwise have thought possible. In the fall of 1974 I became
one of those adolescents, suiting up for the freshman squad.

A lot had changed for me since the seventh grade. I had grown
nearly a foot, and somehow the baby fat had melted away. I was still a
bit gawky and uncoordinated, but I *looked* like an athlete, and when I
joined my new teammates for fall practice, I said I was a receiver and
defensive back—two positions I had never played, but which I considered to be far superior to blocking on the line.

I didn't immediately thrive, footballwise, at Aurora Central. I wasn't
in shape, and I wasn't used to the tempo and intensity of those boys,

some of whom had been playing full-contact football since the fourth grade. I wanted to quit in the beginning and would have but for several long conversations I had with Pat Langan (like Coach Dunn, an Irishman), one of the freshman coaches who gave me advice that was a revelation to me then but that basically boiled down to "one day at a time." I walked to school in the morning sometimes with Coach Langan, and we would discuss things like mortgage down payments and car loans—which also weighed heavily on his mind, though he had the excuse of having a young wife and new baby. I wouldn't have dreamed of talking to my father about those things: When I asked him what he thought about my leaving the team, he just rolled his eyes and snapped, "Quit if you want, but not until the season's over. We Waltons stick things out."

High school athletic coaches are often portrayed in the media as near-misfits who couldn't quite cut it anywhere else—"those who can't do, teach, those who can't teach, teach gym"—but as I get older I am more and more amazed by the job they do as quasi-shamans, initiating young people into the world. Though he probably wouldn't remember them, my whining talks with Coach Langan were crucial to me because I was able to talk things out with a man who had my best interests at heart *at a time when I could not talk to my father.* We now have a joking, familiar, and easy relationship; but in my teens I think my father, who had left home at thirteen and who, with the exception of five years in the military, has worked brutal low-echelon jobs ever since, saw through my gallant facade to the soft, dissembling skirt-hugger I was, and couldn't understand how we were related. And, tough as he was, he wasn't crazy about football, except as an occupier of male teenage energy and time. Football, in his mind, was a luxury, an abstraction; he believed in toughness in the real world. He thought I could be out making money, or better, studying, preparing myself to be chairman of Caterpillar or president of Continental Illinois Bank. He thought the coaches were giving me a big head that I couldn't live up to in life.

I didn't have much to do with Coach Dunn on the football field the first year. In fact, I didn't even realize that my freshman history teacher was the legendary coach until, while I was trudging to the practice field one day after school, he came sprinting up behind me, clapped me hard on the shoulder pads, and yelled "Walton!" Continuing on, he looked back over his shoulder and smiled, "How you like school? I hear you got a pretty good history teacher," then bolted over to the varsity field. All that school year, though, he paid very special attention to me, giving me his *Chicago Tribune*s and *Time* magazines to read when he was finished with them, and assigning several special projects in class that allowed (or forced) me to do research on arcane (to a ninth grader) subjects like Frederick Douglass and the Abraham Lincoln–Stephen Douglas debates.

The freshman season was one of the enduring triumphs of my life. We rolled through the fall, thrashing all of our opponents, including such bigger schools as Batavia and Aurora West Blue (Aurora West was such a big school, over 4,000 students, that they had two freshmen teams). The season was delicious for me; I started at defensive back, leading the team in interceptions, and got in a lot of work on offense (though mostly as a decoy and blocker). Getting on the yellow school buses to ride to away games brought to my romantic and overly imaginative mind the thought of warriors sailing for Troy.

The crowning glory of that season for me was that the boys I had known around town and up and down the valley, my childhood friends and cousins—most of whom had dismissed me as an egghead—were forced to acknowledge me as an athlete. I had been fighting with some of these guys since Little League, and had almost always been on the losing end.

In fact, football became the largest part of my life outside of school, more important to me than anything else. I began lifting weights and doing serious workouts three or four days a week, and the other sports I pursued, basketball and track, I rationalized as being de facto training modes for football. I began to buy sports magazines in earnest, especially those that focused on football, and mailed away to college sports information offices for the media guides of my favorite teams. In 1975, before cable and satellite television, before the World Wide Web and homesites, I could tell you, in detail, about the offensive-line needs at Texas A&M, the quarterback situation at Mississippi State, whether that sophomore flanker at Nebraska was living up to his high school billing or was only a pale imitation of Johnny Rodgers.

. . . . . . . . . .

I don't know what I hoped to accomplish by all this. I suppose I thought that all this information would somehow make me a better player. I was too inexperienced to know that the vast majority of the guys who became great college football players—as I had secretly started hoping I would—didn't read enough material to serve as sports editors at the Associated Press. I didn't know that, for the most part, they rarely read anything at all. What I had found in football, in being one of the fifty or so boys who got to wear the blue-and-gold "Charger Football" jackets that we so prized, was a way of being in the world, an identity. I was a football player.

Sophomore year I was ready. As we entered two-a-days, the brutal preseason rites of August, with ninety-five- and one-hundred-degree practices meant to winnow down the team and condition the survivors, I felt the equal of any boy my age (I reiterate, *my* age), and was scraping to take them all on. Then, one afternoon about a week in, something happened that I've since come to see as one of the two or three most significant events in my life.

We were engaged in "hamburger" drills—one of the harshest rituals of the game, one-on-one tackling maneuvers in which two players lie on the ground, one with the ball, then hop up on the whistle and sprint for the space between two cones, where a tremendous collision occurs. The team had been divided into two circling lines, and we all clapped rhythmically and chanted inanities like "He's a beast!" after particularly stirring smashups.

Standing in line, I had been careful to keep count and make sure that my tackling partner would be Matt Patterson, a fellow sophomore and good friend. We would run the drill as hard as we could and deliver solid licks, but with each other as partners we could also be reasonably sure of surviving the occasion. When my time to step up came, however, the opponent who stood before me was not Matt, but Walt Rodriguez, a senior tight end, two-year starter and universally respected tough guy. He bore me no special animus, and unlike most of the upperclassmen had even deigned to acknowledge my existence a few times. But what could I do? I couldn't just run and let him hit me, because *he* had the ball. *I* had to tackle *him*. How had Matt messed up?

Had I lost count? I pondered the psychic costs of sprinting off the field and transferring to another school.

Coach Dunn blew the whistle. "Come on, Tony," he said. "Show him what you got." I lay down on the hot grass, sweat drenching my face, closed my eyes, and waited. And waited. With the whistle I vaulted to my feet, sighted the cones, slammed my eyes shut and threw every single thing I had at that space, praying primarily that I wouldn't miss him completely, that I would bounce off, that he would run over me, but that I would at least have had the honor of sacrificing my body without fear. I could live with being humiliated, even with being brutalized, but not with being seen as the coward, in truth, that I was.

I wasn't humiliated. Eyes still shut, I ran full force into Walt, hit him with my left shoulder square in the solar plexus, followed through by lowering my helmet and, *shazaam!*, popped the ball loose from his grip as I strained to wrap my arm around him. I was expecting to be dragged on the ground and laughed at, but instead I felt him yield, stumble backward, and collapse, taking me down with him. We lay there tangled for several seconds until Coach Dunn ran up screaming, "Did you see that! Did you see that!" and pulled me—in a daze—to my feet, with my teammates cheering and seeing me, I think, for the first time as a serious person. I could hit.

And that became my reputation, the most cherished reputation of football players everywhere, *a hitter*. My fellow sophomores looked at me with something approaching awe the next few days (I omitted telling them how terrified I had been). The thing snowballed. That moment somehow became a model for manly conduct on the field, and I had to live up to it, though I didn't always want to.

During a practice before a big game a couple of weeks later when the regular punt returners were having a bad day, fumbling the ball several times, Coach Dunn yelled out, "Put that Walton kid back there, he'll catch it!" I remember, to this day, looking around for another guy named Walton, the one he was referring to. But I did it, I went and caught punts, including many fair catches in one critical and close game, and including running two back for touchdowns in other games (but only because I'd had no choice after mishandling fair catches; when a player signals for a fair catch he must be allowed to catch the ball unmolested; if he drops it, it's a free ball, precipitating a free-for-all. I had no choice after missing the catch but to scoop the ball up and run for my life.) After one of the runbacks, one of our coaches ran onto the field and congratulated me by screaming, "You've got cast-iron balls!" I still didn't understand what was going on, only that I was more afraid of looking foolish from failure than I was of whatever pain or punishment would come from not living up to expectations.

But that was a life lesson I learned in football—if you can just hang on, things have a way of working out. Half of being pretty good was in understanding the flow of a play or a game, knowing that this or that *tended* to happen; the other half was, as Woody Allen says, just being there, just showing up. Punt coverage by your opponents was planned based on the ball being in the air for a certain length of time, but if you dropped it and then picked it up and ran, or caught it cleanly, counted to two, and sprinted in the opposite direction, often the first wave of defenders would overrun you—as you would take longer to start moving than they'd counted on—and as if by magic you would have open field.

Coach Dunn showed me a similar trick for the classic counterplay (which is run to the opposite guard-center hole from the hand off). He said, emphatically, "Hit the hole, keep your head down, count three steps, then break against the grain. It'll be wide open." The first few times I blew it badly, then he smacked me on the helmet and said very evenly, "*Don't look, don't think, just do it.*" I did, and that play began to feel like the parting of the Red Sea.

I slowly came to understand why Coach Dunn won all the time. He practiced and prepared constantly and was a disciple of, among others, Vince Lombardi, who said, "Winning isn't everything, it's the only thing." Coach Dunn was a rationalist; he believed that you could analyze situations, draw parameters, assess your capabilities against your opponents', and implement plans. There was no excuse for losing; you just had to plan. We watched hours of film on our opponents each week, spending much of practice running their plays, learning their identifying ticks and tendencies. We studied them so fully that when it came to the actual game we would often know what they were going to do before they did it. This sort of intensity may be routine today in prep sports, but it wasn't in 1976; it gave us an almost supernatural advantage.

And I needed it, I needed any kind of edge I could get as I was still something of an impostor in my new incarnation as tough guy and enforcer. I was also beginning to learn that no matter how well I did, no matter how skilled I became, there were levels of players above me, guys who were born for the contained violence and mayhem of the football field. I wasn't one of those guys; I was a half-step slow and ten pounds too light.

As I see it now, my sin as a football player was that I thought too much, I wasn't what I would call a meat eater, a psycho. I could hit and liked it, but I wasn't like the guys I would later know at Notre Dame who routinely beat each other bloody, smashed their fists through windows, smashed lightbulbs with their teeth (a friend of mine who was All-American and All-Pro did this as a party trick), and other assorted kinds of mayhem. Another friend of mine at Notre Dame told me that the way to imagine what college ball was like was to think of the absolute hardest hit you had suffered in high school, from a guy like DeKalb's Mel Owens (later a Michigan and then L.A. Rams star) or Elgin's Mel Cole (later an Iowa star), and imagine that level of violence on every play. I couldn't. I cringed thinking about it. Taking a hit from one of those guys was enough to make me start considering what else I might be good at.

I had a headache during much of my sophomore year from being hit so much and I sometimes wondered whether it was worth it. But I admit it, I liked being seen, in that small circle, as a man among men; I liked being feted with the candy-bar signs the cheerleaders and poms made for us every Friday; I even liked being teased, as happened one day when I was limping up the stairs between classes, and a wiseass classmate called out, "Walton, you're even slower here than you are out on the field!" The way everybody laughed, with pleasure, told me that this wasn't an insult.

Junior year, I played "The Victor," a position on our defense that was roughly analogous to the University of Michigan's "Wolfman," which is to say, a position of honor. The Victor was a kind of floating safety whose job it was to line up into the opposition's strength, read the play as it developed, and get to the ball with decisive force. The Victor was also supposed to be able to defend the run or the pass with equal skill and ferocity; and when the coaches counted blue helmets around the ball at the close of a play in the game-film frame, the Victor's head had better have been there, preferably planted firmly in the middle of the ball carrier's chest.

I was doing quite well, the team, surprisingly, less so, when the unimaginable happened. I suffered a separated shoulder, an extremely painful injury (the arm bone tears out of the shoulder socket) that was to occur to me twice more. But adhering to the cult of toughness, I missed only a week of practice, though I moved for a while to less demanding positions. I felt driven to prove to the coaches and my teammates that I could cut it. Signs were posted in our training room and over the last door we walked through on the way to the field: "Pain is a badge of courage, wear it with pride," and "Those who stay will be champions." I believed both.

We weren't champions that year, however, not even making the state play-offs. Coach Dunn had pointed to that year, 1976, as the one in which we would have the balance, speed, and size to win the state championship. He had gone so far as to take a large contingent of us down to Normal, Illinois, home of Illinois State University, for the state championships the year before so we "would know what it felt like to be down there in that atmosphere" the next year and would be equipped to avoid its distractions. He also hoped that seeing the festivities would inspire us. Coach had achieved everything but a state-championship win (during the first part of his career there hadn't been football play-offs in the state of Illinois), and wanted one desperately.

But we fell apart as a team that year; I've never understood why. My closest guess is that the guys were changing, that they could no longer believe in the simple pieties of work, practice, and victory. Sex, drugs, and rock and roll seemed to make more sense than hamburger drills. The malaise of irony, soon to paralyze the country, was settling into even our quiet corner of the Midwest; the old ways could no longer be believed. But Coach thought we had merely "gone flat," that he had failed us and himself, and he redoubled his efforts.

And, for a year, they paid off. My senior year we rolled from one triumph to the next, including a tremendous victory at Ottawa Marquette, a downstate power who had made the mistake of inviting us to be their homecoming opponent (the gravest of insults, as it implies an expected, easy, victory). We shut out an offense that had been averaging forty points a game using pro tricks like timed-pass patterns, in which the quarterback throws to a spot, not a player. We had done our homework, studied the film, and so knew to prevent the player from getting to that spot (by various means fair and foul). We ran blitzes—sending more than the usual number of defenders in attack to hurry the quarterback. On almost every play we kept their All-State wide receiver (who, coincidentally, would later become a good friend in college) from catching any balls. A few weeks later we handily beat another downstate power, Marengo, and it started to seem like 1977 was in fact the year.

A year before the team had been much more talented—several of the seniors went on to play competitive small college ball—but that team hadn't cohered. During my senior year, everyone came together, and we looked like tough, true contenders. One of my sweetest memories is of reading a Wednesday *Chicago Tribune* and seeing my name among the area's scoring leaders after a great game—against archrival New Lenox Providence. My picture had also been in the Sunday paper that year, bulling for extra yardage with several tacklers clinging and trying to bring me down.

But the dreams of glory were not to be fulfilled, not for me or for the team. I was having trouble with my shoulder, and, calamity of calamities, contracted pneumonia after several days of practice in rain and mud. I missed the last game of the regular season. I couldn't help wondering, what *was* the point? I made it back for the play-offs as a backup, only to participate in a decisive loss at home to Benet Academy, an upscale Catholic school from nearby Lisle, in the first round. We collapsed in that game and gave up, the one thing we were not *ever* supposed to do, and I have since wondered whether it happened because we were tired physically and mentally from the long season, or whether we, all of us, were simply tired of football and saw a way out. We were supposed to hate Benet, "rich" boys from Naperville and

. . . . . . . . . .

Wheaton and Hinsdale, and were supposed to teach them a thing or two about intensity and tempo.

But we were the ones who were schooled. We were pitiful. During that year, unlike the previous season, we had maintained the fiction that we were warriors and heroes throughout the regular season; but we folded in the most humiliating fashion, 27–6, when it mattered. And I think Coach Dunn saw something, too, saw that his beloved Catholic boys were succumbing to the culture at large and would no longer believe what they needed to believe—study, contemplation, violence—to be great. He resigned from our school a few weeks later, accepting a job as head coach at a huge public school in a northern Chicago suburb.

We betrayed that man, and I think we broke his heart, but how could we have known? We were supposed to be hitters, but were, in fact, phonies. We were sixteen- and seventeen-year-old boys living in a culture that was loosening up; we wanted to sample slack. Had the rest of my teammates been perpetrating the same masquerade I had?

In the locker room after the play-off loss, I remember sitting on the floor and crying, more from relief, I think, than sadness. Coach walked up to me, knelt before me, lifted my chin up, and said, "One thing: You can be as good as you want to be at anything you want." After a moment he stood up, bent over, and kissed the top of my head; then he straightened, turned, and walked away. I was stunned by this show of tenderness from a man whom, for all his kindness to me, I had always seen as remote, and I didn't understand what he meant. But then I realized (I thought) that he didn't know I had no intention of playing football in college, that I had begun to get recognition for my schoolwork and writing and had begun to meet the kind of girl who thought football was stupid, but that knowing about poetry and jazz was very, very cool. I had started to think football was stupid as well, and I was tired of the pain, of being sore and battered from the middle of August until Thanksgiving.

Years later, however, I don't see any of it as that simple, and I think that Coach Dunn might have known exactly what I was thinking. He was, after all, the man who had taken me, on his own time, to visit various colleges, including Northwestern (where he also arranged for me to meet their coaches and to spend some time with their then-star, Pete Shaw), which was decidedly "up" in our neck of the woods. He was also the one who had told me, when I expressed interest in attending a small local college, "I'm sure _____ is a fine school with a lot of fine Christian folks, in fact the coach is a good friend of mine, but around here we don't think about _____, we think about Southern Cal and Notre Dame." That was the first time I had thought about Notre Dame as a possibility for me. How had this Irishman from Chicago's rough-and-tumble West Side come to see so much in me, a secretive, suburban black kid, a would-be poet pretending to be a football hero, scheming to get out of what he considered to be nowhere? How had he known? Had this been what he meant that afternoon in sophomore practice, "Come on, Tony, show him what you got"?

The tackling drill that afternoon lingers; I have replayed it a thousand times. Something happened to me that day, and in the movie of my life that plays through my mind it is the proverbial first turning point, when the hero, in ignorance and valor, embarks upon the dark road of sorrow that will lead to his redemption. *I was so afraid*, and would remain so for some time. I would be into my late twenties before I was truly sure of myself, partially from implementing lessons — don't look, don't think, just do it, plan, practice, *and don't give up* — that I learned from Coach Dunn and from playing football, lessons I learned before I knew there was a life for men beyond sports and work.

Later in my life I've probably gone too far the other way, away from the timidity I had then and toward a certain ruthlessness — I have often thought that if I had possessed the mental ferocity when I was playing that I have now, bred from surviving long stretches of unemployment without money in hostile New York City and cold, cold Maine, I *would* have been All-American. But on that hot day in August I learned the sort of lesson that is crucial to becoming what we in our culture call "a man," something you must figure out for yourself because no one, not your coach, not your brother, not even, perhaps especially not, your father, will ever tell you: The first step in a man's learning not to be afraid lies in hanging in there, hanging on, not under any circumstances giving up, and, most of all, not under any circumstances giving any hint, clue, or acknowledgment that he is, or might be, afraid.

# Derivative Sport in Tornado Alley

. . . . . . . . . .

*by*
DAVID FOSTER WALLACE

When I left my boxed township of Illinois farmland to attend my dad's alma mater in the lurid jutting Berkshires of western Massachusetts, I all of a sudden developed a jones for mathematics. I'm starting to see why this was so. College math evokes and catharts a Midwesterner's sickness for home. I'd grown up inside vectors, lines and lines athwart lines, grids—and, on the scale of horizons, broad curving lines of geographic force, the weird topographical drain-swirl of a whole lot of ice-ironed land that sits and spins atop plates. The area behind and below these broad curves at the seam of land and sky I could plot by eye way before I came to know infinitesimals as easements, an integral as schema. Math at a hilly Eastern school was like waking up; it dismantled memory and put it in light. Calculus was, quite literally, child's play.

In late childhood I learned how to play tennis on the blacktop courts of a small public park carved from farmland that had been nitrogenized too often to farm anymore. This was in my home of Philo, Illinois, a tiny collection of corn silos and war-era Levittown homes whose native residents did little but sell crop insurance and nitrogen fertilizer and herbicide and collect property taxes from the young academics at nearby Champaign-Urbana's university, whose ranks swelled enough in the flush 1960s to make outlying non sequiturs like "farm and bedroom community" lucid.

Between the ages of twelve and fifteen I was a near-great junior tennis player. I made my competitive bones beating up on lawyers' and dentists' kids at little Champaign and Urbana Country Club events and was soon killing whole summers being driven through dawns to tournaments all over Illinois, Indiana, Iowa. At fourteen I was ranked seventeenth in the United States Tennis Association's Western Section ("Western" being the creakily ancient USTA's designation for the Midwest; farther west were the Southwest, Northwest, and Pacific Northwest sections). My flirtation with tennis excellence had way more to do with the township where I learned and trained and with a weird proclivity for intuitive math than it did with athletic talent. I was, even by the standards of junior competition in which everyone's a bud of pure potential, a pretty untalented tennis player. My hand-eye was OK, but I was neither large nor quick, had a near-concave chest and wrists so thin I could bracelet them with a thumb and pinkie, and could hit a tennis ball no harder or truer than most girls in my age bracket. What I could do was "Play the Whole Court." This was a piece of tennis truistics that could mean any number of things. In my case, it meant I knew my limitations and the limitations of what I stood inside, and adjusted thusly. I was at my very best in bad conditions.

Now, conditions in Central Illinois are from a mathematical perspective interesting and from a tennis perspective bad. The summer heat and wet-mitten humidity, the grotesquely fertile soil that sends grasses and broadleaves up through the courts' surface by main force, the midges that feed on sweat and the mosquitoes that spawn in the fields' furrows and in the conferva-choked ditches that box each field, night tennis next to impossible because the moths and crap-gnats drawn by the sodium lights form a little planet around each tall lamp and the whole lit court surface is aflutter with spastic little shadows.

But mostly wind. The biggest single factor in Central Illinois' quality of outdoor life is wind. There are more local jokes than I can summon about bent weather vanes and leaning barns, more downstate sobriquets for kinds of wind than there are in Malamut for snow. The wind had a personality, a (poor) temper, and, apparently, agendas. The wind blew autumn leaves into intercalated lines and arcs of force so regular you could photograph them for a textbook on Cramer's Rule and the cross-products of curves in 3-space. It molded winter snow into blinding truncheons that buried stalled cars and required citizens to shovel out not only driveways but the sides of homes; a Central Illinois "blizzard" starts only when the snowfall stops and the wind begins. Most people in Philo didn't comb there hair because why bother. Ladies wore those plastic flags tied down over their parlor-jobs so regularly I thought they were required for a real classy coiffure; girls on the East Coast outside with their hair hanging and tossing around looked wanton and nude to me. Wind wind etc. etc.

The people I know from outside it distill the Midwest into blank flatness, black land and fields of green fronds or five-o'clock stubble, gentle swells and declivities that make the topology a sadistic exercise in plotting quadrics, highway vistas so same and dead they drive motorists mad. Those from IN/WI/Northern IL think of their own Midwest as agronomics and commodity futures and corn-detasseling and bean-walking and seed-company caps, apple-cheeked Nordic types, cider and slaughter and football games with white fogbanks of breath exiting helmets. But in the odd central pocket that is Champaign-Urbana, Rantoul, Philo, Mahomet-Seymour, Mattoon, Farmer City, and Tolono, Midwestern life is informed and deformed by wind. Weatherwise, our township is on the eastern upcurrent of what I once heard an atmospherist in brown tweed call a Thermal Anomaly. Something about southward rotations of crisp air off the Great Lakes and muggy southern stuff from Arkansas and Kentucky miscegenating, plus an odd dose of weird zephyrs from the Mississippi valley three hours west. Chicago calls itself the Windy City, but Chicago, one big windbreak, does not know from a true religious-type wind. And meteorologists have nothing to tell people in Philo, who know perfectly well that the real story is that to the west, between us and the Rockies, there is basically nothing tall, and that weird zephyrs and stirs joined breezes and gusts and thermals and downdrafts and whatever out over Nebraska and Kansas and moved east like streams into rivers and jets and military fronts that gathered like avalanches and roared in reverse down pioneer oxtrails, toward our own personal unsheltered asses. The worst was spring, boys' high school tennis season, when the nets would stand out stiff as proud flags and an errant ball would blow clear to the easternmost fence, interrupting play on the next several courts. During a bad blow some of us would get rope out and tell Rob Lord, who was our fifth man in singles and spectrally thin, that we were going to have to tie him down to keep him from becoming a projectile. Autumn, usually about half as bad as spring, was a low constant roar and the massive clicking sound of continents of dry leaves being arranged into force-curves—I'd heard no sound remotely like this megaclicking until I heard, at nineteen, on New Brunswick's Fundy Bay, my first hightide wave break and get sucked back out over a shore of polished pebbles. Summers were manic and gusty, then often around August deadly calm. The wind would just die some August days, and it was no relief at all; the cessation drove us nuts. Each August, we realized afresh how much the sound of wind had become part of the soundtrack to life in Philo. The sound of wind had become, for me, silence. When it went away, I was left with the squeak of the blood in my head and the aural glitter of all those little eardrum hairs quivering like a drunk in withdrawal. It was months after I moved to western MA before I could really sleep in the pussified whisper of New England's wind-sound.

To your average outsider, Central Illinois looks ideal for sports. The ground, seen from the air, strongly suggests a board game: anally precise squares of dun or khaki cropland all cut and divided by plumb-straight tar roads (in all farmland, roads still seem more like impediments than avenues). In winter, the terrain always looks like Mannington bathroom tile, white quadrangles where bare (snow), black where trees and scrub have shaken free in the wind. From planes, it always looks to me like Monopoly or Life, or a lab maze for rats; then, from ground level, the arrayed fields of feed corn or soybeans, fields furrowed into lines as straight as only an Allis Chalmers and sextant can cut them, look laned like sprint tracks or Olympic pools, hash-marked for serious ball, replete with the angles and alleys of serious tennis. My part of the Midwest always looks laid down special, as if planned.

The terrain's strengths are also its weaknesses. Because the land seems so even, designers of clubs and parks rarely bother to roll it flat

. . . . . . . . .

before laying the asphalt for tennis courts. The result is usually a slight list that only a player who spends a lot of time on the courts will notice. Because tennis courts are for sun- and eye-reasons always laid lengthwise north-south, and because the land in Central Illinois rises very gently as one moves east toward Indiana and the subtle geologic summit that sends rivers doubled back against their own feeders somewhere in the east of that state, the court's forehand half, for a rightie facing north, always seems physically uphill from the backhand—at a tournament in Richmond IN, just over the Ohio line, I noticed the tilt was reversed. The same soil that's so full of humus farmers have to be bought off to keep markets unflooded keeps clay courts chocked with jimson and thistle and volunteer corn, and it splits asphalt courts open with the upward pressure of broadleaf weeds whose pioneer-stock seeds are unthwarted by a half-inch cover of sealant and stone. So that all but the very best maintained courts in the most affluent Illinois districts are their own little rural landscapes, with tufts and cracks and underground-seepage puddles being part of the lay that one plays. A court's cracks always seem to start off to the side of the service box and meander in and back toward the service line. Foliated in pockets, the black cracks, especially against the forest green that contrasts with the barn red of the space outside the lines to signify fair territory, give the courts the eerie look of well-rivered sections of Illinois, seen from back aloft.

A tennis court, 78′ × 27′, looks, from above, with its slender rectangles of doubles alleys flanking its whole length, like a cardboard carton with flaps folded back. The net, 3.5 feet high at the posts, divides the court widthwise in half; the service lines divide each half again into backcourt and fore-. In the two forecourts, lines that run from the base of the net's center to the service lines divide them into 21′ × 13.5′ service boxes. The sharply precise divisions and boundaries, together with the fact that—wind and your more exotic-type spins aside—balls can be made to travel in straight lines only, make textbook tennis plane geometry. It is billiards with balls that won't hold still. It is chess on the run. It is to artillery and airstrikes what football is to infantry and attrition.

Tennis-wise, I had two preternatural gifts to compensate for not much physical talent. Make that three. The first was that I always sweated so much that I stayed fairly ventilated in all weathers. Over-sweating seems an ambivalent blessing, and it didn't exactly do wonders for my social life in high school, but it meant I could play for hours on a Turkish-bath July day and not flag a bit so long as I drank water and ate salty stuff between matches. I always looked like a drowned man by about game four, but I didn't cramp, vomit, or pass out, unlike the gleaming Peoria kids whose hair never even lost its part right up until their eyes rolled up in their heads and they pitched forward onto the shimmering concrete. A bigger asset still was that I was extremely comfortable inside straight lines. None of the odd geometric claustrophobia that turns some gifted juniors into skittish zoo animals after a while. I found I felt best physically enwebbed in sharp angles, acute bisections, shaved corners. This was environmental. Philo, Illinois, is a cockeyed grid: nine north-south streets against six northeast-southwest, fifty-one gorgeous slanted-cruciform corners (the east and west intersection-angles' tangents could be evaluated integrally in terms of their secants!) around a three-intersection central town common with a tank whose nozzle pointed northwest at Urbana, plus a frozen native son, felled on the Salerno beachhead, whose bronze hand pointed true north. In the late morning, the Salerno guy's statue had a squat black shadow-arm against grass dense enough to putt on; in the evening the sun galvanized his left profile and cast his arm's accusing shadow out to the right, bent at the angle of a stick in a pond. At college it suddenly occurred to me during a quiz that the differential between the direction the statue's hand pointed and the arc of its shadow's rotation was first-order. Anyway, most of my memories of childhood—whether of furrowed acreage, or of a harvester's sentry duty along RR104W, or of the play of sharp shadows against the Legion Hall softball field's dusk—I could now reconstruct on demand with an edge and protractor.

I liked the sharp intercourse of straight lines more than the other kids I grew up with. I think this is because they were natives, whereas I was an infantile transplant from Ithaca, where my dad had Ph.D.'d. So I'd known, even horizontally and semiconsciously as a baby, something different, the tall hills and serpentine one-ways of upstate NY. I'm

. . . . . . . . . .

pretty sure I kept the amorphous mush of curves and swells as a con-
trasting backlight somewhere down in the lizardy part of my brain, because the Philo children I fought and played with, kids who knew and
had known nothing else, saw nothing stark or new-worldish in the
township's planar layout, prized nothing crisp. (Except why do I think
it significant that so many of them wound up in the military, performing smart right-faces in razor-creased dress blues?)

Unless you're one of those rare mutant virtuosos of raw force, you'll
find that competitive tennis, like money pool, requires geometric thinking, the ability to calculate not merely your own angles but the angles of
response to your angles. Because the expansion of response-possibilities
is quadratic, you are required to think $n$ shots ahead, where $n$ is a hy-
perbolic function limited by the sinh of opponent's talent and the cosh
of the number of shots in the rally so far (roughly). I was good at this.
What made me for a while near-great was that I could also admit the differential complication of wind into my calculations; I could think and
play octacally. For the wind put curves in the lines and transformed the
game into 3-space. Wind did massive damage to many Central Illinois
junior players, particularly in the period from April to July when it
needed lithium badly, tending to gust without pattern, swirl and back-
track and die and rise, sometimes blowing in one direction at court level
and in another altogether ten feet overhead. The precision in thinking
required one to induct trends in percentage, thrust, and retaliatory
angle—precision our guy and the other townships' volunteer coaches
were good at abstracting about with chalk and board, attaching a
pupil's leg to the fence with clothesline to restrict his arc of movement in
practice, placing laundry baskets in different corners and making us
sink ball after ball, taking masking tape and laying down Chinese boxes
within the court's own boxes for drills and wind sprints—all this theo-
retical prep went out the window when sneakers hit actual court in a
tournament. The best-planned, best-hit ball often just blew out of
bounds, was the basic unlyrical problem. It drove some kids near-mad
with the caprice and unfairness of it all, and on real windy days these
kids, usually with talent out the bazoo, would have their first apoplec-
tic racket-throwing tantrum in about the match's third game and lapse

.    .    .    .    .    .    .    .    .

into a kind of sullen coma by the end of the first set, now bitterly *expecting* to get screwed over by wind, net, tape, sun. I, who was affectionately known as Slug because I was such a lazy turd in practice, located my biggest tennis asset in a weird robotic detachment from whatever unfairnesses of wind and weather I couldn't plan for. I couldn't begin to tell you how many tournament matches I won between the ages of twelve and fifteen against bigger, faster, more coordinated, and better-coached opponents simply by hitting balls unimaginatively back down the middle of the court in schizophrenic gales, letting the other kid play with more verve and panache, waiting for enough of his ambitious balls aimed near the lines to curve or slide via wind outside the green court and white stripe into the raw red territory that won me yet another ugly point. It wasn't pretty or fun to watch, and even with the Illinois wind I never could have won whole matches this way had the opponent not eventually had his small nervous breakdown, buckling under the obvious injustice of losing to a shallow-chested "pusher" because of the shitty rural courts and rotten wind that rewarded cautious automatism instead of verve and panache. I was an unpopular player, with good reason. But to say that I did not use verve or imagination was untrue. Acceptance is its own verve, and it takes imagination for a player to like wind, and I liked wind; or rather I at least felt the wind had some basic right to be there, and found it sort of interesting, and was willing to expand my logistical territory to countenace the devastating effect a 15- to 30-mph stutter-breeze swirling southwest to east would have on my best calculations as to how ambitiously to respond to Joe Perfecthair's topspin drive into my backhand corner.

The Illinois combination of pocked courts, sickening damp, and wind required and rewarded an almost Zen-like acceptance of things as they actually were, on-court. I won a lot. At twelve, I began getting entry to tournaments beyond Philo and Campaign and Danville. I was driven by my parents or by the folks of Gil Antitoi, son of a Canadian-history. professor from Urbana, to events like the Central Illinois Open in Decatur, a town built and owned by the A. E. Staley processing concern and so awash in the stink of roasting corn that kids would play with

· · · · · · · · · · ·

bandannas tied over their mouths and noses; like the Western Closed
Qualifier on the ISU campus in Normal; like the McDonald's Junior
Open in the serious corn town of Galesburg, way out west by the River;
like the Prairie State Open in Pekin, insurance hub and home of Caterpillar Tractor; like the Midwest Junior Clay Courts at a chichi private
club in Peoria's pale version of Scarsdale.

   Over the next four summers I got to see way more of the state than
is normal or healthy, albeit most of this seeing was a blur of travel and
crops, looking between nod-outs at sunrises abrupt and terribly can-
dent over the crease between fields and sky (plus you could see any
town you were aimed at the very moment it came around the earth's
curve, and the only part of Proust that really moved me in college was
the early description of the kid's geometric relation to the distant
church spire at Combray), riding in station wagons' backseats through
Saturday dawns and Sunday sunsets. I got steadily better; Antitoi, unfairly assisted by an early puberty, got radically better.

   By the time we were fourteen, Gil Antitoi and I were the Central Illinois cream of our age bracket, usually seeded one and two at area tournaments, able to beat all but a couple of even the kids from the Chicago
suburbs who, together with a contingent from Grosse Pointe MI, usually dominated the Western regional rankings. That summer the best
fourteen-year-old in the nation was a Chicago kid, Bruce Brescia
(whose penchant for floppy white tennis hats, low socks with bunny-
tails at the heel, and lurid pastel sweater vests testified to proclivities
that wouldn't dawn on me for several more years), but Brescia and his
henchman, Mark Mees of Zanesville, OH, never bothered to play anything but the Midwestern Clays and some indoor events in Cook
County, being too busy jetting off to like the Pacific Hardcourts in Ven-
tura and Junior Wimbledon and all that. I played Brescia just once, in
the quarters of an indoor thing at the Rosemont Horizon in 1977, and
the results were not pretty. Antitoi actually got a set off Mees in the national Qualifiers one year. Neither Brescia nor Mees ever turned pro; I
don't know what happened to either of them after eighteen.

   Antitoi and I ranged over the exact same competitive territory; he
was my friend and foe and bane. Though I'd started playing two years
before he, he was bigger, quicker, and basically better than I by about

age thirteen, and I was soon losing to him in the finals of just about every tournament I played. So different were our appearances and approaches and general gestalts that we had something of an epic rivalry from '74 through '77. I had gotten so prescient at using stats, surface, sun, gusts, and a kind of Stoic cheer that I was regarded as a kind of physical savant, a medicine boy of wind and heat, and could play just forever, sending back moonballs baroque with spin. Antitoi, uncomplicated from the get-go, hit the everliving shit out of every round object that came within his ambit, aiming always for one of two backcourt corners. He was a Slugger; I was a Slug. When he was "on," i.e. having a good day, he varnished the court with me. When he wasn't at his best (and the countless hours I and David Saboe from Bloomington and Kirk Riehagen and Steve Cassil of Danville spent in meditation and seminar on just what variables of diet, sleep, romance, car ride, and even sock-color factored into the equation of Antitoi's mood and level day to day), he and I had great matches, real marathon wind-suckers. Of eleven finals we played in 1974, I won two.

Midwest junior tennis was also my initiation into true adult sadness. I had developed a sort of hubris about my Taoistic ability to control via noncontrol. I'd established a private religion of wind. I even liked to bike. Awfully few people in Philo bike, for obvious wind reasons, but I'd found a way to sort of tack back and forth against a stiff current, holding some wide book out at my side at about 120° to my angle of thrust — Bayne and Pugh's *The Art of the Engineer* and Cheiro's *Language of the Hand* proved to be the best airfoils — so that through imagination and verve and stoic cheer I could not just neutralize but use an in-your-face gale for biking. Similarly, by thirteen I'd found a way not just to accommodate but to *employ* the heavy summer winds in matches. No longer just mooning the ball down the center to allow plenty of margin for error and swerve, I was now able to use the currents kind of the way a pitcher uses spit. I could hit curves way out into cross-breezes that'd drop the ball just fair; I had a special wind-serve that had so much spin the ball turned oval in the air and curved left to right like a smart slider and then reversed its arc on the bounce. I'd developed the same sort of autonomic feel for what the wind would do to the ball that a standard-trans driver has for how to shift. As a junior

·    ·    ·    ·    ·    ·    ·    ·    ·    ·

tennis player, I was for a time a citizen of the concrete physical world in a way the other boys weren't, I felt. And I felt betrayed at around four-teen when so many of these single-minded flailing boys became abruptly mannish and tall, with sudden sprays of hair on their thighs and wisps on their lips and ropy arteries on their forearms. My fif-teenth summer, kids I'd been beating easily the year before all of a sud-den seemed overpowering. I lost in two semifinals, at Pekin and Springfield in '77, of events I'd beaten Antitoi in the finals of in '76. My dad just about brought me to my knees after the Springfield loss to some kid from the Quad Cities when he said, trying to console me, that it had looked like a boy playing a man out there. And the other boys sensed something up with me, too, smelled some breakdown in the odd détente I'd had with the elements: my ability to accommodate and fash-ion the exterior was being undercut by the malfunction of some inter-nal alarm clock I didn't understand.

I mention this mostly because so much of my Midwest's communal psychic energy was informed by growth and fertility. The agronomic angle was obvious, what with my whole township dependent for tax base on seed, dispersion, height, and yield. Something about the adults' obsessive weighing and measuring and projecting, this special calculus of thrust and growth, leaked inside us children's capped and bandan-na'd little heads out on the fields, diamonds, and courts of our special interests. By 1977 I was the only one of my group of jock friends with virginity intact. (I know this for a fact, and only because these guys are now schoolteachers and commoditists and insurers with families and standings to protect will I not share with you just how I know it.) I felt, as I became a later and later bloomer, alienated not just from my own recalcitrant glabrous little body, but in a way from the whole elemental exterior I'd come to see as my coconspirator. I knew, somehow, that the call to height and hair came from outside, from whatever apart from Monsanto and Dow made the corn grow, the hogs rut, the wind soften every spring and hang with the scent of manure from the plain of bean-fields north between us and Champaign. My vocation ebbed. I felt un-called. I began to experience the same resentment toward whatever children abstract as nature that I knew Steve Cassil felt when a soundly considered approach shot down the forehand line was blown out by a gust, that I knew Gil Antitoi suffered when his pretty kick-serve (he was the only top-flight kid from the slow weedy township courts to play serve-and-volley from the start, which is why he had such success on the slick cement of the West Coast when he went on to play for Cal-Fullerton) was compromised by the sun: he was so tall, and so stubborn about adjusting his high textbook service toss for solar conditions, that serving from the court's north end in early afternoon matches always filled his eyes with violet blobs, and he'd lumber around for the rest of the point, flailing and pissed. This was back when sunglasses were unheard of, on-court.

But so the point is I began to feel what they'd felt. I began, very quietly, to resent my physical place in the great schema, and this resentment and bitterness, a kind of slow root-rot, is a big reason why I never qualified for the sectional championships again after 1977, and why I ended up in 1980 barely making the team at a college smaller than Urbana High while kids I had beaten and then envied played scholarship tennis for Purdue, Fullerton, Michigan, Pepperdine, and even—in the case of Pete Bouton, who grew half a foot and forty IQ points in 1977—for the hallowed U of I at Urbana-Champaign.

Alienation-from-Midwest-as-fertility-grid might be a little on the overmetaphysical side, not to mention self-pitying. This was the time, after all, when I discovered definite integrals and antiderivatives and found my identity shifting from jock to math-wienie anyway. But it's also true that my whole Midwest tennis career matured and then degenerated under the aegis of the Peter Principle. In and around my township—where the courts were rural and budgets low and conditions so extreme that the mosquitoes sounded like trumpets and the bees like tubas and the wind like a five-alarm fire, that we had to change shirts between games and use our water jugs to wash blown field-chaff off our arms and necks and carry salt tablets in Pez containers—I was truly near-great: I could Play the Whole Court; I was In My Element. But all the more important tournaments, the events into which my rural excellence was an easement, were played in a different real world: the courts' surface was redone every spring at the Arlington Tennis Center, where the National Junior Qualifier for our region was held; the green of these courts' fair territory was so vivid as to distract, its surface so new and rough it wrecked your feet right through your shoes, and so bare of flaw, tilt, crack, or seam that it was totally disorienting. Playing on a perfect court was for me like treading water out of sight of land: I never knew where I was out there. The 1976 Chicago Junior Invitational was held at Lincolnshire's Bath and Tennis Club, whose huge warren of thirty-six courts was enclosed by all these troubling green plastic tarps attached to all the fences, with little archer-slits in them at eye level to afford some parody of spectation. These tarps were Wind-B-Gone windscreens, patented by the folks over at Cyclone Fence in 1971. They did cut down on the worst of the unfair gusts, but they also seemed to rob the court space of new air: competing at Lincolnshire was like playing in the bottom of a well. And blue bug-zapper lights festooned the lightposts when really major Midwest tournaments played into the night: no clouds of midges around the head or jagged shadows of moths to distinguish from balls' flights, but a real unpleasant zotting and frying sound of bugs being decommissioned just overhead; I won't pause to mention the smell. The point is I just wasn't the same, somehow, without deformities to play around. I'm thinking now that the wind and bugs and chuckholes formed for me a kind of inner boundary, my own personal set of lines. Once I hit a certain level of tournament facilities, I was disabled because I was unable to accommodate the absence of disabilities to accommodate. If that makes sense. Puberty-angst and material alienation notwithstanding, my Midwest tennis career plateaued the moment I saw my first windscreen.

Still strangely eager to speak of weather, let me say that my township, in fact all of East-Central Illinois, is a proud part of what meterologists call Tornado Alley. Incidence of tornadoes all out of statistical proportion. I personally have seen two on the ground and five aloft, trying to assemble. Aloft tornadoes are gray-white, more like convulsions in the thunderclouds themselves than separate or protruding from them. Ground tornadoes are black only because of the tons of soil they suck in and spin around. The grotesque frequency of tornadoes around my township is, I'm told, a function of the same variables that cause our civilian winds: we are a coordinate where fronts and air masses converge. Most days from late March to June there are Tornado Watches somewhere in our TV stations' viewing area (the stations put a little graphic at the screen's upper right, like a pair of binoculars for a Watch and the Tarot deck's Tower card for a Warning, or something). Watches mean conditions are right and so on and so forth, which, big deal. It's only the rarer Tornado Warnings, which require a confirmed sighting by somebody with reliable sobriety, that make the Civil Defense sirens go. The siren on top of the Philo Middle School was a different pitch and cycle from the one off in the south part of Urbana, and the two used to weave in and out of each other in a godawful threnody. When the sirens blew, the native families went to their canning cellars or fallout shelters (no kidding); the academic families in their bright prefab houses with new lawns and foundations of flat slab went with whatever good-luck tokens they could lay hands on to the very most central point on the ground floor after opening every single window to thwart implosion from precipitous pressure drops. For my family, the very most central point was a hallway between my dad's study and a linen closet, with a reproduction of a Flemish annunciation scene on one wall and a bronze Aztec sunburst hanging with guillotinic mass on the other; I always tried to maneuver my sister under the sunburst.

If there was an actual Warning when you were outside and away from home—say at a tennis tournament in some godforsaken public park at some city fringe zoned for sprawl—you were supposed to lie prone in the deepest depression you could locate. Since the only real depressions around most tournament sites were the irrigation and runoff ditches that bordered cultivated fields, ditches icky with conferva and mosquito spray and always heaving with what looked like conventions of copperheads and just basically places your thinking man doesn't lie prone in under any circumstance, in practice at Warned tournament you zipped your rackets into their covers and ran to find your loved ones or even your liked ones and just all milled around trying to look like you weren't about to lose sphincter-control. Mothers tended sometimes to wail and clutch childish heads to their bosoms (Mrs. Swearingen of Pekin was particularly popular for clutching even strange kids' heads to her formidable bosom).

I mention tornadoes for reasons directly related to the purpose of
this essay. For one thing, they were a real part of Midwest childhood,
because as a little kid I was obsessed with dread over them. My earliest
nightmares, the ones that didn't feature mile-high robots from *Lost in
Space* wielding huge croquet mallets (don't ask), were about shrieking
sirens and dead white skies, a slender monster on the Iowa horizon, jutting less phallic than saurian from the lowering sky, whipping back and
forth with such frenzy that it almost doubled on itself, trying to eat its
own tail. Throwing off chaff and dust and chairs; it never came any
closer than the horizon; it didn't have to.

In practice, Watches and Warnings both seemed to have a kind of
boy-and-wolf quality for the natives of Philo. They just happened too
often. Watches seemed especially irrelevant, because we could always
see storms coming from the west way in advance, and by the time they
were over, say, Decatur you could diagnose the basic condition by the
color and height of the clouds: the taller the anvil-shaped thunder-
heads, the better the chance for hail and Warnings; pitch-black clouds
were a happier sight than gray shot with an odd nacreous white; the
shorter the interval between the sight of lightning and the sound of
thunder, the faster the system was moving, and the faster the system,
the worse: like most things that mean you harm, severe thunderstorms
are brisk and no-nonsense.

I know why I stayed obsessed as I aged. Tornadoes, for me, were a
transfiguration. Like all serious winds, they were our little stretch of
plain's $z$ coordinate, a move up from the Euclidian monotone of fur-
row, road, axis, and grid. We studied tornadoes in junior high: a Canadian high straight-lines it southeast from the Dakotas; a moist warm
mass drawls on up north from like Arkansas: the result was not a
Greek $\chi$ or even a Cartesian $\Gamma$ but a circling of the square, a curling of
vectors, concavation of curves. It was alchemical, Leibnizian. Tornadoes were, in our part of Central Illinois, the dimensionless point at
which parallel lines met and whirled and blew up. They made no
sense. Houses blew not out but in. Brothels were spared while or-
phanages next door bought it. Dead cattle were found three miles
from their silage without a scratch on them. Tornadoes are omnipo-
tent and obey no law. Force without law has no shape, only tendency

and duration. I believe now that I knew all this without knowing it, as
a kid.

The only time I ever got caught in what might have been an actual
one was in June '78 on a tennis court at Hessel Park in Champaign,
where I was drilling one afternoon with Gil Antitoi. Though a con-
temptible and despised tournament opponent, I was a coveted practice
partner because I could transfer balls to wherever you wanted them
with the mindless constancy of a machine. This particular day it was
supposed to rain around suppertime, and a couple times we thought
we'd heard the tattered edges of a couple sirens out west toward Mon-
ticello, but Antitoi and I drilled religiously every afternoon that week
on the slow clayish Har-Tru of Hessel, trying to prepare for a beastly
clay invitational in Chicago where it was rumored both Brescia and
Mees would appear. We were doing butterfly drills—my crosscourt
forehand is transferred back down the line to Antitoi's backhand, he
crosscourts it to my backhand, I send it down the line to his forehand,
four 45° angles, though the intersection of just his crosscourts make an
X, which is four 90°s and also a crucifix rotated the same quarter-turn
that a swastika (which involves eight 90° angles) is rotated on Hitler-
ian bunting. This was the sort of stuff that went through my head when
I drilled. Hessel Park was scented heavily with cheese from the massive
Kraft factory at Champaign's western limit, and it had wonderful expensive soft Har-Tru courts of such a deep piney color that the flights
of the fluorescent balls stayed on one's visual screen for a few extra seconds, leaving trails, is also why the angles and hieroglyphs involved in
butterfly drill seem important. But the crux here is that butterflies are
primarily a conditioning drill: both players have to get from one side of
the court to the other between each stroke, and once the initial pain
and wind-sucking are over—assuming you're a kid who's in absurd
shape because he spends countless mindless hours jumping rope or running laps backward or doing star-drills between the court's corners or
straight sprints back and forth along the perfect furrows of early bean-
fields each morning—once the first pain and fatigue of butterflies are
got through, if both guys are good enough so that there are few un-
forced errors to break up the rally, a kind of fugue-state opens up inside
you where your concentration telescopes toward a still point and you

lose awareness of your limbs and the soft shush of your shoe's slide
(you have to slide out of a run on Har-Tru) and whatever's ouside the
lines of the court, and pretty much all you know then is the bright ball
and the octangled butterfly outline of its trail across the billiard green
of the court. We had one just endless rally and I'd left the planet in a
silent swoop inside when the court and ball and butterfly trail all
seemed to surge brightly and glow as the daylight just plain went out in
the sky overhead. Neither of us had noticed that there'd been no wind
blowing the familiar grit into our eyes for several minutes—a bad sign.
There was no siren. Later they said the C.D. alert network had been out
of order. This was June 6, 1978. The air temperature dropped so fast
you could feel your hairs rise. There was no thunder and no air stirred.
I could not tell you why we kept hitting. Neither of us said anything.
There was no siren. It was high noon; there was nobody else on the
courts. The riding mower out over east at the softball field was still
going back and forth. There were no depressions except a saprogenic
ditch along the field of new corn just west. What could we have done?
The air always smells of mowed grass before a bad storm. I think we
thought it would rain at worst and that we'd play till it rained and then
go sit in Antitoi's parents' station wagon. I do remember a mental ob-
scenity—I had gut strings in my rackets, strings everybody with a high
sectional ranking got free for letting the Wilson sales rep spraypaint a
W across the racket face, so they were free, but I liked this particular
string job on this racket, I liked them tight but not real tight, 62–63
p.s.i. on a Proflite stringer, and gut becomes pasta if it gets wet, but we
were both in the fugue-state that exhaustion through repetition brings
on, a fugue-state I've decided that my whole time playing tennis was
spent chasing, a fugue-state I associated too with plowing and seeding
and detasseling and spreading herbicides back and forth in sentry duty
along perfect lines, up and back, or military marching on flat blacktop,
hypnotic, a mental state at once flat and lush, numbing and yet exquisitely felt. We were young, we didn't know when to stop. Maybe I was
mad at my body and wanted to hurt it, wear it down. Then the whole
knee-high field to the west along Kirby Avenue all of a sudden flattened
out in a wave coming toward us as if the field was getting steamrolled.
Antitoi went wide west for a forehand cross and I saw the corn get laid

down in waves and the sycamores in a copse lining the ditch point our way. There was no funnel. Either it had just materialized and come down or it wasn't a real one. The big heavy swings on the industrial swingsets took off, wrapping themselves in their chains around and around the top crossbar; the park's grass laid down the same way the field had; the whole thing happened so fast I'd seen nothing like it; re-call that Bimini H-Bomb film of the shock wave visible in the sea as it comes toward the ship's film crew. This all happened very fast but in se-rial progression: field, trees, swings, grass, then the feel like the lift of the world's biggest mitt, the nets suddenly and sexually up and out straight, and I seem to remember whacking a ball out of my hand at Antitoi to watch its radical west-east curve, and for some reason trying to run after this ball I'd just hit, but I couldn't have tried to run after a ball I had hit, but I remember the heavy gentle lift at my thighs and the ball curving back closer and my passing the ball and beating the ball in flight over the horizontal net, my feet not once touching the ground over fifty-odd feet, a cartoon, and then there was chaff and crud in the air all over and both Antitoi and I either flew or were blown pinwheel-ing for I swear it must have been fifty feet to the fence one court over, the easternmost fence, we hit the fence so hard we knocked it halfway down, and it stuck at 45°, Antitoi detached a retina and had to wear those funky Jabbar retina-goggles for the rest of the summer, and the fence had two body-shaped indentations like in cartoons where the guy's face makes a cast in the skillet that hit him, two catcher's masks of fence, we both got deep quadrangular lines impressed on our faces, torsos, legs' fronts, from the fence, my sister said we looked like waf-fles, but neither of us got badly hurt, and no homes got whacked—either the thing just ascended again for no reason right after, they do that, obey no rule, follow no line, hop up and down at something that might as well be will, or else it wasn't a real one. Antitoi's tennis con-tinued to improve after that, but mine didn't.

# Being There: The Art of the Black Pool Hustler

. . . . . . . . . .

*by*
CECIL BROWN

When I play pool, I want to win. The challenge is always there even when I'm joking. I love this game, and when I see the green baize and hear the clicking and kissing of the cue ball, I am excited. I love feeling the weight of the stick in my hand and the smoothness of the shaft as I control the cue ball, like she was my toy, a genie ready to do my bidding. I love to watch the cue ball when it spins to the side or caroms into another ball, only to kick a third ball into the pocket. She's my lady luck, or, in street vernacular, my bitch.

One night here in Oakland, I walked into Eli's Mile High Club, a blues club where the blues still thrives; some of the blues players come from as far as New Orleans. There's a pool table right next to the bar, which makes—two major activities of black men frequenting pool halls—drinking and aiming—in easy reach of each other.

I shot a game of pool and won. Then, I shot another game and won; then, I made the mistake of shooting another game and winning again. The pool sharks smelled blood. They thought I was a pool shark, and they wanted to make money. When I won the fourth game, I saw a brother slip from his stool and go out back to the patio. There he would whisper the news to one of the most deadly sharks that the club harbors.

Sure enough, when I won my fifth game, there, standing over the table, waiting to take me on, was Romeo, a known pool hustler. Romeo is always in Eli's, and his main function is waiting until the music starts and then dancing with some of the stray women that show up. Eli's is a black club, but the blues attracts a wide cultural and ethnic range of women. Most of them come to "grind" on the slow tunes. The most typical woman, then, are middle-aged black women who grew up during rhythm and blues times. There are some Saturday nights, however, when the UC Berkeley is on weekend break, that the place is filled with white girls.

If there is a lull in the normal activities in S.F., you will find a crazy party of white, upper-class liberals, who go absolutely bonkers over this blues place. Romeo is not partial to any class of available women. He is an equal opportunity employer. He just wants to spend the night, establish a sexual relationship, and from this the girl "helps him out" with some money, "pocket change." And, he is usually successful. Hence his name, "Romeo." Most pool hustlers pride themselves on hustling women *and* pool.

He watched me drop the eight ball.

"That's nice, man," he said. "You shoot a good stick!"

Yeah, right. All pool hustlers are alike, and they come on the same way. "You shoot a good stick!" was also used in the movie, *The Hustler*.

"Thanks."

I looked at him. Romeo is a nice-looking brother, in his late thirties, but I have yet to understand how any woman would sleep with a brother with Geri Curls.

"You wanna shoot a few games?"

"How much?"

"Five dollars."

"No, let's shoot for fun."

Now, no matter what they say about me, my reputation will stand, because it will never be challenged. I had learned the first rule of pool hustling—when to stop. It is a hard rule to learn. In *The Hustler*, Paul Newman's character, Fast Eddie Felson, beats Minnesota Fats for eleven thousand dollars, and because he doesn't know when to quit, he loses all of it. The rest of the story is about how he struggles to overcome this difficulty. Winning in pool hustler's philosophy is not about skill, but about character.

One of the main obstacles to the game of pool is for the neophyte to

. . . . . . . . .

learn the fine art of recognizing the pool shark. The pool shark is different from other pool lovers. The average guy shoots pool for recreation. The shark shoots pool for a living. Making a living at a sport would seem to be commendable were it not for the fact that pool is different from other sports.

We may look at African American sports in two categories. In one category, the player demonstrates his physical skills, as in boxing, where the appearance of the powerful body is used to discourage opponents. The big, muscular body is still part of the physiological view that the slave South had of the black man. Since strong-bodied black men were connected to the slave economy, the explicit message sent to black men is that you are welcome to participate in the symbolic exchange of work, as long as it's sport, as long as you are using your body. The boxer explicitly shows his body as a display of the capitalist work ethic.

On the other hand, there is a second category of sports in which the player disguises his skills, or as the pool hustlers call it, his "speed."

Unlike the boxer, whose work ethic is explicit, the pool hustlers subvert the capitalist system by not doing any hard work at all. In the explicit sports, the player's intentions are up front. The boxer wants to knock the opponent out and win the cash. But the intentions of the pool shark are always indirect and implicit. He pretends, in fact, to be playing a game just for "fun," but he is really hustling—i.e., he is turning a game of fun into profit.

"The hustler's cardinal rule," wrote Ned Polsky in *Hustlers, Beats, and Others*, "is: *don't show your real speed.*" For this reason the pool hustler is hated by others who are devoted to the game, primarily because they despise the rule upon which the game is based: Once you master the skill of the game, in order to make money at the game you must have a "sucker." A "sucker" is somebody who is stupid enough to believe that his skills are better than yours—and willing to bet on them. If the hustler can give the *illusion* that he is not as good as he really is, he can generate suckers. This is why pool hustlers have to go to different towns where their skills are not known and have not been exposed by word of mouth. Once the word of mouth has been generated that so and so is a shark, the game is finished for that player. In the argot, this oral communication is called "sending a wire."

A look at the history of pool in America will shed some light on how the game has affected the African American player. Although it was published thirty years ago, Ned Polsky's sociological study of the pool player remains, for the most part, valid in its essential facts. Polsky traces the origin of American pool back to billiards in England, where it had two traditions. The first tradition was that billiards was played by the upper classes in private; the second tradition was that it was played by the lower classes in public. "As this second tradition developed," Polsky wrote, "the 'respectable' upper class who played at home or in meeting places restricted to their own kind . . . were immediately concerned to distinguish themselves from [English billiard playing], and in doing so they conceived it as morally deviant."[2] Charles Cotton, an English gentleman, remarked in 1674 that it was bad enough that the upper class—the *hoi aristoi*—wasted its time and money on billiards, but it was much worse for the lower classes—the *hoi polloi*—in this game that lead to a life of dissolute gaming.[3] Polsky claims that this "morally deviant" attitude toward pool began back in England, and that it came with the game when it was brought to America in the seventeenth century. As he makes clear, "poolrooms *always* had 'middle-class morality' very solidly against them, were *always* highly stigmatized." (His italics.)[4] For Americans, the poolroom was a symbol of corruption of moral values. It was also the place where men could be free of the confining world of femininity. It was, as Polsky rightly believes, "a special kind of subculture that has become increasingly rare and unimportant in America—the heterosexual but all-male subculture, which . . . serve[s] as [a] sacrosanct refuge from women. The poolroom was not just one of these places: it was *the* one, *the* keystone."[5] (His italics.)

Polsky wrote his book after seeing Paul Newman's *The Hustler*. He tried to account for the impact that pool had on the general public as a result of the popularity of the film. In the end, he claimed that the film did a good job of showing the world of the pool hustler, but that the world described in the film no longer existed; it was the world of pool players in the thirties.

The recent history of pool in America, Polsky concluded, is how manufacturers of pool equipment and poolroom owners have tried to "upgrade" the "image" of "moral stigma" attached to the game. "In the pool business" this is known as "cleaning up the game." To achieve this, poolroom owners "install[ed] carpets and bright lights and pastel colors, curb[ed] obscene language, and [got] rid of hustlers and hoodlums and alcoholics, and tr[ied] to bring women in." But the mistake they made was to "subscribe to the commonly accepted view that the game's popularity waned because of the growing association of poolrooms . . . with gamblers, loafers, criminals and the like." The real reason that pool declined is "because of certain long-term changes in America's social structure."[6]

Some of the long-term changes in the social structure can be seen in how pool has affected African Americans. If Polsky is right that, in America, pool playing began with the upper classes and "trickled down" to the lower classes, then "moral deviancy" was a legacy for black male players of the game too. The game of pool became, after the Emancipation Proclamation, a way of expressing a need of the African American male to become a "hustler" in almost all aspects of social life in America.

The game taught black males how to pass down their experience and knowledge of how to survive in a white, racist country. It taught the men grace under pressure, perseverance, timing, and rhythm. Out of the oral tradition there came great stories of legendary pool hustlers.

One of my friends who plays pool a lot and considers himself a 'hustler' is Dominick Shannon, age forty-five. He learned to play pool as a teenager in Berkeley pool halls, the most well known of which is called Kips. He was taught the skill by older players. "For me to learn the game was a skill I could always use," he told me recently while we attended the nine-balls tournament at First Place, a pool hall with twenty-seven tables. "Back in the sixties," he said, chalking his cue, "the older men taught me a trade to earn a living off of. That's how I see it. If I couldn't play music, I knew I could play pool."

The three other black men who are shooting with us agree.

"That's how I learned. From the older men," Morris Foster said. Morris is in his late forties and has his own sheet-metal company. "It was like learning a trade."

We are watching a friend of ours, Moe Wright, shoot a game of nine balls in the Monday night tournament. He is playing a white boy, a nerd type, who silently wins the game.

When Moe comes back over after being defeated, he says, "I shouldn't be missing easy shots like that. I work everyday and can only play two or three hours a day. I used to play eight hours a day."

When I ask them why there are so few black men in the tournaments, they laugh. "It's expensive to play in those tournaments," Morris said. "Last year I took my two sons to Vegas where I played in a tournament. It cost me a three-hundred-dollar fee to get in. We stayed in a hotel for about another three hundred dollars. My boys are teenagers, and they eat a lot. In the end, it cost me over two thousand dollars for four days. And I didn't win the tournament."

When I mention that some top white female players, like Vivian Villarreal, received earnings up to one hundred thousand dollars in 1996, Morris shook his head in disbelief.[7] "I know a player been playing over forty years and ain't made that much!"

But Moe disagreed. "It's possible for white women to make that much. But most of the time you see white women playing on television tournaments, they have backers. Somebody is willing to pay their hotels and expenses. You see them advertising in the magazines. But nobody's going to give a brother money to go shoot pool."

But they both insist that there are many black pool players in the Oakland area. Then Morris offered another insight about black pool players and tournaments.

"These guys are really good," he told us, "but you'll never see them at the tournaments, because they don't want to go through all that trouble. They will wait until the guy has won the tournament money, and then clean him out."

He told a story about Preacher Red, a black hustler, who always had his cap pulled down over his face and carried a bottle of booze in his back pocket. "But that was lemonade in the bottle," and he wasn't drunk. He just acted like he was, so that "somebody who thinks he knows how to shoot" will take him on. "Preacher Red would take all their money."

"Oh, yeah, that reminds me of Buck Tooth," Moe said, and tells another funny story about how this pool player used his ugly teeth to

make players think he was stupid. Pool players have an endless number
of stories about pool players, all of them colorful characters.

"I never like to play pool shooters from the South," Morris said.
"They shoot funny, you know. They talk all the time, and distract you.
But a guy told me once that every part of the South had different ways
of shooting pool, and that he could tell just by the way the shooter
played the game where he was from in the South."

"Hey, Morris, what about dumping?" I asked. All pool hustlers
know about dumping. Dumping occurs when one player allows his opponent to win because the spectators are betting against him. Later, the
players split up the money they have won from the spectators. Polsky
gives a good example of dumping, as follows:

> Hustler A played hustler B for $70. A's side bets with spectators
> totaled $100 and B's side bets with spectators totaled $380. Therefore
> A deliberately lost to B, paying him $70 and paying $100 to specta-
> tors, with B collecting $70 from A and $380 from spectators. Later, in
> private, B gave A $310 (the $70 that A had "lost" to B, the $100 that
> A had paid to the audience, plus $140 or one-half the overall amount
> won from the audience). Each player thus made $140 on the deal.[8]

Morris laughed, "I *heard* about it. But I never did it." We all
laughed, knowing that this is exactly what a real hustler would say; he
would never admit to practicing the dump, which is central to the art of
hustling. Hustlers are after the money, and other hustlers know that
and will excuse other players who dump.

Many African Americans remember stories from their childhoods
about legendary black pool hustlers. Yet when we come to think of it,
there are not many such characters in African American literature.
In Anglo-American literature, there have been two books devoted exclusively to the life of the pool hustler: *The Hustler* (1958) and *The
Color of Money* (1983). Both were made into movies starring Paul
Newman as Fast Eddie Felsen in different stages of his career. In these
films, as if to pay some respect to the well-known fact that blacks were
and are great pool hustlers, there are many visual references to black
pool hustlers.

In *The Hustler*, for example, the opening shot of the pool hall,
which is early in the morning when the hall is as quiet as a cathedral,

shows a black man cleaning up. He walks with a limp, and we see him in many scenes as the story unwinds. He doesn't speak, yet his presence haunts the film. In *The Color of Money*, not only do black pool players haunt the film, but one player (Forest Whitaker) hustles the white hero and wins.

I mentioned *The Hustler* to Dominick Shannon. He's an actor. "Remember that brother in the first scene of the film?" I asked him.

"Yeah," he said, "that's Mel. Mel Steward. He lives right down the street in Berkeley." Dominick had seen the film many times, and was influenced by it when it came out in 1961. When I checked the film credits there was no mention of Mel Steward or the role he played, yet the names of other characters in the film were given, even when they didn't have speaking parts. It was interesting to me that while the film fails to recall the name of the player, his name is on the lips of the black men who still play pool in this area. Is the message here that the folk tradition can be relied on when the technology fails to record the name?

"Eddie Felson comes from Oakland and played in the Red Pit," Shannon said, mentioning the most famous pool hall in Oakland during the sixties.

"I never seen him in there," Morris said, "and I was always there."

In *The Hustler*, the hero, Eddie Felson, violates his own principle: He lets himself be hustled because he doesn't know when to stop; he loses his ability to judge the character of the opponent.

The Paul Newman films pay homage to the presence of African American males in the game of pool, yet there are no films or books featuring the world of the black pool hustler, which is surprising given the impact of the game on the lives of African Americans. No, it is not in the world of print or film that you would find the black pool hustler as hero. You would, however, find the folk hero in the African American folk tradition. He is called the pool-shooting monkey. In oral narratives, or toasts, you find the black male expressing admiration for the pool hustler, who could make a living without subjecting himself to any other animals in the jungle. The narrative captures the group's concept of themselves and how they let the pool-shooting monkey become their shadow, allowing the group psychological health.

Pool is an African American male sport that was adopted from the Anglo tradition. From a form that African Americans developed from whites, pool became a sport that allowed black men to express their own world views.

In the black communities before residential segregation, pool hustling in the black community thrived because blacks were not confined into any one section of any given metropolitan area. After the passage of state and city ordinances legally forcing blacks out of neighborhoods that were more than 80 percent white, blacks were forced to live in only certain areas of any given city. Thus, South Side Chicago, the west side of St. Louis, the Harlem area in New York became "ghettos." During the creation of the ghetto and until the Civil Rights movement, pool hustling became an expressive sport for the ethos of the African American male.

Pool reached its peak in the 1930s for whites, but for blacks it went a lot longer, for it still had work to do with the lower-class self-expression. When whites found jobs, there was no longer time to idle away with pool. Because blacks did not get the jobs that whites did, they had more time to shoot pool and develop the aesthetics of hustling, of turning nothing into something. A bluff becomes transformed into solid cash when one is good with his mouth and his pool stick.

Robert Byre, an expert on the game and author of several pool books, claims that the rise in the number of bachelors in America during the 1930s caused the rise of pool halls. "Weddings were bad news for the owners of pool halls," he wrote. "Pool was overwhelmingly a man's game, and when a man got married he tended to hang up his cue. Wife, family, and mortgage required his full attention and it was typical that he was lost to the game until he was widowed, fired, or retired."[9] When black men were out of work, there were more pool halls.

In the sixties, pool players got a boost from the film, *The Hustler*, but this was shortlived. However, with the coming of the second pool film, *The Color of Money*, there was a lasting influence on pool. Since the 1980s pool has ceased to be a lower-class form of entertainment. Pool became upscale during the eighties and remains so today. Back in the old days you could shoot a good long game for a dollar; now the rate is as high as twenty dollars an hour. Once the pool halls were male only; now in the chic San Francisco cafés, the most visible players of pool are women. In Oakland, pool playing has even become a couples sport. There is an association of couples tournaments that meets twice a week. Dates play games in which the aim is not to win but to socialize. The art of the pool hustler is disappearing.

Like other aspects of American cultural life, pool has been appropriated by the white middle class. Last year the ESPN World Open Billiards Championship was televised on ESPN2; it was a cultural performance without any culture. These televised games feature pool players who are usually white women, rarely men or black women, but most definitely never a black man.

In the end, the poolroom owners and pool manufacturers have gotten what they wanted: a rise in the economics of the business and a new era in which people buy equipment, space, and tournaments on television.

To understand the cultural presuppositions about pool, we have to turn to the folk culture. Jelly Roll Morton is widely acknowledged to be one of the founders and innovators of early jazz culture, but few realize that he was an exceptionally good pool player. "I wanted to be the champion pool player in the world," Jelly Roll Morton told folklorist Alan Lomax, "so I left New Orleans, where there were too many sharks, to go to some of these little places where I could practice on the suckers."[10]

As I have said, the game of the hustler depends on suckers. The pool hustler's self-deprecating posture, his betting as it were on his own inability to shoot, is an artful game that mirrors the black man's situation in the social world. The system of the con artist, the general category to which we must place the pool shark, rests on being able to put one's self down in the eyes of one's opponent. "My system," Jelly Roll confesses, "was to use the piano as a decoy." Jelly Roll was one of the great piano players of his time, yet in order to win money at pool, he used the piano to attract suckers. "I'd play dumb," he goes on, "until the bets rolled up high, then I'd clean them out."

The pool hall is depicted in the folklore as a perfect setting for the pool shark. The pool shark is described as somebody who loves to dress well and draw everybody's attention to his taste in clothes.

As Moe, Morris, Dominick, and I gathered up our sticks to leave, I started reciting the toast "Pool-Shooting Monkey," which I had learned back in a Bolton, North Carolina poolroom when I was a teenager.[11] They cracked up with laughter.

"My daddy used to know that one," Dominick laughed.

"Shoot," said Morris, "I still know some of it." When I asked him to recite, he couldn't remember much of it.

> "I don't know but I was told," I began:
> The monkey went out on his morning stroll
> He had on a double-breasted suit and long black robe,
> He had a walkin' stick on his arm and his hair was gassed,
> And everybody could tell by the clothes he wore
> That he was a pool-shooting monkey from Coconut Grove."

The teller makes it clear that this was *one* of the pool-shooting monkeys, not the *only* one. Certainly this toast was created by many speakers. When a teller of the tale is really good, he or she turns the pool-shooting monkey's clothes into symbols. The monkey's "double-breasted suit" is not just any suit, it is symbolic of a special feeling the monkey has when he wears that suit. The suit is really his identity, for you can tell by his clothes that he is a "pool-shooting monkey from Coconut Grove." In real life, suits do tell us a lot about the wearer, but in oral toasts, clothes are symbols of identification.

Not just his clothes, but the pool-shooting monkey's actions are symbolic. Notice that he plays pool with an ease not usually found in real life. His actions are therefore "fabulous," that is, they are entertaining. Symbolic clothes and actions allow the performer to transform mundane existence into distracting images of cathartic laughter. One of the most salient features of African American folklore is its ability to arouse cathartic outburst in the target audience. One can test this principle by reciting the "Pool-Shooting Monkey" toast to a friend. Notice by just reciting the first lines about the pool-shooting monkey's clothes, the smiles grow wide until they burst into cathartic laughter.

Through symbols like clothes and actions, pool husters create and recreate fabulous pool sharks like the pool-shooting monkey and share their world view with real-life pool sharks like Jelly Roll Morton. Essential to the art of the pool hustler is the ability to reconstruct oneself into another more fabulous person. Like the fabulous monkey, pool players rename themselves, redress themselves, and become the fabulous person that is necessary to sell themselves as a commodity.

Morton knew some fabulous pool sharks like "Bob Rowe, the man who didn't know how many suits he had, and his wife, Ready Money, were regulars, also the Suicide Queen, who used to take poison all the time." Whenever Morton talks about a game of pool, he introduces the fabulous pool sharks as if he were introducing the NBA lineup: "In came Chicken Dick," he'd say, talking about a game in which one had to fight to get winnings, "In came Chick Dick, the uptown roughneck, and started yelling, 'Keep the game, hey little boy? You don't know what you doing. I'm goin to keep game.' He hit Morton so hard that he fell on the table with his hands still on the balls. Morton hits him in the face with the balls, but he jumps back like he's made of rubber. But Morton kept hitting him in the face with the cue balls until they had to haul Chick Dick out of there. After that, the boys started calling Morton Winding Boy. 'Don't fool with Winding Boy. He like to kill Chicken Dick.'"[12]

Just like the fabled monkey, pool shooters like Jelly Roll Morton dressed distinctively. "All the smart guys wore overalls and a flannel shirt, busted open at the top with no tie," Jelly Roll said, remembering how the pool hustlers dressed in 1905. "From that dress you was considered a sharpshooter."

While he was hustling suckers, he scatted toasts about "Brother Lion and Brother Monkey."[13]

Ladies and gentlemen, we are now in the jungles.
Every one of you are animals . . .

Once he sets the stage, Jelly Roll Morton (while he takes a break between shots) recites the toasts about the monkey and the lion. The animals have a party and dance, to which the lion is not invited. The lion takes offense:

Well, the Lion came through the door,
Ugh, you could tell that Lion was positively sore.

"Let me in the hall." "What you wine do?"
"I'm gonna wreak up this dogone [sic] animule ball."

This is similar to the lines in the "Party-Time Monkey," in which the animals have a party and don't invite the monkey. The monkey goes home and gets his gun. The lion tries to calm him down:

The Lion said, "I know you all hot and excited,
You mad 'cause you didn't get invited."
He say, "But it was the Coon that told us yesterday about a quarter past noon."
He [Party-Time Monkey] said, "Next time y'all have a party and I get all excited.
There gonna be some bad-assed happenings if I don't get invited."
He say, "I do what I please, talk shit, stay drunk seven days a week."

There is much antisocial behavior associated with pool through the image of the pool player in African American folk culture. Just as the pool-shooting monkey is extolled because he doesn't comply with the nine-to-five work ethic, so Morton saw himself as a hero because he didn't work, he played pool. Already by 1905, pool had become a symbol of rebellion and resistance to a system in which work was corrupted.

Even so, Morton saw himself as different from other pool sharks, like Skinny Head Pete and Florida Sam. "They didn't work," Morton said, "because they were kept up by women." The true shark must put women in second place to pool. As Morton puts the rules, "From time to time, two or three girls fell in love with me, but I didn't pay much attention. I was interested in playing pool."

Morton knew that in order to become a great pool shark, he would have to hang out with pool sharks, and he did. Like jazz, or any art form, pool was often passed down from one generation to the next. Morton realized that pool playing could not be learned in school, at least not the traditional school.

His school was the school of the streets, back roads, and long rides on the rail, often as a hobo. He hung out with the likes of Harry Dunn, a card shark, who almost got him killed. There was another one who was "very black," but his name was "Lily White," a fabulous name for a fabulous man. In fact, it was with Lily White that Morton ended up in jail and eventually on the chain gang. From the chain gang, he ran back to his life as a pool shark and piano player, relieved from the fear that while in prison somebody would break his hands in a prison fight, so that he wouldn't be able to play either again.

While touring the country in 1905, Morton wrote "Alabama Bound," "King Porter Stomp," and "You Can Have It, I Don't Want It." These became classic examples of early jazz. One night, after creating one of his masterpiece jazz compositions, Morton shot a game of pool with the original Pensacola Kid. The Kid was waiting for a sucker, and so was Morton. They found each other, and the match became very tense.

This same event structure is reenacted in the "Pool-Shooting Monkey":

> Now Old Baboon was sittin' inside on a stool
> Waitin' on just any old fool
> The Monkey walks in and says, "You know
> I just love and enjoy to see the eight ball roll;"
> The Baboon says, "Look, Brother Monkey, say, down here we
> shoot the eight ball for fun,
> But now if you got any gold in your clothes, I'll shoot you a
> little sixty-one."

This is precisely the form of challenge the pool shark is looking for. The baboon is truly a shark because he immediately distinguishes this game of sixty-one from "eight ball," which is only for "fun." This dialogue between the monkey and the baboon is a liminal play between the rich (the one who has the money) and the poor (the one who wins the money from the sucker). In *The Hustler*, Eddie, the poor boy, plays the rich man and wins twelve thousand dollars from him. The game of pool unites and mediates these two worlds.

The monkey accepts the challenge, and not only puts English on the cue ball, but a considerable amount of ebonics as well:

> The Monkey said, "Get your cue stick from the wall,"
> Said, "now y'all watch this ugly motherfucker when he
>     bust them balls."
> The Baboon bust the balls and his tarball scratched,
> The Monkey sat back and relaxed.

The monkey has talked the opponent into losing. Before the first shot is made, he tells the onlookers that the baboon is going to scratch, and now that this has happened, he can sit back and relax because he will have a chance to shoot his balls in. And this he does, shot after shot, though he pauses to perform rituals like going to the bathroom, chalking his cue. When he shoots the balls in, he uses a variety of techniques: banking, straight in, combination, and letting the fifteen ball ride. "Raising the cue [stick]" is a metonymy for the massé shot, in which the raised stick enables the player to shoot a ball around the obstacle ball that is standing in the way of his shot.

> The Monkey got up and made the one, two, and three.
> He said, "Watch 'em, horseman, while I go pee."
> He came back from the shitter, and he chalked his stick.
> He made the four, five, and six,
> He made the seven, eight, and banked the nine,
> He played the ten, eleven, and twelve in the side.
> He played a double combination with the thirteen, fourteen,
> He raised his cue, and gave the fifteen a chance to ride.

Just like the pool-shooting monkey, Jelly Roll Morton beat the more powerful opponent; in Morton's case, he played and won a game from the famous pool shark Pensacola Kid, because "all the breaks were with me that day."[14] When he asked for his forty dollars, "the guy holding them was gone." Morton grabbed a chair and told Pensacola Kid that "I would knock his brains out with my cue stick and, quite naturally, the forty dollars came up fast." In real life, many black pool hustlers had to fight for their money, and this is captured, as it were, in the folklore of the "Pool-Shooting Monkey."

Morton escaped death in a comical manner just like the fabulous heroes always do in folk culture. He played a game with the "Bad Man," Aaron Harris, who already had eleven murders to his credit, including his sister and his brother-in-law. The latter were killed in a dispute over a cup of coffee.

Apparently Morton didn't know who he was playing. Of course, he knew of Aaron Harris, and had sung songs about him, but he didn't know that the man he was playing was *the* Aaron Harris. After winning a lot of money from Harris, at two dollars a day, for a few weeks, Harris broke down and told Morton, "If you make this ball on my money, I'm going to take every bit of money in your pocket."

"I said, 'A lot of people go to the graveyard for trying to take what I've got. I got something to stop you with too . . . A hard-hitting .38 special.'" They went on playing the game. Before Morton's next turn he warned Harris that if he made the next shot, Harris's money was going right into his pocket: "I raised my cue high in the air, because my taw [cue] ball was close under the cushion, and I stroked this ball and into the pocket she went. It was then that Aaron Harris found out he had been playing a shark."

Instead of trying to kill him, as he had killed other people when they cheated him in cards, Harris befriended Morton. "Okay, kid," he said, "you're the best. Loan me a couple dollars."

"Now that's the way to talk," Morton said. "Don't try to take anything from me. Nobody ever does."

After the Bad Man left, another gambler, a Bob Rowe, "who wore a diamond stud so big that he never could get no kind of tie that would hold it straight up," told Morton, "Kid, don't play that fellow no more."

"Why should I eliminate playin' him? He brings me money here every day."

"That's Aaron Harris."

"I came near passing out," Morton said. Then he went on to sing a Bad Man ballad about Aaron Harris.

What ever happened to this interweaving of the folklorist and the pool shark in African American folk culture? What is left of the folklore is in the stories told by people who still remember the old pool hall and its function in the African American community. There are two reasons why blacks no longer use pool as a game through which to express a particular black male ethos. First, the pool hall has been invaded by women; it is no longer the sacred area for the ritual of maleness. Second, the pool shark can no longer exist in these shallow economic waters.

What has changed pool is not the disappearance of the "moral de-

. . . . . . . . . .

pravity" issue, but a change in the social structure. In the first place, the pool hall is no longer the meeting place it once was in black neighborhoods. Integration destroyed the culture of the black pool hall and the pool hustler. Pool can be found in most night clubs all across America. Where it is found, there are most likely to be many players who are not African American males. In a similar fashion, blues concerts today are usually attended predominately by whites.

The fact that pool hustling has declined is due mainly to the difficulty of earning a living from it. Although the style of playing pool—the combining of folktales and "talkin' shit" while engaged in playing as a way to influence the game—has nearly died out in black communities, there are still pockets of the old folk culture left in many cities like Harlem, Chicago's South Side, and Oakland.

There are still many pool halls in Oakland, like the Serenade Club that caters to the cultural and psychological needs of the black community. In the Serenade Club there is only one pool table; all you have to do to play is put your name on a chalk board and four quarters in the coin slot. I play there with Ebert and Lawrence. Ebert is from Canada, although he was raised in Oakland. His favorite shot is the carom of one ball into another one. Lawrence can't shoot a straight ball in the pocket, but he is a master of the banking shot.

It is great fun playing at the Serenade Club. The music is soul. Around five o'clock, one of the barmaids puts a large pan of barbecued chicken wings on a table near the pool table. Between shots, we gnaw on the chicken wings and sip from our gin glasses. Lawrence's opponent is shooting while looking around and laughing with the onlookers. His shot goes in the pocket, and he squeals out like an animal.

"Wow!" he laughs. "Watch this!"

He aims to shoot a five ball in the pocket. And he makes it. "Wow!" he screams again and dances around to the other side of the table. Everybody is having fun, for pool is the quintessential black male game. What makes it the quintessential black male game is that it is oral and competitive both verbally and physically; it allows for individual expression while maintaining a group status. In addition to these qualities, it is cathartic: It releases pressure instantly, and revives the flagging spirits of its participants. Furthermore, it is skills displayed and it is skills disguised.

"Remember the picture of Dr. King shooting pool?" Moe said as we walked to our cars. In 1965, *Life* magazine published a photograph of Martin Luther King Jr. shooting pool. He has his sleeves rolled up. But the magazine had some sinister intent, because at that time pool was associated with the lowest dregs of black society. Yet this widely distributed photograph reached many low-income black people. The result was to make Dr. King more popular among blacks who could not read about him because they were illiterate. Because of this photograph they began to relate to him, because pool was a game they knew well.

That pool shooting and the negative connotations associated with it can be appropriated by the white middle-class and by the mass media (in such films as *The Hustler* and *The Color of Money*) indicates how easy it is for the white power structure to infiltrate the most hallowed inner rituals and rites and sites of black male character building. Yet these changes in the social structure have not diminished the interest that African American men feel for pool playing.

To be sure, there is some money to be made in pool, but this doesn't seem to be the real attraction for African American men. The real attraction seems to be the psychological association of pool playing with sex. After all, the pool stick is phallic, and we must not forget that pool has given us many sexual metaphors, too. "Playing pocket pool," for example, means masturbating, and the idea of sliding a pool stick through the fingers is an obvious sexual metaphor. Pool has been primarily a bachelor sport where men are able to talk openly about their attitudes toward women. The term "hustler" was applied to pool players a long time before it was used for prostitution. Therefore, it is reasonable to assume that, in addition to cultural and social reasons, African American males are drawn to pool for psychological, and hence unconscious, motivations.

"Pool is supposed to be the sport of the nineties," Moe shouts to me as he gets in his car and drives off.

The sport of the nineties? But not really. Not like it used to be. For African American males, there was a time when pool was an expressive form that helped them overcome the dehumanizing effects of white racism. During the periods of American history when blacks were segregated, pool hustling was a form for dealing with despair. By using oral narratives like the toasts, pool players created what Berndt Ostendorf calls "a mood of participatory catharsis."[15] While shooting the game, the hustler recreated himself and the hustling world to make it more glamorous than it really was, but also to "overcome both the alleged lack of an alleged past and a viable future by making the most of instant gratification."[16]

However, more recently in pool halls in North Oakland—where they cater to a young dating crowd—one doesn't hear pool shooters telling their stories; one hears rap music playing in the background while the young players study their shots silently. Gone are the bragging and the boasting and the mythmaking. Except in a few places, in some older neighborhoods, the art of the black pool hustler is a fading one.

## NOTES

1. Ned Polsky, *Hustlers, Beats, and Others* (Chicago: Aldine Publishing Company, 1967), 52.
2. Ned Polsky, "Of Pool Playing and Poolrooms," *Hustlers, Beats, and Others* (Chicago: Aldine Publishing Company, 1967), 23.
3. Ibid., 23.
4. Ibid., 17.
5. Ibid., 31.
6. Ibid., 14–15.
7. *Billiards Digest* (December 1996), 74.
8. Polsky, *Hustlers*, 57.
9. Robert Byre, *Wonderful World of Pool and Billiards* (Harvest Original, 1996), 4.
10. Alan Lomax, *Jelly Roll Morton* (Pantheon Books, 1993), 135.
11. My version is from Bruce Jackson, *Get Your Ass Out of the Water and Swim Like Me: Narrative Poetry from Black Oral Tradition* (Cambridge: Harvard University Press, 1974). It was recited in 1965 by a young black man to the author.
12. Alan Lomax, *Mister Jelly Roll: The Fortunes of Jelly Roll Morton, New Orleans Creole and Inventor of Jazz* (New York: Duell, Sloan and Pearce, 1950), 157.

13. Morton claims that it was he and not Louis Armstrong who "invented" scat singing; the example of scatting that he offered is similar to the toast tradition of "The Party-Time Monkey," a version of which is found in Bruce Jackson's *Get Your Ass Out of the Water and Swim Like Me*.
14. This story is in Alan Lomax's *Jelly Roll Morton*, 158.
15. Berndt Ostendorf, *Black Literature in White America* (Brighton Sussex: Harvester Press; Totowa, NJ: Barnes & Noble Books, 1982), 229.
16. Ibid.

# Second Wind

. . . . . . . . . .

*by*
LORRAINE KEE

By the two-minute warning, I'd already ridden the elevator down from the press box with the other sportswriters and was waiting outside the New Orleans Saints' locker room.

I was alone with my thoughts.

Soon Saints players would thread their way under the stands and file victoriously into their locker room after beating up on the St. Louis Rams. It was my job to interview the players on the opposing team, so I was tensely calculating how quickly I could get that done and then bolt across the Louisiana Superdome's carpet in time to catch the Rams players before they showered, dressed and slumped to the idling buses. A deadline loomed. I had two sidebars to write.

Before I was fully aware of who was standing next to me, I heard his voice: "I bet you really like going into the locker rooms."

The intonation of the voice cracked my concentration. It was different from that of the sports fans who'd asked this black female sportswriter more times than I could count, "Do you go into locker rooms?"

No, this sounded more insidious than inquisitive. I whipped my head around. The man was in a uniform. A security guard? He wasn't some "Joe" off the street. Only people with authorization — the teams, reporters, stadium employees, and the well-connected — were allowed down here.

"Get away from me," I seethed through my clenched teeth, instantly resentful of the intrusion and the insinuation.

He backed off. Suddenly the door to the Saints' locker room opened. The herd of reporters spilled inside, splintering off in every direction to interview players.

Done with my interviews, I headed up to the press box, still stewing. I told a male official with the Saints about the encounter. Then I recounted it to a male colleague. They shrugged. What had I expected? I wasn't surprised they weren't outraged. I just wanted someone to share my irritation with, if only briefly.

But there was no time for that because of my deadline.

I was on my own. I would feel that way more often than not until I decided to leave the sports department.

## STRENGTH IN NUMBERS?

Look around in any press box Sundays in the National Football League. You can count the female sportswriters faster than you can say Brett Favre. OK, maybe Fred Biletnikoff.

There are still not enough African Americans covering major beats. Most are African American men. In five years, I met no more than a dozen African American female sportswriters. We'd acknowledge each other with a nod across a crowded press room.

For most of that time, I was a columnist. About ten African American sportswriters have regular columns in this country. From Final Fours to the NFL, I met only one African American female sports columnist. I heard later that she'd left sports to go into feature writing.

I came from the news side.

The traditional route for male sportswriters is working their way through the ranks. Initially they cover high school sports. That might lead to college sports and, if they're good, to professional sports. Good sportswriters are usually years in the making. I took the less-traveled, more accelerated route.

In the spring of 1990, a *St. Louis Journalism Review* article embarrassed the *St. Louis Post-Dispatch* by pointing out the lack of diversity in the newspaper's sports department. Of the approximately thirty staffers, there was only one African American. He covered high school sports.

.    .    .    .    .    .    .    .    .    .

Only one woman wrote at the time. She was covering high school sports. Both numbers were dismal, considering the numbers of African Americans playing amateur and professional sports and the revolution in women's athletics.

At the time of my switch to sports, I was covering the cash-strapped city of East St. Louis. But after about a year of covering that city's gritty politics, I was ready for a change. Besides, since college, I'd had an interest in covering athletics.

Before the *Review* article, I'd expressed an interest in moving to sports. The *Journalism Review* article prompted the editors to approach me rather than hire from outside the newspaper.

It really wasn't that much of a leap, I'd joke later. Winners and losers in politics, winners and losers in sports. Bobbing and weaving in politics, bobbing and weaving in sports.

Actually I can't remember if any of the editors asked me whether I had written sports before. I had in college.

The job called for me to double as sportswriter-columnist. No raise right away. That would come later. After all, the managing editor wasn't sure this Great Experiment would work out. Anxious to get my face in the newspaper, the editors wanted me to start a column right away. I persuaded them to wait for a few months, while I figured out what I wanted to say.

Of course, I never thought that it wouldn't work out. I'm a good reporter. I could do this. Like any reporter, covering a planning and zoning meeting or cops, I would learn. The only thing my white male colleagues had on me was experience.

I never gave much thought to whether they would or would not accept me, or whether my appointment was the result of "affirmative action." It didn't matter to me if there was no rash of invitations to lunch or to grab a beer. If they felt like I was being foisted on the department, made up mostly of white males, I didn't care.

I was more consumed with doing a good job, making myself into a respectable sportswriter. And time would take care of that. Besides I knew what I was wading into: a department of mostly white males who'd worked with very few people like me. It wasn't the first time that had happened.

A raise did, in fact, come a few weeks after I started in the sports department.

When I look back on that time, my thoughts sometimes wander to that one female sportswriter who was plugging away in the department upon my arrival. We had little in common. She was white, had a bubbly personality, had grown up in the business. Her father had been a well-known columnist at a St. Louis newspaper. She'd traversed the traditional sportswriter route.

Yet here we were—two specks in a male-dominated department.

I can recall one particularly poignant conversation she and I had. Several months after I arrived in the sports department I was assigned to cover the women's Final Four. I was very excited at the prospect— our newspaper had never sent anyone to the women's championship before. By right though, I thought, that the other woman should go. She had been in the department longer, had championed women's sports longer.

We had a lump-in-the-throat conversation near the city desk where I offered to tell the sports editor that she should go instead. She told me not to bother or the newspaper would send no one.

I went.

About a year later, Cathie Burnes Beebe died suddenly from an aneurysm.

## PASSION FOR PUNTS

I'd always liked sports. I'd even loved some.

Growing up on air force bases from Louisiana to North Dakota to Massachusetts to Kansas, I would watch games balanced on the arm of my father's easy chair.

My parents had three girls. I was as close to a son as my father was going to get. My sisters had a passing interest in sports. But, for me, it was a passion I could share with my father. On Thanksgiving, while my sisters helped my mother stuff the turkey, I'd be in the living room with my dad.

Sometimes, he would impress the invited guests with his daughter's

. . . . . . . . .

snap football knowledge. In that era, I was affectionately considered a tomboy—a term I've since scrapped because of the limits it imposes on little girls.

I hung around with the boys, played their games, and even wandered into the garage with them to covertly look at *National Geographic* magazines. What's the big deal about breasts? I wondered, as the boys ogled the naked natives on the color pages.

One of the biggest influences on me, outside of my mother and father, was Barbara Jordan. The former Texas Congresswoman, who appeared to be a big woman like myself, possessed a voice that resonated with the richness of molasses.

Outside of her, I revered athletes. I played softball, ran track, bowled. I was cut from the volleyball team. I was never a very good athlete, but I followed those who were.

I loved the Lakers, loathed the Celtics; admired Ashe, abhorred Ainge; imitated Mays, ignored the Islanders; screamed for the Steelers, scorned the Cowboys; rooted for Billie Jean King, reviled Bobby Riggs; dreamed of Kareem, denounced McHale.

I was born about the time that Althea Gibson sat atop the tennis world. I was nine when Tommie Smith and John Carlos raised their fists in defiance and Arthur Ashe crashed the lawn party at the U.S. Tennis Championships. I turned fifteen the year the Cleveland Indians made Frank Robinson the first black manager in the major leagues and Hank Aaron surpassed Babe Ruth's 714 home runs.

As sports editor of the campus newspaper at Wichita State, I would take the first tentative steps on my journey toward becoming a full-fledged sportswriter. And once I joined that club, I would spring from spectator to sportswriter.

No more cheering in the press box.

## MIND OVER MATTER

When you become a sportswriter, the armchair quarterback is transformed into an instant sports authority.

Shortly before I plunged into my new assignment, a former managing editor introduced me during a regular meeting between newsroom staff and a handful of African American readers at the newspaper.

"Now if I can only teach her the difference between a football and a basketball," the editor chortled during an otherwise pleasant introduction. He later apologized. He hadn't meant it the way it sounded.

I knew sports, but covering it meant boosting my appreciation of its history, its statistics, and its personalities. Its elegance, its elan.

Few athletes embodied that more for me than retired heavyweight champion Muhammad Ali, Olympic gold medalist Jackie Joyner-Kersee and Rams wide receiver Isaac Bruce. During my five years in the sports department, I interviewed them all.

Ali was then fifty, his voice down to a whisper because of Parkinson's disease. But he was still pretty, as my mother once told me he was. And Ali still had bounce in his delivery, even if this proud former heavyweight champion was reduced to amusing us with magic tricks or landing playful punches with adoring fans.

The indomitable Joyner-Kersee, the East St. Louis-reared heptathlete already contemplating life after gold medals, was mustering the chutzpah for a final hurrah at the Olympics in Atlanta. Age and asthma weren't on her side. Despite a hitch in her hamstring, she hopped away with a bronze medal in the long jump.

At 185 pounds, the humble Bruce hardly casts an imposing figure in street clothes. Yet, on the field, Bruce is transformed into a steely and strutting stealth receiver.

Beyond them, I grew to admire one man in particular: Bill White, former Cardinals first baseman and the first black president of the National League. The first time I met White was during the Cardinals Centennial Celebration in 1992, though I'd tried several times previously to arrange interviews.

Before the festivities, I approached him on the field: "Don't you know I don't give interviews?" he snarled.

I'd heard that, I said as we fell into step on the field at Busch Stadium. I interviewed him that day and a number of times afterward. A *New York Times* article had cast White as an "angry man." Later, in an

. . . . . . . . . .

interview with me, he insisted he was. But White is also charming, big-hearted, and inspired.

That day he told me that the best thing he could do as the first black to head a professional league was to "do a good job." Just as Jackie Robinson had before him, he added.

What did I like about covering sports? The athletes.

These people—already endowed with great athletic gifts—rise to be the best of the best on their fields of competition. I was fascinated with their spirituality, how body and mind triumph over 300-pound line-men, pulled hamstrings, and fastball-hurling pitchers.

Moreover, I found an occasional peace, before deadlines would deny it, in Busch Stadium. Sitting in the stadium, I was hypnotized by baseball's leisurely pace under yawning blue skies on 80-degree days as the ballplayers plotted strategy on the surreal green grass.


## LOVE AND WAR

I remember this particular letter because it came from Russ Francis.

This Francis, not the former tight end for the New England Patri-ots, was from Fenton, MO, a small town outside St. Louis. But, be-cause of the name, the letter stuck with me. Francis also wrote his letter to an editor rather than to me. A colleague deemed it so wretched at first that he whisked it away before I could read it. He eventually relented. I've kept it.

In any case, Francis saw my addition to the sports staff as tanta-mount to reverse discrimination, grounds for revolt. He threatened to cancel his subscription. His venom wasn't particularly shocking to me—I'd learned a painful lesson about racists riding to school as the only black on a bus full of white kids in Wichita, KS. I was simply amused that he was so riled by my hiring.

Was it an affirmative-action hire? Yes. But I still had to do the work.

People often asked me whether my take on sports was different be-cause I was a woman and African American. The whole question smacked of the old debate about whether you're a black journalist or a journalist who happens to be black. I refuse usually to engage in that debate.

Of course, I was different.

I could no more separate myself from my womanhood and blackness than Maya Angelou could escape truth in her poetry. It's who I am. My experiences are mine, just as I speak here for no other sportswriter than myself.

Still I was offended when a colleague suggested I was at some advantage by being an African American woman covering African American athletes.

It sounded as if he expected the black athletes and me to share some special bond, a secret handshake or code. Yes, we had some shared experiences. That was something I could bring to my writing. No, that did not imply some color-coded cohesion. I had to earn my props just like the next sportswriter.

I read sports history books, consulted other news stories, learned intricacies of free agency from team officials and hitting from hard-nosed safety Toby Wright. When I wanted to know about the wrinkles posed by left-handed quarterbacks, I repeatedly circled the perimeter of the football field as the quarterbacks coach gave me the benefit of his experience. They were happy to oblige. The players were never patronizing. But I made it a point of being informed, asking intelligent questions. When I didn't know something, I didn't feel the need to fake it. I simply asked.

As I struggled as a new columnist to find my voice, I wrote more often about women than my male colleagues. I felt it was my duty.

I wrote more often about African Americans. I felt it was my responsibility.

And I tried to write about them as not only athletes but also as individuals. I never asked them about how it felt to be tall when men preferred their dates shorter. Black athletes were not hostages of the 'hood, imbued with innate abilities to run faster and jump higher. I didn't judge women's basketball by whether the players could dunk. My barometer went more toward how competitive a program was, whether it could make the NCAA tournament.

. . . . . . . . . .

Once upon a time, I wrote a column about the lack of African Americans on the team the Rams had selected to do its broadcasts. Ten were appointed. None was an African American. It made perfect sense to me that the broadcasting should be more diverse considering that about 65 percent of the Rams players were African American and about 50 percent of the city's residents were.

For weeks afterward, I was accused of being a racist. One irate reader went to the trouble of finding a picture of a jackass, Xeroxing my face on top of that and then attaching the words: "asshole of the month." I was flattered that he'd gone to so much trouble.

One caller gathered some of his coworkers together and called me. Why, he complained, did I have to write about race so much? Why, I wondered, didn't he complain that the white sportswriters didn't write about it enough?

Another caller accused me of glorifying welfare because I wrote about an unwed mother of two who was coaching her son's Little League team. Why, the caller asked, didn't I say she was black? To this day, I can't recall her race. I interviewed her over the telephone. And what did race matter in this instance?

Funny thing is, there was no hue and cry when I wrote about women. And nobody asked the male sportswriters why they weren't writing enough about women.

There were demonstrations of support, much more positive than negative. They came in letters and calls to me at the office. I was flattered when I was among a group of women honored with the St. Louis Sports Commission's first-ever women of sports achievement award.

I took up for women treated like second-class citizens on golf courses, groused about the topless bar ads in my own sports section, and reminded readers of a coach's responsibility to graduate players as well as choreograph plays.

The column was the most visible expression of my take on sports. But, on Sundays, the arena became the weekly NFL picks by the staff. Some fans, of all stripe, pulled for me to beat the guys. I was just happy never to finish last.

Early on, when I led our band of pigskin prognosticators, an editor inquired with a colleague if he was making my picks for me.

He wasn't.

Didn't it occur to a colleague that I would also be offended when he suggested that a black sports columnist in another city was an argument against affirmative action? That I would be offended when an editor used me in a photograph to promote a new project at the newspaper when there was a question about whether I would even be a part of the changes?

## CROSSING PATTERN

I'm an African American woman.

Normally, for me, they're one and the same. But sometimes those two sides of my whole seemed at odds. It happened when I wrote columns about O.J. Simpson, boxer Mike Tyson, or Rams running back Lawrence Phillips.

Simpson had been accused of murdering his ex-wife, Nicole Brown Simpson, and Ronald Goldman. Tyson served time for raping a Miss Black America contestant. And Phillips was placed on probation for assaulting his girlfriend at the University of Nebraska.

African Americans have a justifiably skeptical view of the criminal justice system. At the July convention of the National Association of Black Journalists, I sat rapt as former Black Panther Geronimo Pratt told the story of his release after twenty-seven years of imprisonment.

Pratt, who'd been accused of murder, said he'd been railroaded. A judge released him, citing the prosecution's failure to tell the defense that the key witness against Pratt was a paid informant for the FBI and police.

As a woman, I believe strongly that there is no excuse for domestic violence. Yet, I was uncomfortable about criticizing the brothers in print. I felt out of step, at times, with other African Americans. After all, the polls said most African Americans believed Simpson innocent. I had doubts.

In the end, I wrote what I believed was right, or at least I took a posi-

. . . . . . . . .

tion consistent with the values that my mother and father had instilled in me.

I wasn't sure about Simpson's guilt or innocence. I wrote about the plight for the Simpson children. I condemned domestic violence, those who put athletes on pedestals, and how an American success story had shrouded an American tragedy.

## ONE-ON-ONES

Illinois football coach Lou Tepper hugged me. Twice.

The hugs were innocent enough.

The first one came after the University of Illinois football team shut out East Carolina in the Liberty Bowl. The team had hoped to do better than the Liberty Bowl.

The second time came after he'd coached his final game in Champaign. He'd been fired. And he swept his family and myself into a emotion-tugging embrace at midfield.

I grew unbearably uncomfortable, wondering what my male colleagues would think. I doubted whether he'd ever hugged a male sportswriter.

Later, Tepper and I talked. I told him why I pulled away. A sensitive, enthusiastic coach, he understood.

I always tried to act professionally, as I trod this most testosterone of turfs.

That was partly out of a sense that I was under a microscope—one letter writer once complained that I was paid more than the other sportswriters at the newspaper. How would he know? I chuckled. For the record, I wasn't.

I didn't dillydally in the locker room. I knew when I entered who I wanted to interview. I knew where their locker stalls were. I left.

Sure, I was uncomfortable at times. But I was uncomfortable in women's locker rooms too. There's something awkward about standing clothed in a room of unclothed people, whether they be male or female.

I never encountered the animosity Lisa Olson met with in the New

England Patriots locker room a few years ago. The former *Boston Herald* reporter charged that she had been sexually harassed by some Patriots players.

But women reporters in the locker room aren't the issue they once were simply because there are more of them.

To head off criticism, I acquainted myself on everything from the subtleties of pass routes and special teams to the hardness of artificial turf and free agency. The players, the coaches, the games were the fun part of the job.

Less fun for me was a strained relationship with the sports editor.

Even in hindsight, I'm not sure where we went wrong. We seemed to have a million differences. By themselves, none appeared fatal. Together, they were why I left sports.

He might disagree, but I always thought our deep-seated differences—which occasionally drove me to church to pray for a resolution—were more about style than substance. No, our differences were philosophical too.

## A ROLE MODEL

I was a hit on career day.

For the most part, my nine-year-old daughter was proud that her mother was a sportswriter.

Her mommy did something different from the other mothers—the other fathers too. After a man in the International House of Pancakes asked me to autograph his placemat, she chortled, "You're famous."

We went to games together. I encouraged her as she took her first foray into the wide world of organized sports. She plays basketball. She was tickled the day I surprised her at school with baseball tickets to a Cardinals play-off game. I took her to a closed Rams practice for "Take Our Daughters to Work" day.

For me, there was always a bit of irony in that daughters celebration. Why? Because way too often I took my work home to her.

On a couple of occasions, after I did interviews on my home phone, we ate supper at 9 P.M. I'd sometimes run to her school, stop at the McDonald's on the way back to work where she'd eat at my desk

.    .    .    .    .    .    .    .    .    .

while I clattered the keys on the terminal. She was remarkably toler-
ant, until she'd finished her Happy Meal, unwrapped her toy prize, rearranged my cluttered desk, colored my scrap paper, unraveled a
grease pencil, rifled through the drawers.

Then she'd utter a variation of every parent's bane on a long car ride
home.

"Are you done yet?"

No.

"Can I get a snack out of the vending machine?"

Guilt-ridden, I'd point to the change multiplying in the bottom of
my purse. Take it. No licorice, I warned.

At least, on school nights now, she goes to bed at 9 P.M.


## ON THE SIDELINES

A few months ago, I left the sports department and went back into
news.

Why?

I was tired.

Tired of the battles from within and without. Tired of battling
alone. Tired of being Super Mom and sportswriter. Tired of looking
around and seeing too few people who looked like me. Tired of being
the token. Tired of waiting for people to change. Tired of being angry.

I will miss the games, the players, the coaches. The laughs I shared
over dinners with some of my colleagues on Saturday nights before
games. I will miss what, to me, was one of the best jobs in the newspaper. Where else do they pay you to watch a game?

But my time there had expired. I'm working on getting my second
wind.

# Rodeo, Racing, and Sumo Wrestling: A Confession

. . . . . . . . . . .

*by*
JONIS AGEE

Who can say why it begins? Who even names it out loud? It's in the very nature of obsession to be hidden from the self until after the fact.

"I'm having other people's dreams," I complained after the move to Michigan two years ago.

"What do you mean?" people asked.

"It's exhausting to spend the night with strangers in places you've never been. What about my people, my memories?"

They just looked at me, apparently thinking I was only speaking in metaphor.

By early December, new friends noticed a steady decline in my appearance and health, to say nothing of my conversation. They suspected a new lover or something worse. Such is the nature of friends. But when I turned on the TV to tape the National Rodeo Finals in the middle of a party that Saturday night, at least part of the secret came out. Or maybe it was the fact that for ten days I kept the word Rodeo and the time it would appear on ESPN printed in ballpoint on the back of my hand.

"Is that the stamp they used at an actual rodeo that you just didn't want to wash off?" George asked.

"No," I told him. "It's the Finals." He stared at my hand for a moment and walked away. When I turned on the TV at midnight in that room crowded with happy wine drinkers, a strange thing happened. Although I'd kept the sound off, it was only a matter of half an

.   .   .   .   .   .   .   .   .   .

hour before the crowd had thinned out and a group of people ringed the TV staring at the steer wrestling.

"Doesn't it hurt to have your head twisted that way?" Tish asked as the steer got up and trotted off without a blink.

"Look, did you see that?" George said. "The cowboy patted the steer. Like he was thanking him. You never see that from the audience, you're not close enough. He patted him as if he liked the steer." George was to continue to bring this up for the rest of the evening. He was the only person in the group who had ever been to a rodeo aside from me, and he had the distinction of having been the announcer in Spanish at the Houston Stock Show one night years ago. It was never clear how someone in advertising who knew virtually nothing about rodeo ever got this job. He seemed equally confused on that point, but it gave me new respect for him.

Six of us sat there until one-thirty in the morning watching saddle broncs and calf roping, barrel racing and team roping, and the biggest event of them all, bull riding. Between world champion All Around Cowboy Ty Murray, the other cowboy announcers and me, we explained rodeo. We watched a black cowboy, Fred Whitfield, the world champion calf roper, having a tough night while the new kids flashed out of the chute to rope and tie calves in under ten seconds. Trying to infuse the event with danger, I told my friends how one of the toughest competitors had a finger almost ripped off last summer when it got caught in the rope. Then the three Etbauer brothers who began rodeoing by pooling all their money as they traveled from place to place, all rode their saddle broncs, twisting and bucking through the air. Some men whose horses got too droppy were bucked off, landing hard, bouncing on shoulders, backs, and heads, having to be helped out by the medics waiting at the gate. By the finals, almost everyone in the rough-stock events competes with some kind of injury: cracked and broken fingers, wrists, arms, and feet; twisted knees; torn groin muscles and elbow ligaments; broken ribs; and more.

Watching the lightning-fast team roping where the header loops a steer's horns and the heeler has to catch the two hind legs, my friends gasped at the speed and precision. During the barrel racing, they hollered the horses home. Generally, they were having a surprisingly good time. They were reluctant tourists, uneasy about getting off the boat to wander on this island that at first glance seemed completely uninhabited. After a while they could only bring themselves to replenish food and drink during commercial breaks, which were in themselves worth seeing since the ads showed cowboy life so remote from their own they laughed uneasily.

While I enjoyed the rodeo that evening, I was equally interested in my friends' reactions. I'd recently moved to Ann Arbor to teach writing at the University of Michigan where there was nothing remotely cowboy or western going on. For a person who owns twenty pairs of cowboy boots, this could be a lonely place. When I told people I was staying up half the night because ESPN didn't broadcast rodeo until one or two in the morning, my students stared at me with that expression that says they haven't read the book, and my colleagues gave that same short, derisive chuckle I was hearing during the commercials for Pemmican Beef Jerky, Wrangler jeans, and cowboy cab trucks you could sleep in. What is it that makes us this way? I wondered, until the bull riding came on.

While most rodeo events such as calf roping and saddle bronc riding grew out of actual ranch life, bull riding smacks of everything that is unnecessary and dangerous—strapping a cowbell on a piece of rope around the flanks of a bull and pulling a rope around his girth that you hang onto while you try to ride him with one hand. Then there is the suicide wrap of the rope around the hand, which means getting hung up tied to the bull trying to stick, kick, and fall on the bucked off rider. I like to imagine the beginning of this event as a bunch of guys sitting around the corral one day bragging how they could ride anything with fur on it, and then someone brings out a bull. It's such a totally useless thing to do that it possesses its own absurd beauty. Bull riders are battered, scarred, limping, taped up, and determined men. And unlike the other events, it's not even enough to stay on for eight seconds, you have to get off and start running before the bull butts, tramples, or gores you. In fact, the event is so dangerous, there are men dressed as clowns whose real job is to distract the bulls from the riders who climb, crawl, or are dragged away. Rescued by clowns, what better paradigm for life?

. . . . . . . . . .

By the middle of ten straight days of riding bulls, there are black eyes, stitches, broken bones, and concussions. But every night they get back on. Wrapping the rope carefully around the gloved hand and winding it between the fingers, each man in his own particular ritual, tugging down the hat, slapping his cheek, grimacing, and giving the nod, jumps out of the chute on 2,000 pissed-off pounds of rock and roll meat. This is an equal-opportunity job. The bright chaps and color-coordinated shirts don't make a damn bit of difference if you can't hold your spurs in that loose hide and keep the bull from bucking you off the end of your arm or pulling you down in the well as he spins with enough g-force to give you the kind of whiplash ambulance-chasing lawyers only dream about. Bulls are smart. They feel exactly where the rider is, how he's tipped, which way he shifts to keep up with the motion, and they use it all against him. Then there's the scramble on the ground, with the clowns dancing in front of the charging bull while the rider's trying to shake off last night's concussion and jump for the fence rails.

During the bull riding, my friends made more noise than usual. It wasn't that they weren't watching, it was something else. They were disturbed, maybe even outraged, the way you are when you see other people's children playing dangerously close to the traffic. You want to stop them, make them behave. "Why would anyone do that?" Betty asked. "After the first time, I mean? I'd never get back on." Even the men nodded without envy.

Because that's where the money is, I wanted to quote Willy Sutton on why he robbed banks, but that isn't exactly true of bull riders. Billy Etbauer makes more in saddle-bronc riding, and he only has to contend with the chance of horses falling on him or wrenching him up and flinging him to the ground. Horses only step on a rider by mistake. Maybe Willy Sutton's words are useful though because their very simplicity makes you think harder than you would, as if he had robbed banks in a state of purity. Something about the nature of direct action. Bull riding fascinates and disturbs because the rider is so clearly overmatched. Announcers like to say, "It's not a matter of if you'll get hurt, it's a matter of when and how bad."

Watching Tuff Hediman ride that night with my friends, I remembered a year ago when Bodacious, the rankest bull in the country, smashed his face and knocked him out. Tuff's face looks different now, more a mask with severed nerves, knitted bones, missing mobility. I don't want him to get on any more bulls, and I cringe every time a hoof glances off a shoulder, lands too close to his head, or he gets hung up in the rope and whipped around and around while the bull tries to catch him with its horn and kick him to pieces. Lane Frost died riding bulls. Maybe the same thing that makes people ride bulls, makes us watch them.

I used to wonder if it was just vicarious, if I wanted to see more disaster, but that's not it. My friends' protests would be my own in the coming week as Scott Breding climbed on night after night with a separated shoulder that meant he couldn't raise his free arm enough to counterbalance the bull's motion and save himself from being bucked off. Wearing a face mask because he'd been knocked out by Bodacious in that same event a year ago, Scott managed to ride only a couple in ten tries. He was going for the day money, earned for the highest scores on a given day, although we're not talking the hundreds of thousands of dollars of other professional athletes. But toward the end even that seemed impossible, and it was like watching an old soldier going into a battle he knew he was going to lose. It wasn't even the glory. He had it to do, so he did it. Courage, it seems, is always the result of some form of foolishness.

As my friends left that night, they thanked me for the rodeo although during the days to come when I was too groggy from sleeplessness to make sense, they laughed, called me weird, eccentric. I tried to make them understand what I was doing in the middle of the night watching TV, but they weren't convinced. "Obsessed," they muttered. To them, the small visit had sufficed. They appreciated the explanations of events I'd given them, but they weren't going any further. Some nights at 2 or 3 A.M. I did get lonely though, wishing I knew one other person still awake, someone I could talk to about my favorites in the bareback riding who take such beatings lying back, heads bouncing up and down like balloons on the bucking haunches, the nights they used the eliminator pen. Or the finals night when so many of the riders were simply too sore and hurt to stay on. And when Fred Whitfield, the calf roper, described losing interest in the event after he'd won the world title last year, only to come back to recognizing his need to use his gift, I wanted to turn to someone else and point out how that holds true for so many of us, how once you've achieved something great, it's hard to stay as hungry.

There were clearly lessons to be learned here, and stranded as I was with other people's dreams in a new life, I began to pay attention to every single moment on that screen. After all, how hard the horses and bulls buck are a percentage of the rider's score. No chance of just talking your way out of it.

And rodeo is a team sport in the oddest sense. A rider, roper, wrestler teamed with a total stranger who happens to have four legs and fur. Sometimes there are other members of the team helping too — the barrel racer, roper, and wrestler's horses, the hazer keeping the steer in a straight line for the wrestler, the pickup men on horses in the rough-stock riding events, the clowns in bull riding. In addition to championship awards for the cowboys, there are year-end awards for best horses, clowns, and bulls, too, respect given where deserved.

Following the move to Michigan, I noticed that while my nights were preempted for someone else's life, my waking hours were flooded with the debris of my own childhood days. Dislocation, being unhomed, unbound is provocative to the psyche, it turns out, as if memories, like carefully packed old china, are jostled and broken open in the moving process. For instance, I remembered that in fourth and fifth grades I loved the Yankees every time they were in the World Series, and that the boys and I smuggled the scores from one kid to another on those hot fall afternoons. None of the other girls were interested in sports, except for Judy Mason who was famous for being the best athlete in the school. While we girls played softball and soccer at recess, Judy preferred football. Then one afternoon after school, she decided to teach me how to play. For two hours we ran up and down the block-large park across the street from my house, Judy pitching the football to me then chasing me down with a bone-thumping tackle. Over and over and over, I ran like a dog from the fatal embrace of an oncoming truck. I never much liked football or Judy Mason after that. Not until I moved to Ann Arbor.

For most of my adult life, I treated sports and an interest in them as a kind of fast food for the soul. Not nourishing, adding fat from empty calories, making the self pouchy, bloated. Although as a kid I read all the horse stories, westerns, baseball and football stories I could find in the library, I thought those were subjects you outgrew, especially if you were female. At least that's what Mr. Rice, my first high school English teacher, said as he presented me with a reading list of "great literature." He was right about the list. I'm still not sure about the rest. I'm not trying to fool myself too much with the illusion that sports are some great metaphor. No, I think it's different and more complicated than that. I find the language, terminology, inventions of a world specific to itself, authentic, refreshing, even nourishing. What I'm discovering is perhaps mostly about myself, more than anything else, but I can't swear that's true either. Maybe it's the act of letting something outside myself, so far outside myself as to be almost virtually unimaginable, arrest me. Make me put the brakes on and pay attention. Even obsess me.

In a college town there is usually one big sport. Forget the fact that the hockey team won the NCAA championship two years ago, the Michigan football coach is paid better than most college presidents. And every Saturday there's a home game, I'm trapped in my house from morning till dark by the stadium five blocks away. Buying a big red truck and moving here may not have been the best idea I've ever had, but starting over in another state offered a certain appealing sense of adventure at a point when my life had grown hopelessly predictable. If someone had offered me a ride on a bull at that moment, I probably would have taken it too.

The first fall here I learned the harsh lessons of living five blocks from the Big House with the second largest football seating capacity in the country. You grocery shop the day before or the day after the game. You don't try to sneak out to the movies at Briarwood Mall on game afternoons unless you like spending an hour and a half browsing Blockbuster Videos with the suspicious eyes of clerks supervising you while the exiting game traffic blocks the streets. You don't plan on going out to eat or having food delivered until Sunday night of a football weekend. Don't even consider trying to leave or enter town by Interstate 94 when the game lets out because your ramp will be closed, and the cop will not be even remotely interested in your problem.

You'll spend the next week fantasizing him with tire tracks across his bored expression. And most of all, you don't try to discuss the game with your university colleagues because most of them don't give a damn about the game.

At first I didn't care either, but that changed. When you're in a one-trick-pony town, you better learn to like the pony. I began to seek comforting talk over the drubbing by Northwestern or the way we slammed Ohio with the new butcher at the meat market or the cab driver taking me back from Detroit Metro Airport at one in the morning after a Kafkaesque series of plane delays that leave me dragging two suitcases through utterly deserted corridors in search of just one person who could point to transportation. A normal thirty-dollar ride became fifty at that hour, but as long as he didn't deliver me into the blown-out bowels of Detroit itself and kept the conversation on how the mighty blue and gold was doing, I would have gladly paid a hundred.

It was only a few weeks before I discovered that one of my colleagues shared more than the casual or condemning interest in the game. Maybe it was because we were both nominally from Minnesota. At least that was the pretext. Steve had season tickets though, which was a dead giveaway. So it began that on Saturday mornings we would find ourselves on the phone having the same desultory conversation lamenting the faults of our team and magnifying the strengths of the other team, trying to get a fix on the outcome. Sometimes we called each other at halftime if it was an away game—almost certainly after the game was over—to recite our favorite moments.

I've never completely grasped the rules of football. But I'm better at them than with hockey though I dated an ex-college goalie and spent several Minnesota winters in the empty gray cold of late-evening ice arenas cheering the abbreviated play of the adult league with the other women, none of us able to look each other in the eye as we prayed for game's end when our men would come bursting out of the locker room fired up and ready for other kinds of games. Well, that's another story, and not completely understanding the rules of a game has never stopped me from taking part in it.

On those late fall afternoons, I could hear the crowd roaring and chanting while the air smelled of crisp burning leaves—I'd like to say that but it hardly ever happened. These days our leaves are collected and hauled away like garbage. And the Big House is really a giant bowl scooping the sound up and shooting it directly into the wild blue yondering sky. Sometimes I imagine the feet-stomping yahooing waves continuing endlessly out there in darkest space, streaming over the debris of abandoned wrenches, cables, and defunct satellites on its eternal journey, as determined as ever, toward the great black holes waiting like giant mouths at the other end of the galaxy. But like I said, I never heard the cheering or announcing in my house with the windows and doors closed, and therefore it was the television that made the game five blocks away a reality.

After a while, I found myself planning Saturdays around the TV game. Discovered any number of tasks including writing a novel with one ear cocked for big plays that required a dash to the other room.

It wasn't until one of the last home games in November that Steve invited me to come along on his tickets. That was when I discovered that for all my participation through the television, I didn't know the protocol of how to dress, when and how to arrive so I wouldn't seem like a first-timer. It was nerve-racking watching the cars crowd the streets around my house, while I waited anxiously inside for the right moment, and having to run past everyone at the last minute when I realized I was going to be late.

As soon as we settled into our seats, the sun departed behind the kind of heavy blue-black eggplant clouds that by Midwestern standards mean a cloudburst if you're lucky and a tornado if you're not. But when the Minnesota team took the field, the wind switched sides like it had a bet down against us, and cut through my thin raincoat as if it were made of Kleenex. I sat on my hands to keep my fingers from turning into Popsicles. Only the fact that each numbered space on the metal bleachers was six inches wide, making us line up like spawning frogs in a roadside ditch, kept heat in any part of my body. Crossing my legs almost required surgery on the entire row, and I came within inches of strangling the small boy wriggling next to me.

But we're here, I kept telling myself, the picture on my TV perfectly replicated down to the single-engine planes buzzing like mosquitoes as they circled the field pulling ad banners. I even located the ABC cameras

and felt the same inexplicable thrill as the first time I saw the ABC
Sports semis parked in the stadium lot days before the opening game in
late August when I had to stop myself from pulling over to admire them.
I immediately went home that day and called my sister in California
telling her to watch the game so she could maybe see me or my house. I
don't know what she thought I was going to do—stand outside the stadium waving until they came over to take my picture maybe. I didn't
know about regional broadcasting yet either, although a doubt as to
why the entire country would find the Michigan football team so wonderful did surface.

The game started with Steve and me cheering for both sides and
spreading the criticism evenly. At halftime the woman I'd been digging
my knees into all afternoon turned around and said, "It's lucky for you
Michigan's ahead." We all laughed, but I could tell she meant it. Being
new, my loyalties were splintered, broken things I hadn't had time to
repair yet.

That first fall, I floundered to some degree, sorting my identity into
new categories, finding so little intact it shocked me. Originally from
Nebraska, I had secretly rooted for Big Red football for years. Now, I
read sports pages daily in two papers, checking Monday morning
rankings as carefully as my horoscope, lingering over the possible fates
of bowl bids the way I used to worry about life after death. After
Christmas, I holed up with a week's worth of food, some videos, and
the bowl schedule. People kept calling to see why I didn't want to leave
the house. Was I sick, did I need food or medicine? I'm working, I
announced, hoping Steve wouldn't let on that we'd bet on every game.

However, since neither of us knew that much about other teams, our
betting had this other dimension. He bet against Ohio because they
weren't gentlemen. Florida because they played dirty. The list of social
and ethical offenses was minute and thorough.

Lacking all kinds of judgment when it came to human behavior
(people from Nebraska had to take a lot of ribbing about the "felony
squad"), I chose my favorites on much closer and more personal
grounds. I never liked Notre Dame because everyone else did. Besides,
Lou Holtz came to Minnesota, said he'd leave if they didn't build the
domed stadium so he could play indoors, they did, and he left anyway.

They were my tax dollars. I liked Alabama because I almost took a job there, but even before that, I liked their nickname: The Crimson Tide. Steely Dan liked it too, and I liked them. It's always Texas because I always meant to drive there on vacation but ended up going other places. "States nobody else wants to go to," my sister announces each summer as we climb in my truck and head for Missouri or Mississippi, South Dakota or Kansas, avoiding big cities and tourist traps. Moreover, I bet on any team with a sad story. Any school or state connected to anybody I've ever loved, unless it ended badly. For me, that was. Even then, it might get the bittersweet vote. There weren't really standards involved here. My sponsorship was completely and arbitrarily personal, created out of a web of mythology that defied most explanation. I had to wonder if this was the pattern of my whole life. As Sallust said: Myth never happened but is.

The good thing about football-filled holidays, which I never understood as a child watching men clustered around the TV as intent as sparrows on bushes in winter, is that you're so tired by New Year's Eve, you can hit the sack early and avoid all the fuss and depression. And you have something to look forward to the next day: more bowl games.

As I pulled away in the bowl sweepstakes, I began to feel real positive about the year to come. Especially when Nebraska rolled over Florida like Judy Mason that long ago afternoon chasing me up and down the park with her superior speed and strength. But this time I was on the right side of it and could only wish by the fourth quarter that the other team would grin and say okay, we've had enough, and they'd all clap each other on the backs and go home. It doesn't happen that way, though. A player has to stand there reaching up to catch a ball knowing that the minute his fingertips receive that first caress, something the size of a John Deere tractor is going to plow right over him. This is the part I can't bring myself to believe in. In my story, I could never make myself catch that ball, knowing what I know. In truth, I can't even make myself stop and look downfield for the receiver to throw the damn thing to either. There are times I have to get up and walk out of the room watching this game.

As a woman, I'm not alone in this obsession either. In early January this year I was at Nick's house for dinner. As usual, the men exchanged their Super Bowl remarks in the corner over appetizers, but later in the kitchen we women got to discussing football more thoroughly. Elena said that she just has to "walk into the room with a game on and no matter who it is or what it is, within minutes I'm rooting for one side or another as if my life depended on it."

Mary said figure skating did it for her. "Those lean bodies." We began stacking dirty plates and listing all the sports we loved. Tennis and skiing. Any team sport.

"The entire Olympics," I bragged, "except synchronized swimming." Elena turned on the disposal and pushed the dinner scraps in the hole with a spatula. Then Linda confessed to liking synchronized swimming, so I backed off. We were seeking consensus in our kitchen admissions. Probably a lot of important secrets are revealed in this setting, and certainly after an evening discussing the latest fiction, the best restaurant in New York, the wine, and the latest political scandal at the dinner table, we were ready for something loaded with ordinary quirkiness. A certain relief accompanied our talk; we had risked our credentials as women in coming out of the closet as sports fanatics. Finally we moved on to the Super Bowl, shy yet eager to declare our choices and opinions. That's when we discovered that we were all rooting for Green Bay because the town owned the team. For women, that had the appeal of good domestic economy, like grocery shopping on a budget. The individual-team-ownership deal seemed "more like a pissing contest," Linda said. "The teams should all be owned by their cities and answerable to the people who support them," Elena said. We'd had enough wine to solve a lot of problems with major sports in that kitchen session.

While it surprised and pleased me to realize that other women were hooked too, I still haven't publicly revealed the extent of my involvement yet, how I am being tutored on a weekly basis. Oh, I do drop a few hints here and there, trying people out with something like, "Hey, can you believe that Tiger Woods?" Even my sister who is willing to spend her hard-earned vacations in unlikely places with me, balks at some of this. She's heard his name, but can't be brought to the TV for golf. I admit that until this last fall, I never watched a game of golf in my life. I couldn't have told you the difference between a birdie and that thing people do with their middle fingers in rush-hour traffic. I still can't name the irons or their specific uses. Lately though, I've realized certain truths about the game. In golf, for instance, you have one of the ultimate individual sports. And while I used to think that the caddy was an atavistic symbol of class, listening to the gray-bearded guy advising Tiger on the lay of a shot, I learned the truth—there is no such thing as a truly individual sport. Tiger Woods has more talent than anyone has seen since Arnold Palmer, yet he's had his father and mother, coaches and caddies surrounding him with information and advice his whole life. Sure, it's his ass on the line, but a lot of people have helped him haul it there.

Actually, I discovered, there was a lot of wisdom-getting in televised sports, and since my dream life was being operated by someone else's remote control, I became willing to look and learn. Having thrown out twenty years of living in St. Paul, Minnesota and watched it being hauled away like curbside trash on Friday morning, pieces blowing from the truck barreling down the street, I kept wondering what I was doing here in Michigan. The gift of starting my life over was turning into the kind of thing my ex used to give me for Christmas: potholders, a plastic spice rack, and why all those books on frozen deserted places, I always meant to ask him.

Then in May the Michigan 500 was held right down the road in Brooklyn (Irish Hills for true insiders). It started with the splintering of the Indy Racing League and CART (Championship Auto Racing Teams). I'm always a sucker for a debate. I'll take sides on anything. It was easy to begin reading about the drivers and Indy cars and to watch the qualifying runs for both the Indianapolis 500 and the Michigan 500, and Memorial Day became one of the most enjoyable holidays in recent years, switching back and forth between the races. That was the beginning. All summer I followed Greg Moore, the Canadian rookie working for his first win, and veteran Jimmy Vasser running for the championship, from race to race, trying to pick up enough to understand the complexity behind the beauty and speed of those cars. Although listening to race announcers was like being stranded at the railway station in a foreign country whose language you know only a

. . . . . . . . . .

few words of, certain repeated terms became key: pop-off valves and flat spotting, turbulence and taking downforce, camber and telemetry. There was something terribly important at stake in each quarter turn of a rear wing, or whether the car made a turn on the point of cohesion, and while I didn't understand exactly what it was, the urgency became startlingly clear as cars spun and flipped, smashing into one car after another, caught fire and rolled over and over down the track, splattering against the wall.

The critics are wrong about racing fans. It isn't only the crashes we wait for. It's the moment of relief seeing the driver climb out of the car, the utterly pure truth that the track and the racing cars lay bare for us: Merely surviving a race is sometimes the equivalent of winning. An Indy car covers the length of a football field in one second. Our futures are deliberate and potentially violent forces bearing down on us. Anything can happen: A tire can go down, the engine can blow, the car can suddenly lose downforce and spin, other cars can lose control and spin in your path. The smallest adjustment of the car affects how it handles. The weather, sun and clouds, heating and cooling the track can change the setup on the car and speed of the track. As in life, it's the most minute calibrations that produce the most profound results in the face of the dispassionate and accidental nature of events.

The problem with Indy racing was that it only happened every other week at most, and my summer Sundays were too long without it. Everyone I knew was out of town for the summer. I always meant to go outside and do something, but it was too hot. I was too tired. So it was by default that I sat through part of a NASCAR Winston Cup race. The cars were heavier and slower and bumped each other in a way that would launch a lighter Indy car to Jupiter. "Bunch of rednecks," I muttered, but kept watching. Cars would spin out, kiss the wall, wash down the track, then limp off to pit row, where teams in matching jumpsuits laden with sponsor labels would swarm over them, taping, patching, riveting until the car roared off again. Even several laps down, reduced to one gear; steering marginal; back end, sides, or front end stove in; metal flapping; the cars continued to race because points are awarded for finishing as well as winning and placing. Besides, the sponsors pay to have their names in front of the spectators all afternoon. After a while, I started rooting for cars ten laps down as well as those chasing the leader. Racing luck seemed like luck in general—you had to be able to survive it.

Dale Earnhart, The Intimidator, drove with a broken collarbone and ribs, in so much pain he didn't want to climb out of the car again. Terry Labonte drove the last two races to win the championship with a badly broken finger crucial to steering. Ernie Irvan came back from a nearly fatal crash wearing an eye patch to finish many races in the top ten. At the Southern 500, Dale Jarrett skidded on oil, hit the wall, and came back to finish even though he'd missed the Winston Million bonus. By the end of races, drivers were battered, exhausted, and calling for oxygen to fight the carbon-monoxide poisoning. This was closer to bull riding and rodeo than anything I'd ever seen. I fell in love. I started thinking in terms of tire temperatures and track surfaces, pitting under green, getting too loose or too tight, moving the track bar, and drafting. Fridays I could watch the pole testing for the fastest lap, although the pole car only won 15 percent of the races. Saturday, practice laps and "happy hour," where the teams pull out the stops to make a perfect marriage of car and track and weather to get the car "hooked up." Sundays, the race with all the accidental grace and terror that seemed a hallmark of life itself.

But I couldn't confess this new obsession to anyone around here. It was like joining a cult with its own unique language and rituals. I could only make vague excuses about needing to work when people called or stopped over. While the academic world may allow a certain degree of football fanhood, clothed in communal ideals about leadership and courage and team spirit, to permeate its corridors, nobody has ever suggested that any such accommodation could be made for these renegade stock-car racers. Although car racing is the fastest growing sport in America with new tracks being built every year, it has nothing whatsoever to do with anything recognizable on a college campus where being able to fix your own car is seen as something of a social liability. You use cars to go places. You're in school so you can get a job and pay someone else to change the oil, tune the engine, rotate the tires.

So these days, it's my eleven-year-old nephew, Talbot, in California I talk with about Dale Jarrett, our favorite Winston Cup driver, whose father Ned is a former driver himself who announces racing. Last week we spent an hour on the phone ranking our other favorites: Mark Martin in the Valvoline car, Bobby and Terry Labonte who race for different teams, Rusty Wallace in the Miller Lite car, The Intimidator in the number three car, but disagree on Jeff Gordon, the young hotshot. We dream about going to see a race next summer together. He remembers the numbers and sponsors of the cars, and I remember the race courses and drivers. I wonder if I should rent a camper for the weekend, if I'll be able to see as much as I do on my big TV, if the drone of the engines as lazy and comforting as garden bees on TV will drive me crazy in person. There's something sanitized about sports on TV.

I've noticed that there's a kind of schizophrenia in the world of sports, the same one that underlies our culture as a whole. We are a classless society with classes, and our sports fall into class lines too. Despite the fact that I can speak openly about football and baseball and golf around Ann Arbor, mostly I keep my mouth shut about car races and rodeo. Since stock-car racing grew out of the dirt tracks of the South and the rural areas of the Midwest, it retains a homegrown flavor, lacking the international glamour of Indy and Formula One racing with their sleek cars and accents. Reflecting its roots, Winston Cup is a family sport, a hybrid cross of demolition derby and drag racing in the family sedan. The drivers' families travel with them as much as possible and cluster around them before and after races. It's also big, burly racing full of physical contact and enough patience, cunning, and teamwork to survive on the track. The 3400-pound cars can go 200-plus miles per hour on the straightaways and still trade paint. Very American, I realized as soon as I learned the language. Every sport seemed to constitute a language then, a means of describing, of locating, of replicating its own culture and reality.

Visiting western Nebraska last fall to conduct some particularly tricky negotiations regarding Sandhills land I own out there, I found it the greatest benefit finally to have the kind of access to discourse I'd previously disregarded—through football. Brad, the Nebraska Power Company rep, and I started our meeting with baseball but continued through twenty minutes of football before we came to the essential business, which only took fifteen minutes. Five years ago, even two years ago, our business would never have been settled so easily. Finally, I understood.

The following day the more delicate discussion with Mike, my neighbor, took place at breakfast. Both of us were facing some painfully expensive and necessary concessions to each other. Fortunately, we began by discussing Michigan and Nebraska's recent football losses. First we shared the shock of Nebraska's first loss in over two years to Arizona, which seemed to make the next negotiation go somewhat more smoothly, neither of us reaching for the angry words that were lurking like bad actors on the outskirts of the play. After a period of silence during which we licked our wounds, we came back to football. For an hour we tried to calculate the bowl and national championship chances for Nebraska, agreeing finally that Michigan would have to beat Ohio, and Nebraska would have to go unbeaten. When we parted, we were smiling, having come back to common ground, as if we momentarily pulled the strings of the universe between us.

So it is that lately I have discovered that I happen to like being in new places, or being in old places becoming strange again. In the moment of simultaneous dislocation and recognition, the world becomes remarkable again, every nuance fraught with sparkling possibility. What more could I ask for? Whoever abducted my old dream life, I've decided, can have it, because sumo wrestling is more interesting on the International Channel narrated in Japanese than on ESPN in English.

## ABOUT THE AUTHORS

. . . . . . . . . .

GERALD EARLY is the Merle S. King Professor of Modern Letters in Arts and Sciences and director of the African and Afro-American Studies Program at Washington University in St. Louis. He has edited a collection of Countee Cullen's work as well as *Speech and Power*, an anthology of African American essays, and *Lure & Loathing: Essays on Race, Identity, and the Ambivalence of Assimilation*. He is the author of *Tuxedo Junction*, a collection of essays on American culture, *Daughters: On Family and Fatherhood*, and a book of poetry, *How the War in the Streets Is Won: Poems on the Quest for Love and Faith*. His most recent book is on Motown Records called *One Nation Under a Groove: Motown and American Culture*. His book, *The Culture of Bruising: Essays on Prize Fighting*, won the 1994 National Book Critics Circle Award. He is the recipient of a Whiting Writer's Award, a General Electric Foundation Award, and the Washington University Distinguished Faculty Award. In 1995, he organized the first conference on Miles Davis and American Culture. His essays have appeared in *Harpers*, the *New Republic*, *Civilization*, and *Hungry Mind Review*. He is currently finishing a book about Fisk University.

JONIS AGEE teaches fiction in the M.F.A. program at Michigan University. Her most recent book of fiction is *South of Resurrection*. She is also the author of *Bend This Heart*, *A .38 Special & a Broken Heart*, *Strange Angels*, and *Sweet Eyes*.

TERI BOSTIAN is a recent graduate of the Nonfiction Writing Program at the University of Iowa, where she teaches workshops in the essay and literary journalism.

CECIL BROWN is a novelist, screenwriter, and teacher. His most recent book, a memoir, is *Coming Up Down Home*. He earned a Ph.D. in African American Literature, Folklore, and Narrative Theory from the University of California-Berkeley. His book, *Stagolee Shot Billy: The Buried History of the Black Man in American Culture,* will be published in 1998 by Harvard University Press.

WAYNE FIELDS is a professor of English and director of American Culture Studies at Washington University. He is the author of *Union of Words: A History of Presidential Eloquence, The Past Leads a Life of Its Own,* and *What the River Knows: An Angler in Midstream.*

LORRAINE KEE is a general assignment reporter at the *St. Louis Post-Dispatch*. She has worked for newspapers in Missouri, Connecticut, and Kansas.

PHILLIP LOPATE is the editor of *The Art of the Personal Essay* and author of the essay collections *Portrait of My Body, Against Joie de Vivre, Bachelorhood, Being with Children,* and of the novels *The Rug Merchant* and *Confessions of Summer.* A recipient of Guggenheim and National Endowment for the Arts fellowships, he is the Adams Professor of English at Hofstra University.

JAMES A. MCPHERSON teaches at the Writers Workshop at Iowa University. He is the author of *Elbow Room,* which received the Pulitzer Prize, and *Hue & Cry.* His newest book, *Crabcakes,* was published in February 1998.

VIJAY SESHADRI was born in India and came to America at age five. He grew up in Columbus, Ohio. He is the author of *Wild Kingdom,* his first collection of poems. His work has appeared in the *Threepenny Review,* the *New Yorker, Shenandoah, Antaeus,* and *AGNI.*

KRIS VERVAECKE is a recent graduate of the Iowa Writers Workshop in fiction. Currently she teaches writing and literature courses at a small college. She has essays forthcoming in *The Healing Circle* and *Between Mothers and Sons: Reflections by Women Writers.*

. . . . . . . . .

A MacArthur Prize Fellow, LOÏC WACQUANT is an associate professor of Sociology at the University of California-Berkeley, and a re-
searcher at the Center for European Sociology of the Collège de France.
He is the co-author, with Pierre Bourdieu, of *An Invitation to Reflexive
Sociology*, and of the forthcoming *Urban Outcasts*. He has published
numerous studies on race and urban marginality, violence and the
body, culture and economy, and the carceralization of social policy in
the United States. "Sacrifice" is based on a four-year ethnography of a
boxing gym in Chicago's ghetto during which he took up the trade and
earned the nickname "Busy Louie" in the ring.

DAVID FOSTER WALLACE is the author of *Infinite Jest* and *Girl with
Curious Hair* and most recently a book of essays, *A Supposedly Fun
Thing I'll Never Do Again*. He teaches at Illinois State University.

ANTHONY WALTON currently lives in Brunswick, Maine. He is the
author of *Mississippi: An American Journey*. He has written for a
variety of publications including the *New York Times, 7 Days,* and
the *New York Times Magazine*. He studied at Notre Dame and Brown
University.

This book was designed by Will Powers. It is set in Sabon and Formata type by Stanton Publication Services, Inc., and manufactured by Edwards Bros., Ann Arbor, on acid-free paper.